The Jola (Diola) are intensive wet-rice cultivators in the Lower Casamance region of Senegal. In this study, the author examines the reasons behind startling contrasts in the organization of agricultural tasks among three Jola communities located within a 45 kilometer radius from Ziguinchor. In Sambujat, situated in the non-Islamisized region south of the river, wet rice is a monocrop cultivated by both men and women. In Jipalom, in the Kajamutay region north of the River, Islam and cash cropping have been adopted; and in Fatiya, in the so-called "Mandingized" region of the Kalunay, social relations have become hierarchical and this has had profound effects on the cropping system and on the division of labor.

The author examines the shift of power relations over time, and their effects on the way in which production has been organized by age and gender, kin and class. Larger issues dealt with are Islamization, women's labor, and the introduction of cash cropping. A concluding section places the history of Jola labor relations within the context of the political economy of Senegal.

Cambridge Studies in Social and Cultural Anthropology

Editors: Ernest Gellner, Jack Goody, Stephen Gudeman, Michael Herzfeld, Jonathan Parry

82
Power, Prayer and Production

A list of books in the series will be found at the end of the volume

POWER, PRAYER AND PRODUCTION

The Jola of Casamance, Senegal

OLGA F. LINARES
Smithsonian Tropical Research Institute

CAMBRIDGE UNIVERSITY PRESS
Cambridge
New York   Port Chester
Melbourne   Sydney

CAMBRIDGE UNIVERSITY PRESS
Cambridge, New York, Melbourne, Madrid, Cape Town, Singapore, São Paulo

Cambridge University Press
The Edinburgh Building, Cambridge CB2 8RU, UK

Published in the United States of America by Cambridge University Press, New York

www.cambridge.org
Information on this title: www.cambridge.org/9780521401326

© Cambridge University Press 1992

This publication is in copyright. Subject to statutory exception
and to the provisions of relevant collective licensing agreements,
no reproduction of any part may take place without the written
permission of Cambridge University Press.

First published 1992
This digitally printed version 2007

A catalogue record for this publication is available from the British Library

Library of Congress Cataloguing in Publication data
Linares, Olga F.
Power, prayer, and production: the Jola of Casamance, Senegal / Olga F. Linares.
  p. cm. – (Cambridge studies in social and cultural anthropology; 82)
Includes bibliographical references and index.
ISBN 0 521 40132 1 (hardback)
1. Diola (African people) – Agriculture. 2. Diola (African people) – Economic conditions. 3. Diola (African people) – Politics and government. 4. Rice – Senegal – Casamance. 5. Casamance (Senegal) – Economic conditions. 6. Casamance (Senegal) – Social conditions. 7. Casamance (Senegal) – Religious life and customs.
I. Title. II. Series.
DT549.45.D56L55   1992
966.3–dc20   90-26070
                                                                              CIP

ISBN 978-0-521-40132-6 hardback
ISBN 978-0-521-04035-8 paperback

For Afo and Ajien, who lived a long life.
And for Bana and Benji, who died young.

Contents

List of illustrations   *page* xii
List of tables   xv
Acknowledgements   xvi
Note on orthography   xviii

INTRODUCTION: IDEOLOGY AND AGRARIAN CHANGE   1
The problem   3
The setting   5
The approach   7
The organization   10

PART I: THE POLITICAL ECONOMY OF SAMBUJAT   13
Chapter 1: The power of the spirit-shrines   15
The people and their rice-growing system   17
Ideational aspects of "power": the spirit-shrines   23
The authority of elders   28
Waxing and waning powers: the "priest–king" or *ai* and the chief   38
Women's "strength": the *Sihuñ* shrines   45

Chapter 2: Rice fields and labor relationships   52
Huteendukay, the labor shrine   53
Marriage and the formation of the conjugal family unit   54
The conjugal family and the gender division of labor   58
Cooperative patterns: the "extended" family or *buaju* unit   61
Associative work: the *hank*, the elders, and the village   65
Female associations   69
The role of religion in the palm-produce trade   71

x   Contents

Conclusions to Part I   74

**PART II: AT THE CROSSROADS: THE KUJAMAAT JOLA
OF JIPALOM**   81
Chapter 3:   Islamization and the introduction of a cash crop   83
Bañuñ history and Jola territorial expansion   84
The trade in forest products   90
Threats to Jola autonomy   92
The Islamization of the north-shore Jola   94
Adopting groundnuts as a cash crop   98

Chapter 4:   The impact on social and productive relations   103
The history of a community: Jipalom in the Kajamutay   104
Agnatic filiation versus uterine ties   105
The girls' excision rite   109
The demise of the *sináati*   111
The female shrines: contrasts with Sambujat   113
The minimal Muslim   115
Productive forces: land "ownership" and "usufructuary" rights   118
Conflicts over borrowed land   123
Gaining access to land on the plateau   127
The conjugal family and the labor process   130
Men's associative labor   132
The women's associations   136
Changing forces and relations of production   138

Conclusions to Part II   140

PART III: MANDING MODELS AND FATIYA MORES   145
Chapter 5:   Ideology and legitimation   147
The Manding: a brief history   149
Salient features of Manding society   151
The role of Islam in Fatiya society   154
Legitimating ideologies: social hierarchies and status asymmetries   161
Land tenure: those who own and those who borrow   166

Chapter 6:   Social relations of production re-structured   172
Constructing gender relations   172
Domestic relations and resources   179
Marriage and the circulation of women   181

The labor process: kinship and seniority	186
Women's work in the rice fields	191
Associative work in the three Jola communities: a comparative note	199
Conclusions to Part III	204
EPILOGUE: THE JOLA IN THE PRESENT NATIONAL SCENE	209
Epilogue	211
Jola communities in 1990	212
On the political economy of the Senegalese State	217
Notes	223
References	243
Index	253

Illustrations

Figures *page*
1 Map showing the approximate location of our three study areas (Esudadu, Northern Kajamutay and Kalunay) and the communities and towns mentioned throughout the book. 12
2 Map indicating the present-day distribution of neighboring ethnic groups, including remnant Bañuñ communities. 86
3 Section of the *biit*, or rainfed rice fields, in Jipalom. Each parcel is permanently surrounded by a low bund or dike. Clusters of parcels in different parts of the *biit* are owned individually. A gentle gradient goes from the *seentam*, which have sandy soils and are fairly shallow, to the *kuyelen* which have clayey soils that retain the water runoff. The *sibaaf* can no longer be cultivated because salts accumulated in them after the drought of the 1970s. Not shown are the *kuyolen* or nursery area behind the *seentam* and the *weng* or deep fields near the *marigot* which have been abandoned. An even more complex pattern of rice-field categories exists in Sambujat (Part I), whereas the rice fields in Fatiya (Part III) are little differentiated. 120
4 Map of a region in the Northern Kajamutay surrounding Jipalom. Since the 1960s, when the map was done, the surface cultivated in groundnuts has increased while that in paddy rice has shrunk. 128

Plates
1 Aerial view of a large Esudadu community. (Courtesy M. and G. Bracher).

List of illustrations xiii

2a	Father and son ridge the paddy fields.	21
2b	Wife and daughter transplant upon them.	21
3	The *Hupila* shrine guards the entrance to the courtyard.	27
4	A ritual elder (*ai*) with his peace-enforcing broom.	39
5	The chief (center) and the men drinking palm-wine together after doing the *kawasen*.	44
6	The in-married women sing at an agnate's funeral.	46
7	A Sambujat man and his wife often work side by side.	59
8	Elders and junior men in Sambujat cultivate together in the same work-group.	66
9	In Sambujat, women of all ages often transplant together.	69
10	The entrance to an *eluup* or House unit. Rice granaries are on the right. The open hut on the left is where women pound the daily rice.	106
11	In some Kajamutay areas, the *kurimen* come together every few years to perform the village-wide *Ebune* festival.	114
12	A visiting marabout.	117
13	Two Jipalom closely related conjugal families working together. (Courtesy, J. David Sapir.)	130
14	Before the introduction of animal traction, Jipalom men prepared each other's groundnut fields by associative labor (the *ekáf*). (Courtesy J. David Sapir.)	133
15	The in-married women's *ekáf* works for a resident male agnate. They are beating the dried plant to detach the nuts. (Courtesy J. David Sapir.)	137
16	Aerial view of Fatiya: (1) the highway to Dakar, (2) ward A: houses with enclosed orchards, (3) ward B: houses with enclosed orchards, (4), (5) groundnut/millet fields, (6) palm groves, (7), (8) rice fields. (Courtesy, Service Topographique, Dakar.)	155
17a	The Arabic school: 17a: a *talibé* teacher writes Arabic on his tablet.	157
17b	his students display their skills.	157
18	Transporting the rice harvest to the chief's compound.	162
19	All the village men do a day's work for a renowned marabout. They dig up his ripe groundnuts (19a), and stack them up to dry (19b).	190
20a	Past and present technologies: men still use the short-handled Manding hoe (*eronkatoŋ*) in light tasks such as weeding.	192
20b	They prepare their plateau fields with the ox-plow.	192

xiv *List of illustrations*

21 The married women's *comité* works for one of its members.
They turn the soil in the rice fields using the long-handled
Manding hoe (*ebara*).   194

Note: All the photographs except numbers 1, 13, 14, 15, and 16, were taken by the author.

Tables

Ia	Principal steps in rice cultivation: Sambujat	*page*	20
Ib	Labor inputs by gender for rice cultivation in Sambujat		60
Ic	Sambujat: household "types" according to two criteria		63
IIa	Area, exclusive of nurseries, cultivated by six Jipalom conjugal households		119
IIb	Flow of labor from different sources for Bojas agnates in *Yentam* (i.e. rain-fed rice fields) preparation during one agricultural season		134
IIc	Labor input by gender in Jipalom (adult days/ha)		139
IIIa	Fatiya household types according to two criteria: co-residence and co-production		163
IIIb	A comparison between female labor inputs in agriculture: Fatiya compared with two other villages		196

Acknowledgements

Every author approaches the acknowledgements with mixed feelings of pleasure and trepidation; pleasure at being able to thank the dozens of people who have given their time, and the various institutions that have given their funds, so generously; dread that one might have left out a helping hand. Then there is the added problem in anthropological fieldwork of not being able to reveal the actual name of field assistants and friends for fear that the information they have given so freely could, unwittingly, be used against them. It should go without saying, however, that this book is a tribute to the Jola, whose courage, competence and contributions shall outlive us all. While I have been away, several of my closest friends have died. This book is dedicated to them, and to Benji.

The following funding agencies made possible the research: The National Science Foundation (1965–1966), the Wenner Gren Foundation (1970, 1980), The Smithsonian Institution (1975, 1979, 1980, 1985, 1988–1990).

While in Senegal, work during the 1960s was greatly facilitated by IFAN (Institut Fondamental d'Afrique Noire), and during the 1970s by the Secrétariat d'Etat à la Recherche Scientifique et Technique. Their enlightened attitude towards research makes it a pleasure to work in their country. Logistic support was also provided by ORSTOM, the French overseas research center. S. and I. Amin, C. and B. LeCour Grandmaison, C. and M. Meillassoux made my visits to Dakar during the 1964–1966 season special events.

J. David Sapir, foremost among Jola scholars, has continued to provide data, advice and critical commentary throughout the years. His willingness to share his knowledge – and five splendid photographs – is greatly appreciated. Martin H. Moynihan, my husband, has been structuring

Acknowledgements xvii

important research problems in Coraciiformes bird behavior around the Jola habitats where I also lived.

I owe a great debt of gratitude to the Smithsonian Tropical Research Institute (STRI), the sub-branch of the Smithsonian in Panama, to which I belong. Its director, Ira Rubinoff, has always been unwavering in his moral and financial support. Our former librarian, Sylvia Churgin, and our present librarian, Vielka Chang-Yau, plus their devoted staff, have gone to great lengths to help me. The printing of my negatives was done in the photographic service laboratory at STRI under the expert direction of C. Hansen.

A very special thanks goes to Roberta Rubinoff, Director of Scholarships and Grants at the Smithsonian in Washington D.C. Roberta has always followed my research with a keen interest and real understanding.

To my colleagues, anthropologists and historians, who have worked in other Jola (or Jola-related) areas, notably M. Schloss, F. Snyder, J. Lauer and R. Baum, many thanks for constructive comments and commentaries. Discussions with J. Irvine and P. Weil who have worked in different sectors of Senegal have been especially fruitful. Through the years, Jack and Esther Goody have provided much intellectual stimulus and moral support.

It is through my parents, siblings, nephews and in-laws that I have learned the real value of cognatic and affinal ties. I must give special thanks to my mother, O. T. de Linares, who has suffered through this book with me, and to my father, F. Linares D., who has shown a lively interest in, and respect for, the Jola rice-growing system.

This book was begun while I was at the Center for Advanced Study in the Behavioral Sciences at Stanford, California, was continued while I was Overseas Visiting Fellow at St. John's College, Cambridge University, and was completed in our house in the Tarn, in southwestern France. I should like to thank the anonymous external reader for his insightful comments, and Con Coroneos, my "creative editor," for making this a much better book.

A sequel to this volume – a more technical and detailed discussion of the history and present status of the Jola rice-growing system – is currently under preparation.

A note on Jola orthography

Throughout the book, I have intentionally followed a mixed strategy in rendering place-names. The names of important cities and towns are written the way they appear in the official 1/200,000 map for Senegal (Institut Géographique National: Paris, Centre en Afrique Occidentale, Dakar, 1970). Thus, Ziguinchor rather than the phonetic transcription Zigicor, Bignona rather than Biñona, Oussouye rather than Usuye, Sindian rather than Sunjan etc. This may facilitate locating these places on a map. The names of the smaller communities, however, are not "Frenchified." They are transcribed phonetically from the Jola. Hence, Telum rather than Talloum, Jugut rather than Diogout, Ñankit rather than Niankit etc. When appropriate, I have given in parentheses an alternate written form the first time it occurs in the text. The three regions discussed, namely the Esudadu, Kajamutay and Kalunay are also transcribed from the Jola. Incidentally, Kajamutay refers to the region, Kujamutay refers to the language and Ajamaat (sing.) / Kujamaat (pl.) refers to the people. Vowel length and tense vowels are marked, respectively, by repetition (aa, ii) and acute accent. However, with long and tense vowels, only the first vowel is marked: e.g. óo, áa, etc. Hence, *sináati*. The symbol ŋ is for the velar nasal. c–k, j–g are not contrastive before front vowels, hence *kucilum esúk*, "those who own the village." See also Badiane and Doneaux n.d.

For a note on Jola Kujamutay grammar and spelling consult J. David Sapir, 1965. *A Grammar of Diola-Fogny.* Cambridge: Cambridge University Press, and J. David Sapir, in preparation, *Dictionnaire Jóola Kujamutay avec traduction française et anglaise.*

I take responsibility for spelling Jóola as Jola. It would be confusing to change, once again, a name that has been variously spelled in the existing literature as Diola, Jiola, Djola. The word is probably derived from Wolof. The various Jola sub-groups call themselves Esudadu, Kujamaat, Jugut etc.

INTRODUCTION

Ideology and agrarian change

The problem
Let us assume for the moment that a visitor to Senegal is driving at the height of the rainy season (July–August) to Lower Casamance (Basse Casamance) in the southwestern corner of the country. Having crossed the Gambian frontier and proceeded along the lower reaches of the Soungrougrou river dividing Lower from Middle Casamance, our visitor will observe Jola (Diola, Jóola) women, singly or in groups, doing all the agricultural work in flooded paddies with the aid of a long-handled, V-shaped hoe. Not a man is to be seen in the alluvial depressions covered with rice fields that separate the villages of the Kalunay (Kalounaye). But, elsewhere, young and mature men can occasionally be seen working alone on the slightly raised ground of the plateaus, where they prepare the sandier soils to receive the millet/sorghum and groundnut crop that only men grow. They use a short-handled hoe or, more often nowadays, an oxen and a plough. Under the shade of grand silk cotton trees, next to the village houses and the highway, old and middle-aged men dressed in white Muslim robes relax on platforms, conversing with each other and greeting passers by.

Once our visitor reaches Bignona, however, and either travels north-west in the direction of the southern Kajamutay (Kadiamoutaye), or crosses the bridge to reach Ziguinchor and continue on to Oussouye and the Pointe St. Georges regions, he or she would notice that in one community after another it is the Jola men of all ages – not the women – who are knee-deep in mud, ridging the rice fields with the aid of a long, straight-handled shovel capped by a metal blade. These men are not alone, however. Their wives are with them, transplanting rice plants along the ridges as their husbands prepare the land. Driving past the palm groves that separate the villages around Oussouye, our visitor can see a Jola man here, another there, clad in a loincloth, suspended like a telephone repairman from the top of a tall palm tree, collecting a liquid sap into gourds. Hence, in a distance of less than 200 kilometers, our visitor has witnessed dramatic differences in the tasks the Jola perform, the tools they use, the crops they grow, and the sex and age of the persons who work the land.

These arresting differences are touched upon in two classical works – the two-part study by L-V Thomas, *Les Diola* (1959), and the section "Paysages et populations des Rivières du Sud" by P. Pélissier in *Les Paysans du Sénégal* (1966: *Livre* III, 623–910). These studies can hardly contrast more in content and approach. The first is by a philosopher turned anthropologist. It is a somewhat "abstract" account of Jola "technology," "psychology," and "social morphology" (volume 1), followed by a discussion of Jola art, music, theories of knowledge and science, moral notions, and religion (volume 2). The second study is by a geographer. It is a descriptive account of Jola technology and agricultural production in the context of history and regional transformations in economy. Even though Thomas touches upon certain aspects of Jola technology, and Pélissier refers in passing to Jola beliefs and ritual practices, by and large the first author focuses upon the spiritual, the second upon the material, side of Jola social life.[1]

Either of the two approaches by itself is incomplete. The first imposes the author's own analytic framework upon a universe of ideals and concepts that is somehow removed from material realities. The second suggests that it is possible to analyze how people act upon the physical world apart from what they believe about it. In giving priority to either "culture" or "nature" these authors understate the essential mediating role that social relations play in the processes of the "appropriation" of nature for community use. And they loose track of the fact that this "appropriation" is done through cultural constructs and shared ideas, as well as through physical, productive activity (Godelier 1984, Ortner 1984).

By contrast, the present study argues that these two ways of looking at the human condition – the ideological and the productive – are deeply connected. The Jola agricultural system that Pélissier describes in such competent detail must also be looked at and analyzed as a moral system, a body of legitimating ideas and beliefs. The ways in which human beings organize themselves to act upon the physical environment are ideologically structured, and ideologies in turn are forged in interaction. The system is constituted not only by the forces and relations of production, but also by a body of beliefs and ritual practices. These beliefs may go under various labels – ideology, religion, superstructure – but the point to remember is

Ideology and agrarian change 5

that they are at one and the same time social responses and ways of organizing the natural world. In these terms, productive processes are never value-free or neutral, but always informed by vested interests, personal motives and power relationships. I will have more to say about power below; here, it is enough to state that this concept includes legitimating notions as well as more coercive interactions.

The setting

It is necessary first to situate the more social–symbolic aspects of Jola production within the immediate physical and demographic environment, then to show how these relations of production are part of a larger political economy of the Senegalese State.

The Jola are a very heterogeneous population of historically related subgroups occupying the Lower Casamance region between the Gambia and Guiné Bissau. Here, they comprise 80–90 percent of the population, although it is impossible to be certain of the total number of Jola who live in Lower Casamance. Estimates range from 200–250,000 (Mark 1985:6) to 400,000 (Baum 1987: 1). I prefer a figure of somewhere between 260,000 and 340,000 persons.[2] Be that as it may, in terms of the total Senegalese population the Jola are a minority of only six to eight percent. They are, however, a unique minority. In a country dominated by ex-slave-owning, state-organized peoples – the Wolof, Sereer, Toucouleurs (Tukulor), Manding (Malinké, Mandinko) – the Jola are often described as "acephalous," for they lack the socially stratified and politically centralized structures that have characterized some (though not all) of their neighbors in the recent past. And, contrary to other Senegalese farmers whose general practice is the bush-fallow cultivation of millets, sorghum, and groundnuts, most Jola, except those that our visitor encountered before reaching Bignona (pronounced Biñona) are famous for practicing an intensive wet-rice agriculture on diked fields that are inundated and transplanted upon year after year.

Overwhelmingly a peasant society, the Jola live amidst their rice fields, in more than 500 separate and largely independent villages or communities, ranging in size from a few hundred to a few thousand inhabitants. This territorial atomization into hundreds of separate communities has affected linguistic developments. Although the Jola language group, together with two other languages, Manjaku (Mandjak) and possibly Balanta (Balante, Doneaux 1975), form part of the Bak sub-family of West Atlantic languages (Sapir 1971), the Jola group itself is very heterogeneous. It is divided into an extended dialect cluster comprised of some ten dialects – several of

6   *Introduction*

which verge on mutual unintelligibility – and four independent languages. Sapir (1971: 59) sums up the linguistic state of affairs as follows:

In any one area what one tends to find is a "layering" of speech forms: a "home" dialect that is very particularistic, an area dialect used by adjacent villages, then one of the regional dialects, Fogny and Kasa, and finally a kind of Kasa–Fogny pidgin that seems to be emerging in market and trade situations.

It should be added that the Jola themselves were once upon a time (before the fifteenth century) concentrated in the region south of the Casamance River. This is why the Kasa dialect spoken in the Esudadu (Esulalu) sub-region, and the Foñi (Fogny) dialect spoken in the southern Kajamutay sub-region – areas discussed in this book – are still mutually intelligible to a large extent. Despite wars, social upheavals and foreign intrusions, the Jola have spread dramatically from their homeland south of the river north to the Gambia, and as far east as the Soungrougrou River, which divides them from their Manding neighbors. Lower Casamance covers about 7,340 square kilometers north and south of the river (see part I: chapter 1). This gives an average Jola population density of 32 per square km in rural areas (Cheneau-Loquay 1988: 116).

As Pélissier (1966) emphasizes, however, Jola population averages do not mean much. Whereas sub-regions such as the southern Kajamutay have average densities of 40 persons per square km, and some, like the Esudadu of Pointe St. Georges, of 50 persons per square km, other regions, such as the marshy islands of the Blis-Karone (Hitou, Niomoun, Hilol etc.), directly north of the Casamance River mouth, have densities of only 8 inhabitants per square km. The same low densities are found in the northernmost regions of the Kombo (Combo), near Gambia, and in the heart of the Kalunay area. Low densities are a product as much of ecological factors (the marshy nature of the terrain) as of historical factors (the Manding religious wars of conversion which ravaged the regions north of the Casamance River).

Profound historical transformations in political economy and national ideology have marked the history of all Senegalese peoples. Among key changes in precolonial times were the Islamization of many rural Senegalese populations and the introduction of cash crops. These changes occurred much earlier and had a more sweeping effect upon other Senegalese societies than they did upon the Jola. Among the Wolof farmers of the Groundnut Basin discussed in p. 219, for example, groundnut production became completely organized along religious lines. Within the Murid (Mouride) brotherhood to which they now belong, wide asymmetries of power and differential control over resources mark the relations between the marabouts, or religious teachers, and their disciples, or *talibés* (*taalibes*; from Arabic *tālib*, meaning disciple).

Among the Jola sub-groups, the adoption of Islam in conjunction with groundnut cultivation has not led to such radical experiments as among the Murid brotherhood. None the less, the changes wrought in Jola society have been considerable. As the Islamicized Jola of the north bank of the Casamance River readily recognize, Islam and cash-cropping have produced profound transformations in their social and political relations – relations that extend out from domestic organization to embrace the whole of community life.

At the same time, neither Islamization nor the adoption of cash crops could by themselves bring about a total transformation of the factors and the actors that influence productive relationships. Political relations of authority and dependency forged between particular Jola sub-groups and neighboring African peoples have also played a key part. It is these neighbors, and not the colonial authorities, or the representatives of world market forces, who have provided the models to be followed. As the old moral order came under scrutiny and rejection, new social relations of production based on a Manding Islamic model of religious comportment began to be adopted by some Jola sub-groups in the Kalunay. Among some other groups like those of the Kajamutay, the absence of appropriate models of religiously sanctioned productive behavior have led to serious dislocations in political economy.

Approach

The diversity in Jola cultural patterns, and the complexity of the historical transformations they have undergone, are not simply the direct unproblematic consequence of the penetration of world market forces, or capitalist relations of production (Snyder 1981). They are also a result of the often contradictory ways in which ideological processes have negotiated between old practices and new economic opportunities. It is this element of contradiction – of ideologies and material forces working in separate directions – which informs the approach adopted in the present study.

By far the most important of the ideological processes at work among many rural peoples of Africa, including the Jola, is religion. By religion is meant "all phenomena that are seen as having a sacred or supraempirical quality" (Morris 1987: 3–4). At the same time as rapid change and destabilizing forces have affected the political economies of Africa, foreign religious groups, with very diverse ideologies, have penetrated the countryside. Islam with its numerous brotherhoods, Catholicism with its various missions, and Protestantism with its separate sects have provided fertile ground on which to explore the thesis that religious conversion can have very uneven effects upon the conduct of economic life. Yet the relationship between religious and economic change has been analyzed from the sophisticated, yet somewhat instrumental, perspective of how new beliefs and ritual practices can provide strategies for economic advancement. Thus, in the context of Hausa traders in Ibadan, A. Cohen (1969) argues that many Hausa converted to the Tijaniyya mystic order of Islam during the 1950s because it reinforced Hausa identity, autonomy and, most important, monopoly of long-distance trade. Long (1968) has also discussed how Zambian farmers who became Jehovah's witnesses were able to develop their links with fellow churchmen. In so doing, they forwarded their own economic aims, while at the same time rejecting customary kinship relationships which were on the whole economically unprofitable. J. D. Parkin (1972) has argued that emerging entrepreneurs from the Giriama group of coastal Kenya would become possessed by Islamic spirits which required them to abstain from participating in "traditional" rituals. In this way they distanced themselves from their kin and neighbors who were likely to constitute a drain on their limited resources. In addition, Webster (1963) has described how the Agege cocoa planters of Western Nigeria provided financial support to African missionaries in return for the latter's effort to recruit labor for the former's plantations. More recently, Martin (1988) has touched upon the effects of conversion and cassava on the gender and age-related division of labor among the Ngawa Igbo of southern Nigeria. Cassava became a female crop offering a lucrative market to local Ngawa women. Christianity, and the educational forms it ushered in, altered authority relations between junior and senior men, and ultimately opened up the door for wage-work in the non-agrarian sector.

These discussions have one thing in common: they emphasize the practical and facilitating functions provided by conversion to a new religion. In so ascribing to a coherent set of functions they shift the focus away from the often contradictory process of ideological change itself into what new religious experiences can do in solid economic terms. But new religions are not adopted simply because of the trauma of conquest, manpower losses, famine and so forth, as Martin herself points out. And they are not adopted either simply because they are readily available, as she herself seems to argue. In fact they are never adopted as a seamless whole, but in a patchy, discontinuous manner. This book argues, therefore, that an approach to the problem of the relationship between religion and economic

Ideology and agrarian change 9

change must take into account processes of accommodation but, crucially, discontinuities between old beliefs and new ritual practices (Berry 1968).

At the same time, however, the impact of new ideologies on economic institutions is always mediated through changing relations of production. Thus, a second emphasis in the present study is on the consequences for social institutions of shifts in the labor process brought about by the impact of religious beliefs and practices. Again, many discussions of how labor relations among African cultivators are organized have been too narrowly conceived, tending to focus solely on the gender division of labor. Thus, according to Boserup (1970), African farming is dominated by extensive systems of bush fallow cultivation in the hands of women employing a rudimentary hoe technology. She contrasts this situation with that in Asia, where intensive systems of cultivation are the rule and are in the hands of men or hired labor employing animal traction and the plough. A similar exclusive tendency is apparent in many otherwise excellent discussions of the gendered division of labor (e.g. Brown 1970, Burton and White 1984, Lancaster 1976, Sillitoe 1985, White *et al.* 1981). But, in fact, within the Jola region alone a greater variation in the division of labor exists than female-centered theories would suggest. In a 45 kilometer radius,[3] practices ranges from a system where men and women, and all the generations, participate in wet-rice production to the best of their abilities, to a system where women do most of the subsistence farming, men grow crops for cash, elders stop working altogether in the fields and marabouts have people to do the work for them.

In other words, changes in productive relations belong to wider structural divisions of which gender is only one – important – aspect. As La Fontaine (1978) carefully points out, in all societies the allocation of social roles is based, not on gender alone, but on such other principles as age, birth-order and relative status. These processes have worked in very different directions among various Jola groups. The single-minded concern with one dimension of role opposition in the agrarian systems of Africa has obscured the diversity of possibilities of adjustment and change.

Age is a particularly important principle in the process of social differentiation in power relationships. To use La Fontaine's own words, it is as much a "cultural transformation of a process of human physiology" as is gender. A good case can be made for the fact that the two principles are often interconnected, not only in practice, but also in cultural logic. For instance, elderly women in one Jola region may re-marry even if they are past reproductive age because they still have an important conjugal role to play in the rice-growing system. In another Jola region, however, a widow who has reached the menopause never remarries even if she is capable of producing rice. For the concepts surrounding gender, age, and the meaning of marital relations have shifted, from being focused on women's productive abilities in one area to being focused on women's reproductive abilities in another area. Hence, distinctions based on gender within the social division of labor frequently depend upon, and often work in parallel with, other social distinctions, especially those made between young, mature, or elder members of society. Yet the consequences of age for the social division of labor have been scrutinized less closely than gender (see Swindell 1985: 18).

In the present study, therefore, the conventional focus on gender is broadened to embrace other social phenomena. Age, status, kinship and ethnic identities are all axes along which changes in the social division of labor can take place. In the case of the Jola these variables, although dialectically related, have been very differently combined into new role models and status relationships. Furthermore, these models and relationships depend upon changes in legitimating notions, and must thus be seen in the context of the power relationships that inform them: "Ultimately, the role played by power . . . may only be that of a proximate cause, but understanding this role is crucial for a process analysis of the division of labor" (Rueschemeyer 1986: 13).

A host of important works (e.g. Hart 1982, Bates 1983 and Clammer 1985) have focused on the monopoly of power by urban bureaucracies and the impact of urban ideologies upon peasant producers. Clearly, the same focus on the distribution of power and legitimacy can be extended to the study of very different agrarian structures within small-scale communities. For here, also, it is essential to understand the nature of the connection between forms of social control and the organization of productive activities. Politics is not solely about ways of dictating policies through the use of force, but also concerns how people may be directed, through mild forms of ideological persuasion and coercion, to perform socially-sanctioned tasks. Finally, then, this study explores precisely how, and through what particular politico-religious concepts, social control is formulated and acts of appropriation legitimated.

The organization
The three parts of this study provide a detailed account of forms of social control and labor organization in Jola communities (whose names have been disguised), located in three contrastive regional social formations – areas that have been sites of significantly different historical currents. Part I

is on Sambujat, a community in the Esudadu area south of the Casamance River. It attempts to relate pre-Islamic indigenous ideas about the power of the spirit-shrines to the sources of authority that elders and women command. Part II traces the impact of Islam, and new forms of cash cropping, on the structure of control, and on the social division of economic tasks, within a second community called Jipalom in the Kajamutay region to the north of the Casamance River. Here, it is important to draw a distinction between the simple passing of time and social change (Giddens 1979: 198–233). The adoption of Islamic practices and commercial crops did not lead to significant adjustments in social relations of production; it simply encouraged the uneasy combination of old with new practices. This resulted in internal contradictions in the ways in which human and material resources were geared to social ends. Part III is an attempt to understand these transformations. Here, changes that have been referred to as the "Mandingization" of Jola society, will receive special attention. Some attempt will be made to show how, why, and in what particular manner the Jola have come to adopt particular aspects of Manding religious culture and organizational forms. Most of this data is drawn from a Jola located at the edge of Manding territory, half-way between two cultural worlds.

The Epilogue conveys some idea of the startling speed with which some recent developments are changing the religious orientation and the political economy of the three Jola communities. Its purpose is to show that ideology and economic life are indeed interactively linked so that changes in one sphere may have dire consequences for the other sphere. The last part is an attempt to place local processes in the wider framework of Senegal's political economy. The emphasis will be on the role of the marabouts in the groundnut trade and the lack of political and economic integration between two very different economies of scale. Local groups will be given proper credit for resisting, restructuring, and reconsidering the forces of capitalism and the world economy.

In trying to analyze the events and transformations that have occurred in three separate Jola villages of Lower Casamance in the last decades, we will be covering a great deal of ground. It is my hope that our hypothetical visitor to Lower Casamance will some day pick up this book and from it learn about the complex interplay of forces lying behind the apparently simple regional differences that he or she observed.

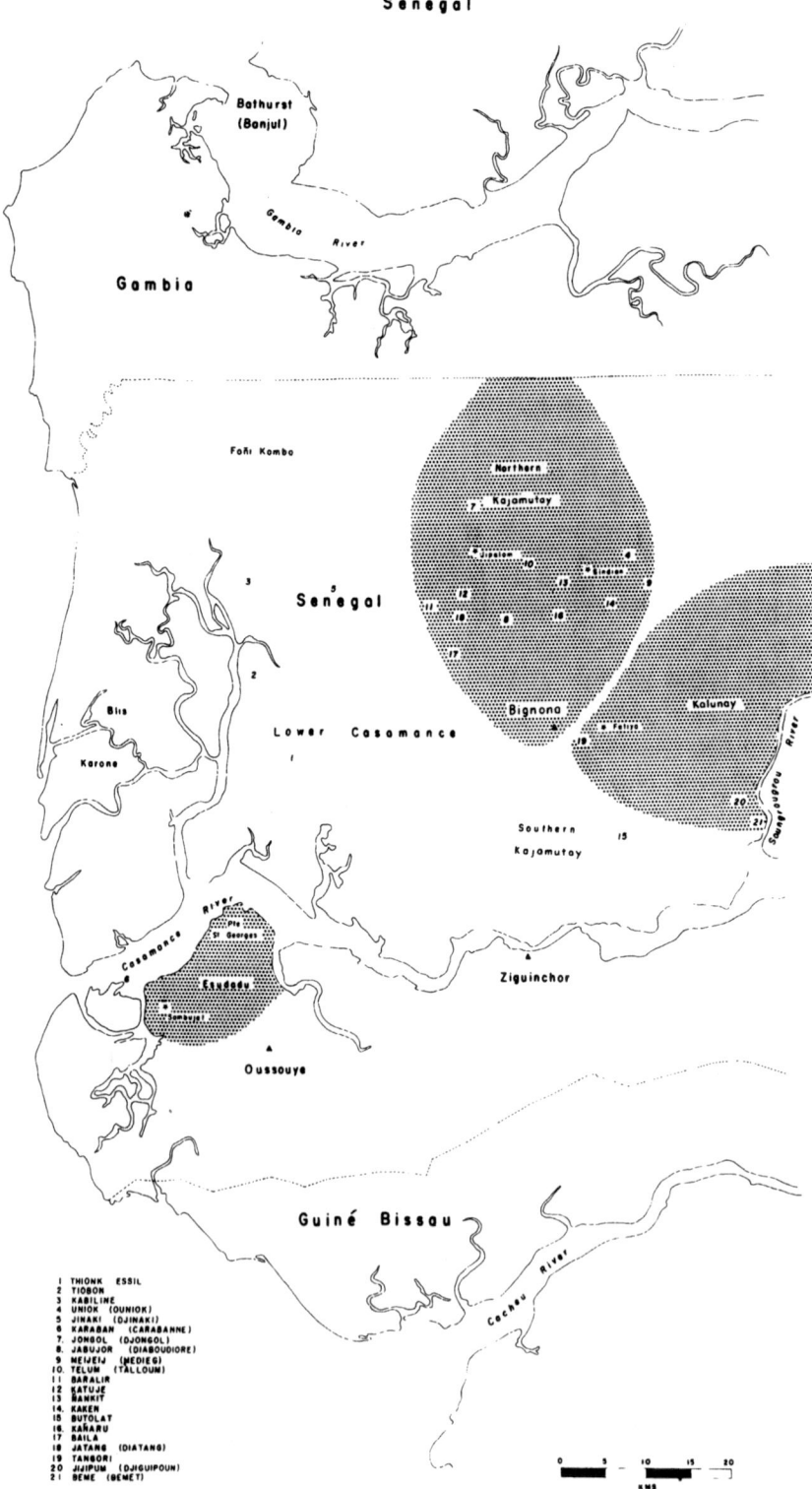

Figure 1: Map showing the approximate location of our three study areas (Esudadu, Northern Kajamutay and Kalunay) and the communities and towns mentioned throughout the book.

PART I
THE POLITICAL ECONOMY OF SAMBUJAT

1

The power of the spirit-shrines

Scholars have remarked upon two striking features of Jola society: the highly developed wet-rice system, and the greatly elaborated *ukiin* (*bakiin*, sing.) or spirit-shrine system. These features are inextricably connected. Although some effort has been made to relate Jola economic behavior to their religious beliefs and ritual practices (most successfully by Baum 1987), a great deal remains to be done. There is still a need for a working theory that can adequately model this interaction.

Political economy can provide such a theory (see Staniland 1985). For it departs from the premise that politics and the economy are dialectically related through complex chains of mutual causation. And it places power where it should be, as the legitimating force shaping productive arrangements and labor relationships. Legitimation is a political process. It can be achieved through consensus and shared ideals; it does not require outright coercion nor the use of force. In societies where bureaucracies are missing and there are no standing armies, as among the relatively self-sufficient rural communities of Africa, religious beliefs and ritual practices often reinforce many aspects of political economy. Cultural ideologies and symbol systems usefully provide a legitimating idiom for the values and aspirations surrounding the economics of role behavior.

Among the Esudadu Jola land is individually "owned" and inherited, and it is also largely worked by household labor. This creates its own problems and contradictions. Rice that is grown in standing water, in fields that are under permanent cultivation, requires a great deal of technical expertise. But, equally important, it also requires a great deal of human management. Although the land can be made to yield an abundant crop, this is only because people are willing to spend long hours in improving their paddy fields. In the Jola rice-growing system people do not simply cut down a patch of forest, grow crops on it, and leave the land to rest for a few years. They cultivate the same parcels year after year. By virtue of the immense effort that is put into improving the land, rice fields have become "private" property. The same is true of land among other societies employing intensive methods of permanent cultivation. Where an intensive wet-rice technology was developed on the basis of "individual skills and experience," as in Asia, the household, rather than a centralized institution such as the State, became the basic property owning and productive unit (Bray 1986: 175–180). Other intensive systems of farming, such as exist among the Kofyar of the Jos Plateau of Nigeria, have also encouraged the emergence of private ownership of land; once land is improved, people are reluctant to part with it (Netting 1965, 1968). In the case of the Esudadu Jola, rice field ownership is a source of friction between individuals and groups who must otherwise cooperate in numerous daily endeavors.

As a result of improved techniques, yields from the Esudadu Jola rice fields tend to be high by any standard. Not only is land "owned" individually and largely worked by household labor, but the crop is also stored separately and consumed separately by each conjugal family. All this encourages an individualistic and competitive outlook towards property and product. But it also has its own contradictory effects. During some periods in the yearly cycle, large groups must coordinate their efforts in accomplishing such tasks as preparation of the land and harvesting. Otherwise the rains may stop early, or the birds may eat the crop before it is harvested. Recruitment to work-groups pose problems. The way in which these problems are resolved reveals the manner in which politics and the economy interact in Esudadu society. How do political processes affect economic relationships in the Jola Esudadu community of Sambujat? Who exerts social control at the local level? Through what channels are power and authority relations expressed? How do age, gender and relative status shape the productive activities of various categories of persons? These questions are worth exploring in the context of the Sambujat rice-growing system. For they reveal the ideological premises upon which social relations of production are often negotiated in many agricultural societies.

People and land frame the basic conditions of production in all agricultural systems. The relationship between available resources and the many ways they can be put to social use generates its own dynamics. Thus, before we turn to wider questions of how religion, politics and the economy are integrated, it seems necessary to examine the setting in which the Esudadu Jola have developed their remarkable wet-rice technology.

The people and their rice-growing system
Sambujat lies on the southern slopes of the Casamance River Delta, on a broad peninsula known as Pointe St. Georges, located within the Department of Oussouye. The people who recognize themselves as Esudadu live in five "pure" Jola villages ranging in size from a few hundred to a few thousand inhabitants. With a population of just over 400, Sambujat is the smallest of the Esudadu communities. It is roughly the size of the wards that make up the larger Esudadu villages: "each township [i.e. large village] is comprised of a series of independent quarters [wards] each with its own government chief, its own loyalties, and its own positions on matters of township concern" (Baum 1987: 346). Within Pointe St. Georges there are nine other villages with substantial non-Jola populations of Wolof, Manding and Sereer in them. These "strangers," predominantly Muslims, were allowed to settle in Esudadu-owned lands at the turn of the century in exchange for protection against slave raiders originating in the Jugut (Djougout), the region directly north of Esudadu (Baum 1987: 251–263). To this day, there is little sustained contact between Jola and non-Jola populations.

In the years that I was there, there were no other outsiders – either Jola born elsewhere in Esudadu, or other Jola, or representatives of other ethnic groups – living in Sambujat. The only "strangers" present were Fulani (Peul, Fula) herders who had been allowed to camp in village lands while guarding the community's cattle.

In 1972, the official Senegalese population census (Direction de la Statistique 1972) gave the population of the *arrondissement* of Loudia-Ouoloff (Luja Wolof) with jurisdiction over the Esudadu villages, as being 16,499. The Esudadu population itself was given as nearly 8,000 persons. More recent estimates (Baum 1987: 10) put the Esudadu population at about 12,000.[1] With densities of more than 60 persons per square kilometer, the Esudadu Jola are densely settled, especially by comparison with other West African rural peoples.

The land which the Esudadu farm is low lying and poorly drained. It is criss-crossed by numerous tidal creeks known in the geographical literature as *marigots*. These winding waterways are lined with mangrove vegetation that is well adapted to the brackish waters that ascend and descend the *marigots* with the daily tides. Formed by recent alluvial deposits, the *marigots* are broken up by two primary formations: sandy, slightly raised plateaus where the inhabitants construct their villages, pasture their animals and tap their palms for wine, and extensive depressions or low alluvial fans where the Esudadu Jola have their rice fields and their fishing ponds. Because of its low relief and coastal location, the Pointe St. George's area is continually exposed to saline conditions. Hence, the inhabitants are entirely dependent on the rains that fall from June to October to flush out the salts from their fields. In a good year, rainfall may be 2000 mm. or more, although during years of drought it is much less. When this happens, the fields usually become too salty. To keep tidal waters out of their fields, the Esudadu people must construct huge dikes along the bank of the *marigot*. To keep rainwater in their fields, they must surround each paddy with a low dike or bund. This involves much earth moving, draining and diking, which is done by slicing open or closing up the bunds, or by letting in freshwater

Plate 1: Aerial view of a large Esudadu community. (Courtesy M. and G. Bracher.)

through conduits made out of the trunk of the Borassus palm. Not surprisingly, the rice-growing system of the Esudadu Jola is extremely labor-intensive and full of risks.[2]

Unlike the Jola north of the Casamance River, the Esudadu grow rice as a monocrop. Because they get their cash from the sale of palm wine during the dry season (pp. 71–73), they need to cultivate little else. Jola wet-rice grows in standing water, in fields that are first inundated by the rains, then transplanted upon. There are different types of fields depending upon the type of soil, their location *vis-à-vis* the main drainage canals, their proximity to the *marigot* or to a freshwater spring, and so forth (Linares 1970, 1981). Table Ia lists the terms the inhabitants of Sambujat employ to refer to their agricultural practices. This list should give some indication of the degree to which the Esudadu system is specialized. Without this terminology it would be difficult, perhaps impossible, for them to explain, and for an outsider to understand, what is actually being done, where and by whom. The Esudadu use these terms regularly, in order to coordinate task-sequences in different sections of the rice fields, tasks which all have specific names. Thus they might say: "today I will do the *jaginden* [the building up of the bunds] in the *Dikosau* [an area used for nurseries]; my wife will pull out the weeds."

Rice cultivation follows a series of well-defined steps. First comes the preparation of the nurseries on which the rice seedlings are to be initially grown. Men build up the old bunds, and ridge and furrow each nursery with the *kanata*, a broad variant of the *kajandu* or fulcrum-shovel that all Jola men employ. It is rested on the knee while lifting up heavy clods of earth. The men also broadcast the rice seed and bury it. Their wives pull out the weeds and fertilize the nurseries with dung that has been head-loaded on baskets from the place where the cattle are corralled. Forest nurseries are somewhat simpler to prepare, for they lack dikes and are fertilized by palm fronds that are burned each year. One month to six weeks after nursery preparation has been completed, the seedlings, more than 30 cm high, are pulled out and taken to the fields, where they are transplanted. Because seedlings must be pulled out carefully lest their roots be damaged, this activity may take from one third to one half as much time as the actual transplanting.

In the literature on rice cultivation, transplanting is often described as the most labor-consuming and onerous task. The Esudadu Jola, however, consider transplanting to be more pleasurable than harvesting because it is done in watered fields, where the sun is less scorching. Transplanting may in fact take slightly less time per unit area than harvesting, even though both

Table Ia: *Principal steps in rice cultivation: Sambujat*

I. Steps in the cultivation process:

1. *Seeding and fertilizing the nurseries (female and male)*

    a. *basul elalak*: to pull out creeper-like weeds (*elalak*) (women and men by hand)

    b. *egáp*: to bury out grassy weeds (*essel*) (men with *kanata*)
    c. *etún*: to carry fertilizer (women)
    d. *kaliñen*: to spread fertilizer (women)
    e. *eyolen*: to "throw" or broadcast seed, (men)
    f. *ehuok*: to bury the seed (men)

2. *Bunding or diking (men with fulcrum shovel)*
    a. *jaginden*: to scrape off the inner side of a bund, lift earth and weeds and turn them over on top of the bund.
    b. *jakeel*: to scrape old vegetation from sides and top of bund, and throw it in the furrow.
    c. *jabet*: to split up the old bund and make it narrower by cutting it down on the sides.

3. *Cutting the sluices (men with fulcrum shovel)*
    a. *ephalen*: to slice bunds to remove a chunk of earth 15 cm. or 80 wide; water usually rushes out.
    b. *katoij*: to replace the chunk of earth in order to plug up the bund.

4. *Ridging and furrowing (men with fulcrum shovel)*
    a. *ewañ* (*kawañer*): general word for cultivating with any of the fulcrum shovels; to split the old ridges down the middle, dig a shallow furrow on the sides, lift the earth and bury the weeds on top of new ridge; results in a flat, broad preliminary ridge.
    b. *emeheng*: to add earth and bury weeds.
    c. *ehuok* or *kahuoy*: to dig into the furrows, lift up the earth and build up ridges higher.

5. *Pulling out plants and transplanting (women by hand)*
    a. *ebuc*: (to "pull out") rice from the nurseries
    b. *ekoiñ*: to transplant

6. *Harvesting (women and men)*
    a. *eiim*: to cut each panicle off the stalk with a knife, gather the panicles on the left hand and place each small handful on the ground. Done by female.
    b. *ekok emano*: to tie (*ekok*) *emano* (rice) using the center vein of the *Borassus* palm leaf into a bundle weighing 3 to 5 kg. Done by male.
    c. *buteb emano*: to carry paddy rice home.

II. Sequence of practices done during each of the main agricultural phases.

   1. Preparation of wet nurseries by technique called *eyolen*: 1a or 1b; 1c; 2a; 4a; 1d; 1e; 4c. Preparation of dry forest nurseries by technique called *bujus*: 1a or 1b; 1d; 4c.
   2. Preparation of paddy land (bunting, sluicing, ridging): 2a or 2b, or 2c; 3a and 3b; 4a and 4b.
   3. Pulling out plants and transplanting: 5a and 5b.
   4. Harvesting, tying up bundles and taking them home: 6a, 6b, 6c.

The power of the spirit-shrines 21

Plate 2: Father and son ridge the paddy fields (top). Wife and daughter transplant upon them (bottom).

activities involve handling each rice plant individually. In transplanting, a person – usually a woman but occasionally also a man – holds a handful of seedlings in the left hand, transfers them one by one to the right hand, and buries each plant with a thrust of the thumb. The seedlings are planted on the ridges, which at this point may be covered by ten or more centimeters of water. The person doing the planting usually walks backwards, burying plants at the average rate of 50 to 60 plants a minute.

Two days to one week prior to transplanting, the men prepare the parcels. Field preparation involves bunding, ridging and furrowing the land. To prepare heavy soils, an Esudadu man uses the other type of fulcrum shovel (the *kaŋom*) having the most curved scoop. He lifts sizeable clods of earth that are still covered with the weeds and rice stubble from the previous year. He then turns them over as he drops them on the ground, thus burying the old vegetation which rots and becomes fertilizer. The purpose of ridging, on the other hand, is to protect the seedlings from excessive salinity. Ridge cultivation of paddy is practiced in many parts of the world where saline tidal lands are used (Grist 1965: 78–79). Some men regularly taste the water impounded in their deep fields, located near the *marigot*, to determine their salinity. If the water is judged to be too salty, it is drained out of the parcel via a sluice in the bund, and rainwater is allowed to come in for a few days. Although the Esudadu Jola prevent brackish *marigot* water from entering their rice fields at all times of the year, it is not unusual for the big dike that serves to contain tidal *marigot* waters to break in spots, allowing salt water to invade some parcels. If this happens, the rice crop is ruined. However, not all water management in the Esudadu area is confined to keeping tidal waters out of cultivated areas. There is also a great deal of impounding, draining and distributing freshwater from rains and springs by means of canals and sluices.[3]

As the rice grows, the water in the parcels dries up until the rice is ready to be harvested. Harvesting is less exhausting than preparing or transplanting the land, but it can be an anxious time for the farmer. The threat of damage by birds, and the fear that rice plants would either lodge (i.e. fall), or become overly ripe if allowed to stand for too long, makes harvest-time the most serious labor bottleneck of the agricultural year. For this reason, it often requires the use of associative (i.e. cooperative or communal) labor. All harvesting is done with the help of a small knife; panicles are cut individually at the rate of 40 to 50 plants a minute, then piled up on the bunds. Once harvested, the handfulls are put on the ridges under the hot sun to dry for two or three days, after which time the panicles are tied into bundles. Each of the resultant bundles (*kukoken* pl., *fukoken* sing., from the verb *koken*, to attach something) weighs anywhere from 3.0 to 4.5 kilograms (kgs,) depending on the rice variety being harvested. Tied in this fashion, the piled-up rice bundles can be carefully guarded from birds. Left in the Esudadu fields to dry for several days to several weeks, the rice bundles are taken back home in baskets to be stored in the granaries. I have calculated that in a "normal" (non-drought year) the Esudadu fields yield an average of 2,000 to 2,500 kg. of rice per hectare, which compares favorably with yields obtained in much of the Far East and Southeast Asia before the Green Revolution.

However, since the Esudadu Jola do not employ draft animals or the plough, their rice-growing practices require a great deal of manual labor to be invested during a relatively short rainy season lasting five months. I have calculated that women invest an average of 105 work-days a hectare, and men an average of 108 work-days a hectare, during the rainy season in all tasks connected with their rice fields (except walking back and forth from home).[4] Since a couple cultivates from 1 to 1½ hectares of land each year, they have to invest a great deal of time in production during peak periods. And this is without taking into account the long hours they spend doing associative work for others.

Ideational aspects of "power": the spirit-shrines

Few of us would disagree that power is one of the most overworked, fuzziest, and as Max Weber put it, "sociologically amorphous" concepts in the social sciences. Yet it can still be made to serve useful ends if some attempt is made to spell out the ways in which this concept is used in particular contexts. For our purpose here, Giddens' concept of power (1979: 88–94) as a relational concept built into all social institutions, is particularly pertinent. It helps to bring actors (i.e. society), resources (i.e. the economy) and social control (i.e. politics) into a dynamic relationship. "Power is the capacity to achieve outcomes; whether or not these are connected to purely sectional interests is not germane to its definition" (Giddens 1984: 257). Power relations unfold through the medium of resources. These can be of two types: "allocative" and "authoritative" (1981: 49–68; 1984: 14–16, 256–262). "Allocative" resources are material resources, which includes raw materials and other features of the environment, the instruments of production, and the objects and artifacts that are produced through human labor. "Authoritative" resources derive from the ability of some actors to harness the activities of other actors. This emphasis on power as guiding strategic conduct through its capacity to transform and re-direct resources is useful in the analysis of forms of social control in Sambujat society.

Within the Sambujat political economy, control over allocative resources is ultimately in the hands of the spirit-shrines (the *bakiin* sing., *ukiin*) and their representatives, the shrine-keepers (*awasen*, sing., *kuwasen* pl.; from the verb *kawasen*, to sacrifice, to pour libations of palm wine). They control authoritative resources. Through the authority that shrine-keepers possess by virtue of being the elders of the community, the spirit-shrines are implicated in the regulation of land, labor and crops. In this role, they can be a medium through which group interests are realized, as when they answer prayers to bring rain and ensure abundant harvests for everyone. Or they can be an instrument of individual promotion, as when they take sides in litigations over land and cattle. Whatever they may do, the effectiveness of the spirit-shrines as agents of social and economic control depends in large measure on the cultural constructs that surround them. That is, on the particular concepts and attributes they are invested with. For the qualities they are thought to possess define the powers they are thought to command.[5]

To my queries concerning what forms the spirit-shrines take I usually received evasive answers. This kind of knowledge is a well guarded secret, especially so if the inquirer is a woman.[6] Nonetheless, several elders were willing to assert that "the *ukiin* were not persons." Rather, they were a "*seytaan kati karamba*" (using a Catholic metaphor, a kind of Satan of the forest), humanlike but not quite.[7] Most important, the spirit-shrines can be male or female. This reflects the kind of gender equality that underlies much of Sambujat social life. Spirit-shrines are polyvalent, multifunctional and able to be courted on both sides of the good and evil continuum. They are certainly not ancestral figures, however, for ancestors do not play an important role in Sambujat culture even though they can hover around on the peripheries when a shrine is being propitiated. Even though there are some shrineless spirits, and some old shrines whose spirits have left them, a spirit is usually closely associated with its shrine. The Jola word for both is the same, and for this reason spirit and shrine are to be used interchangeably, or in combination throughout this discussion.[8]

The inhabitants of Sambujat often disagree over the "real" nature of the spirit-shrines, not because they lack a set of consistent beliefs concerning the nature of men and the world as Middleton (1960: 25) says of the Lugbara of Uganda, but because the spirits are political as well as economic symbols, to be acquired, maintained and manipulated with care. One spirit-shrine may well be more powerful than another, but which is *the* most powerful is not always agreed upon. Not everyone ranks the spirits in precisely the same order of importance, nor are people clear as to when a shrine has passed under someone else's control. Shrines can be "bought," or reluctantly taken over, can be created as well as discarded. Thus they are constantly in a state of flux, not only because they are constantly changing hands, but also because their fortunes may wax and wane. Once a spirit-shrine is set up it should be taken care of regularly. Otherwise it can bring misfortune if it feels it is being ignored. A spirit-shrine may be brought into social prominence, may be neglected, transported to another area, duplicated *sur place*, or may even change form and function. The spirit-shrines can refuse to be reasoned with, cajoled, harnessed or pleaded to. Hence, by their very nature, the *ukiin* must be managed. Their moods and behavior must be interpreted. This makes the authority of elders unavoidable and necessary.

Although Jola elders constantly affirm that the spirit-shrines are few, in reality (if one counts them), they are quite numerous. Baum's own inquiries yielded 48 different types of shrines in one (admittedly large) Kajinol ward. In his own words (Baum 1987: 389-390):

Almost every economic activity of the community has a spirit shrine associated with it, be it palm wine tapping, fishing, blacksmithing, or farming. Other shrines are important for healing, either as diagnostic shrines or for healing specific disorders. Many others are concerned with the perennial problems of rain, crop fertility, and the fertility of women. There are several shrines associated with war, the well-being of the community, and the village councils.

Similarly, my inquiries revealed the presence of numerous spirit-shrines in the much smaller community of Sambujat. But only a few seem to be very powerful. These are approached regularly to ask for rain, a good harvest, lots of cattle. Other important shrines are charged with surveying the rice fields and guarding the herds. Still others protect the rice crop against thieves. Some shrines are approached in case of a dispute between two or more individuals. Yet others punish those who have breached serious moral interdictions. And before there were courts of law, a special spirit was in charge of punishing those who committed the heinous crime of murder.

An actual example may help to clarify the political and economic constructs surrounding an important Sambujat shrine. *Hupila* is the "increase" shrine *par excellence*.[9] It is involved with the productive and reproductive activities of the *hank*, the social group that lives around a common courtyard and shares in most corporate tasks. *Hupila* is thought of as a father with children. The "father" is housed in a small but conspicuous structure at the entrance to the courtyard; the "children" are housed within the particular dwellings of each household head. *Hupila* is concerned with the welfare of the co-resident group of agnates or semi-agnates. Members of the *hank* can ask it for money, a good palm wine harvest, more children. *Hupila* also protects them from evil actions by members of another *hank*. During marriage negotiations, the groom must contribute palm wine and a pig to be sacrificed at the bride's *Hupila* shrine. Within each courtyard group, the eldest functioning male agnate is in charge of the shrine. On its behalf, he continuously performs the libation ritual (*kawasen*) using palm wine. In short, the rituals surrounding *Hupila*, as well as other corporate symbols,[10] enliven and reproduce the social relations that characterize the *hank* as a residential unit (see p. 65).

It would be tempting to interpret the cultural constructs that are built upon such shrines as *Hupila* in terms of Durkheim's influential theory concerning the role of collective representations in building up social consensus. For it is clear that at some level *Hupila* "represents" the *hank* or collectivity of male agnates living around a common courtyard, who act solidarily on many occasions. But, the *hank* is also the focus of much individual competition and small-group dissent. Corporate symbols like *Hupila* do not by themselves perform social work. They do not "bind" all members of the co-resident group into one solidary community. Most rites surrounding *Hupila*, for example, exclude the in-married women. In some circumstances, such as when a married woman is menstruating, she must leave her husband's *hank* lest *Hupila* will "grab" her. These rites also exclude matrilateral kin, temporary visitors and so forth. In fact, shrines cannot operate as common symbols simply because they are ambiguous; they can be courted on all sides. In lining up with one "faction," or with one individual in society, shrines automatically disassociate themselves from another sub-group.

In describing Sambujat's religious system, one must constantly shift the focus back and forth, from the shrines as collective symbols to the shrine-keepers as agents involved in a continuous struggle to mediate in power relationships. Elders provide different kinds of services by interpreting and mediating in spirit attacks upon errant members of the community. For, in the Esudadu context, as well as that of many other African groups, if someone has done something wrong, that is if he or she has committed a breach of the moral or social order, a spirit-shrine is made responsible for the initial punishment. But it is widely recognized that shrine-keepers and other members of the community also play a central role in these encounters. Through rites of redressment, political struggles between

The power of the spirit-shrines 27

power seekers, and individual struggles between wealth seekers, are played out in an open arena. This allows social life to continue by allowing grievances to be aired and resolved temporarily. But it neither "causes" social cohesion at the end, nor makes the underlying social forces that promote conflict to miraculously disappear.

Plate 3: The *Hupila* shrine guards the entrance to the courtyard.

The authority of elders

The sorts of attributes that the Esudadu Jola ascribe to the spirit-shrines are different from the kinds of qualities that they demand from the shrine-keepers of officiants. For though spirits and keepers both have *sembe* (strength, power), a shrine is often praised for being *jakut* (mean, bad or evil) whereas this is never said of its keeper. Certainly, things, or deeds, or even persons may be *jakut* (though this is a terrible thing to say of anyone), but an elder who is a shrine-keeper is thought of as doing his duty. On the other hand, such a person is not ordinarily described as *kasum* (good, sweet) either. What shrine-keepers may be said to have is authority, a quality that requires social skill, legitimacy and political support from the congregation. Insofar as they may be said to have political power, they wield this power in rather subtle ways, as interpreters and intermediaries in spirit attacks and not as independent decision makers.

As cultural constructs imbued with mystical sorts of power, the Sambujat spirit-shrines can bring illness or bestow favors upon individuals or groups. The elders of the community, however, have the earthly duty to mediate in these encounters. They have the ritual authority to diagnose maladies, identify the spiritual agents responsible for them and officiate in rites of atonement. In short, they command authoritative resources. In being thus involved, the elders help to enforce working relations within the community, and by doing so they help to keep the labor force in working order.

No other events lower the productive capacity of individuals or groups more than sickness and, of course, death. Hundreds of working hours a year are lost due to illness. Two days out of every week are spent attending funerals. "Curing" illness and preventing death by mediating between those afflicted and the shrines responsible is a primary duty of elders. Elders also help to reproduce the social relations of production by interceding with the spirits at the time of marriage, procreation and the birth of children. And elders not only officiate in rituals designed to protect resources and improve outputs (larger harvests, better yielding palms, more cattle); they also encourage production and force redistribution by constantly demanding offers of palm wine and animals to be sacrificed at the shrines. Finally, elders encourage overproduction and the storing of large amounts of rice by officiating in life-crisis rituals. In short, in all these contexts, the elders play a crucial role in the political economy of the community.

For these reasons, Jola society south of the Casamance River is often referred to in studies as a gerontocracy. Because only elders can perform a sacrifice, elders have *de facto* control over resources. Once married, a young man must contribute at least one pig, but often two or three, to be sacrificed at the beginning of the rains if he wants to participate in the distributory rituals of the community. This ceremony (the *kaalok*) can be interpreted as a "ticket" for becoming a member of the men's collectivity. If not performed, there will be places where elders go to conduct sacrifices and share in the feasting that junior men cannot go.[11] In "the daily participation in ritual life and the socializing afterwards, the elders become a cohesive group" (Baum 1987: 391). They dictate the rules of inclusion to their "club" and make sure that younger men who are eager to join them go through the proper steps before they are admitted. Though elders monopolize the ritual positions, the existence of several shrines allows for a "broad access to religious authority . . . chances are excellent that any given individual will become an elder or priest of at least one shrine" (Baum 1987: 390).

This does not mean, however, that elders do not compete over the control of some of the most important shrines. The two different versions given in the following extract, recounting how an elder of Sambujat brought the Manga shrine to the village, illustrates how active this competition really is:

I was told by Abel that his paternal grandfather Assimbassen had "made" [i.e. installed] Manga in Sambujat [at the *Kékenin hank*] because he thought Jilamba, another community shrine, was getting too big; it had too many people around it, requiring the sharing of much sacrificial meat and palm wine. However, a different version of why Manga was installed at Sambujat was provided by a non-relative of Assimbassen. He said that on some occasion Assimbassen was not allowed to "talk" at Jilamba. That is, to express his views over a particular incident involving a theft. He had a heated argument with the shrine's officiant as well as with the entire congregation. Then he left for a neighboring village, where he sacrificed a cow and brought Manga here. If someone wants the shrine, they would have to "buy" it from him, and they would have to pay dearly.

Thus, conflict and competition over political space in the conduct of community affairs may be at the root of seeking to attract a shrine. But political ambition also has a price. The person who takes over a *bakiin* must have the means with which to make a sacrifice. Some shrines require heavy payments, over long periods of time:

Jata is in the process of taking over *Bukut*, the powerful shrine associated with the boys' initiation. He was "trapped" by it a few years ago. Jata says he has already sacrificed five pigs; three for the members of the ward or *kalol*, one for the women, and one for people from the neighboring community, who came to teach him how to do the shrine. He still has at least a pig and a cow to go. But he has already begun to do the *kawasen* (the pouring of libations) at the spot in the sacred forest where the shrine has its "head." "If you don't go there and pour palm wine upon it [the *bakiin*], it will leave you," he told me. Jata's assistant, Wosin, owes *Bukut* three pigs but he keeps postponing their sacrifice. I was assured that he will ultimately be forced to do it or the spirit will trap him.

Once a shrine is established, the elder who officiates in its rituals (the *awasen*) comes under the watchful eye of the congregation. When in the cycle of obligatory sacrifices is a particular elder acknowledged to have "taken over" the shrine? How well does he take care of it afterwards? Is he carrying a supplicant's wishes to the spirit effectively? These sorts of judgments are continually being made.

However, it is not only the shrine-keeper or officiant who is dependent upon his "congregation" for legitimacy and support. The spirit-shrines themselves are also dependent upon the expertise of the officiants that attend to them for their prestige. "A particularly wise or adept shrine elder may give the shrine a reputation for power far beyond what it had enjoyed under previous elders" (Baum 1987: 388). Because an elder may bring as much prominence to a shrine as the reverse, succession to the post of *awasen* of a major shrine can be crucial:

The *ai* or ritual elder of Sambujat went by as I was watching a wrestling match between the local youths and those of a neighboring village. A woman spectator from the other village who was sitting next to me remarked: "There goes the *ai*. He has a very mean *bakiin* under control. This time they chose him well."

The moment the acting officiant of a shrine dies, a successor must be found for him. Ritual succession is not automatic, however; there is often more than one incumbent for a position – especially so when the spirit-shrine is a major and well-established one. Within a particular *hank* or courtyard group, the post of shrine-keeper or *awasen* is always passed down in a zig-zag fashion: from brother to real or classificatory brother, or to brother's son; never in a straight linear fashion from father to son; though, of course, it does pass from grandfather to grandson. For father–son succession to take place would be to risk having too much ritual power concentrated within a single family. The following example illustrates how control over the *Hupila* shrine mentioned before has actually devolved:

The *Hupila* spirit-shrine of the Bajetelup *hank* is in the hands of Sisimañ, the oldest functioning elder. The former incumbent was Asumbatin, Jisalo's FFB. When he died, Sisimañ was just a child. So the shrine was held in trust by Salo, his FB. Salo had a son, but he was considered by the elders to be shifty and inept. When Sisimañ was a married man with children, *Hupila* "grabbed" him. His entire body hurt for months. Then he took the shrine over and sacrificed to it; one cow, two pigs and a

The power of the spirit-shrines 31

dog. The dog is there because it bites and growls to protect the house, like *Hupila* should.

Thus, when the elder officiant of a shrine dies, the spirit signals his successor by "trapping" him with an illness. But many potential incumbents can and do fall ill. In the matter of exactly who gets to succeed, the elders who monopolize the shrines have a good deal of say.

In the general course of community life spirits are constantly bringing afflictions by "grabbing" persons (*buyok*, from the verb *kayoken*, to tire, to make someone suffer) with various kinds of illnesses, some major, some minor. When a spirit "grabs" someone, the immediate problem becomes to determine which spirit is responsible. To learn this, the sick person usually consults the officiant of the *Buwinko* spirit, the divinatory shrine *par excellence*. Thomas (1959: 600) has already described this procedure.

In view of the argument I shall be making for the ritual equality of Sambujat men and women, it is important to note here that from 1964, when I first visited Sambujat, to my last visit in 1990, the "chief" of the *Buwinko* divinatory shrine has been a woman. Kina is clairvoyant; she will "dream" which particular *bakiin* has "grabbed" a particular person and urge him/her to approach its officiant, its *awasen*. The latter will prescribe the number of animals (how many chickens, how many pigs, a bull, or perhaps several of these in combination), and the amount of palm wine, which the "culprit" must contribute to be sacrificed. At the propitiatory ritual, the person who has transgressed – who has been trapped by the spirit and is ill – confesses and asks to be pardoned. The officiant speaks to the spirit on behalf of the "culprit" while pouring palm wine upon the shrine. He/she entreats it to "let go" of the person, to be satisfied. Then he kills the sacrificial animals. Together with the palm wine, meat from the sacrificial animals is consumed by members of the ritual congregation represented by the particular shrine.[12]

Obviously, in the sacrifice (the *kawasen*), the principles that determine membership in, or exclusion from, specific social groups are constantly being reinforced and often re-defined by the act of food sharing. In point of fact, the Esudadu Jola tend to describe their shrines in terms of who can, or more often who cannot, be present at a particular libation rite (the *kawasen*), when can he or she eat of the sacrificial meat, where and what kind of morsel? Men (young or old) who have not undergone the aforementioned *kaalok* rite cannot participate in the rituals presided over by the paramount ritual elder or *ai*. And young unmarried women, or women who have not given birth, cannot be present at the ceremonies for the *Sihuñ* or female shrines. Moreover, all mature women and uncircumcised children are excluded from some rituals connected with the principal male-controlled shrines.[13] At these, they cannot be present, nor eat the meat or drink the wine. Nonetheless in many instances, such as the sacrifices that precede taking over the *bukut* or boys' circumcision shrine, they can be given meat from an animal sacrificed expressedly for them.[14] And there are some major, male-controlled shrines at which women and children can and do eat. A woman can always have a male shrine done on behalf of her son. A man can also be present at the rituals conducted at the female shrines on behalf of his offspring. Thus, the overlapping congregations that participate in the rituals surrounding the shrines may, at different times and for different purposes, include all the members of a *hank*, only the men of a certain ward, men and women combined, men plus children and young girls, only members of the patrigroup (the *buayu*), local persons and nearby villagers, all the in-married women, the small circle of relatives of a person who has fallen ill, and so forth.

Sharing food and drink at the shrines is not only a socio-symbolic statement, it is also a material, practical statement. For it is a very effective way of making sure that in this competitive and highly individualistic society resources are circulated. The Jola never kill an animal for home consumption. They insist upon the need to always take a chicken, a pig or a bull to a shrine, to be sacrificed and shared with others. "Each time there is a ritual at a particular shrine, the priests, elders, supplicants, and anyone who has the right to drink at the shrine will gather, perform the rite and then socialize over the palm wine afterwards" (Baum 1987: 391). Hardly a day goes by without one Sambujat shrine or another being propitiated on behalf of someone or another. This means that people are constantly circulating, coming together to share food and drink in groups whose composition varies from one instance to another. These informal occassions provide an ideal setting for the widespread exchange of information and gossip. But they also signify that the decisions the elders have taken concerning particular cases of wrongdoing have been understood and, at least in principle, accepted.

It must be emphasized that elders do not make the everyday decisions of the community. This is done by all mature men in consultation. Elders do not enrich themselves or their kin, nor do they take the law into their own hands. They cannot be said to "police" the actions of members of the community directly. Rather, the role of shrine-keeper is one of mediating in conflictive situations and "translating" the intentions, the wishes, the purposes of the spirits into practical, punitive action. But punishment is not executed through threats or even confiscation of property, ill-obtained or otherwise. What elders do is force public confession, impose redistributive fines, compel persons to realize that they cannot promote their own selfish interests at the expense of the rights of others, or of the public good. Only indirectly can the Sambujat shrine-keepers be said to exert "political" power. Their roles are thus in a sense unique; they do not resemble the roles played by elders in other African societies in all respects. In part, because the Sambujat elders are not ancestors, they operate under particularly severe kinds of constraints. There are stringent checks and balances placed upon their freedom of action.

For example, a person who feels that someone in the community has outraged him can go to a spirit-shrine directly, without passing through a shrine-keeper, and seek retribution. He or she steals into the night and at the designated shrine performs a sacrifice while saying something like this:

Bakiin, I come to greet you. So and so has done me wrong. Catch him, Make him ill. Make his wife ill. Make his children ill. Make his cattle ill, etc. etc.
(Thomas, Luneau and Doneaux 1969: 190–191; my translation)

However, the spirit-shrines do not waste their time with petty disputes, or minor transgressions such as lying. Most of the time they intervene only when serious breaches of the social order have been committed. For this reason, the shrines are described as the "Europeans," the "whites" (*kululum*) of the Jola, because they keep peace. Only when one of the parties in a dispute gets angry and goes to a shrine to accuse someone else of wrongdoing will the spirit intervene. If it does so, it will "trap" whoever is the guilty person. It is only at this point that an elder comes into action. If the person who has socially transgressed and is "trapped" by a spirit refuses to make amends, his agnates will take one of his rice fields, exchange it for a bull and bring it to the shrine-keeper to be sacrificed.

The spirits trap (*bujok*) individuals for a variety of different reasons. I have already mentioned two circumstances: when the shrine needs an officiant because the past incumbent has died, or when a shrine that has been neglected wants to be occupied. These instances of spirit attack reflect the ever present state of competition which characterizes Sambujat social life, including the lives of office holders themselves. There are also other reasons of a less straightforward "political" nature for why a spirit should trap somebody. They have to do with major offenses being committed by ordinary individuals against the moral tenets of the community. More often than not, it concerns breaking a major taboo; something that he or she would die of if a proper sacrifice and libation ritual (the *kawasen*) were not performed on his or her behalf. For example, a man seeing a woman give birth or telling a young boy the facts of life, an uncircumcised youth entering the sacred forest, a woman learning the secrets of the male initiation ceremony or not observing the menstrual taboos. Punishment can be retroactive. A person's father's father may have seen something he shouldn't, or talked to a woman or child about something that happened in the sacred forest, or he may have eaten sacrificial meat or touched a sacred object when he shouldn't, and his grandson many years later may be "trapped" by a shrine and be under the obligation to sacrifice.

Another class of serious offenses are aggressive acts committed by one individual against another member of the community. Frequently, these acts involve property or products, and for that reason they impair directly the proper functioning of the economy. The first offense is stealing, for which the spirits can punish with death. However, it is not easy to steal a person's land, his palm grove or even his cattle. Usually, everyone in the community knows what parcels, which cows, what palms belong to whom. Litigation over rights to land surfaces on those occasions when the situation is unclear. For example, when a man dies leaving only small sons behind, his patrimony should be held in trust by one of his brothers. At the time when the sons become old enough to marry, their "uncle" must turn over the rice fields to them. But the "uncle" may refuse to do so, saying they were his:

Sumbutin was the only surviving son of Assimbajat. He was barely out of the sacred forest [where he was circumcised] when his father suddenly died. As is customary, his father's brother, Akatido, who had married his brother's widow according to the *kataor* or widow remarriage convention, was left as a custodian of Assimbajat's patrimony. When Sumbutin married, he asked his paternal "uncle" Akatido, to return his fields. The latter had been cultivating his deceased brother's fields all along, as is customary. Akatido refused to return the fields, claiming they were his. Since there were no elders alive who had witnessed what had happened, it was Sumbutin's word, backed by his mother (she was in-married agnate), against Akatido's word. Months went by and nothing happened. Then the *bakiin* "grabbed" Akatido. His head ached, he could not move his legs, his stomach swelled. He went to the divinatory shrine, *Buwinko*, and there it was divined that the *Bakiin* Enak was responsible. But he still refused to accept his guilt and sacrifice. His brothers of the *hank* were forced to take one of his heftiest bulls, two of his pigs, and in addition contribute fifty of their own liters of palm wine to the shrine. There, Sulatof, the *awasen* in charge of Enak, conducted the sacrifice. The elders were all present, and many visitors from the adjacent village. Only then did Akatido confess what they already suspected, mainly that he had kept his nephew's fields unlawfully. Once the fields went back to Sumbutin, Akatido began to gain back his strength.

Not only land but also cattle may be "stolen" by a deceased man's brothers. With cattle, it is often another category of spirits, namely the immediate ancestors who have control of the *Kuhuluŋ* shrine, who intervene. The ancestors are not the same as the spirits, though they often hover around at night when a shrine is being propitiated. Otherwise, the dead should stay far away, in Guiné Bissau, the region to which the Esudadu trace their origins. It is not advisable for any person to contact them too frequently. But there are times when an individual must do so (the following case was told to me by a Sambujat elder):

Ndongo of the Esudadu village of Mlomp was very young when his father died. He grew up among his "uncles." One day, while he was in Guiné Bissau tapping wine [during the slack season the men often go to other areas to do the *kawaw*] he entered one of the sacred forests where the Mlomp ancestors are supposed to live. There, he sang his father's song. The father appeared and identified himself. He asked his son "have my brothers given you the cattle I left you"? The son said no, and his father advised him to ask them for it. He gave his son money with which to return and presents for his mother (the deceased's widow). He told his son never to come back. When Ndongo asked his "uncles" to turn over his cattle to him, they tried to give him only half. But when they tried to do so – to separate the herd with one half going to one side of the courtyard, half to the other side – the herd would not come apart. They tried time and time again, but the cattle would not separate. They were finally obliged to give the entire herd to their nephew. "It was Ndongo's dead father who was in the ceiling doing this," I was assured.

[There was a sequel to the story, however. Ndongo's mother, greedy for more presents, told him to go back to his father the next year. Ndongo did so. His father appeared again and "put his hand on his head." Ndongo died two days after he returned. "If you go to Guiné Bissau where the ancestors live, they will put their hands on your head and you will die."]

The case recounted above not only illustrates the fact that brothers and their respective sons are often in conflict over matters of inheritance. It also warns against excessive ambition. The spirit-shrines do not lend themselves readily to being manipulated by greedy individuals who want more than their due. Rather, they are supposed to reward the deserving while protecting the weak and the unsuspecting.

Another occasion when the spirits may intervene is when a person, who seems unable to rear anything, gives someone a heifer to rear for him. If the latter refuses to return the animal once it's grown, the owner goes to a shrine to do the palm wine libation and put a "curse" on the thief.

Besides guarding the rice fields from thieves, the spirit-shrines also protect the rice crop. There are several spirits, not just one, which guard the fields, the crop, the tools used in cultivation, the seed for next year's planting and so forth. They do so wherever these items are, on the fields or in the granary. It should be relatively easy for a thief to steal the bundles of rice that are left on the fields after the harvest to dry. And it would also be possible for a thief to enter a man's granary and steal the rice stored there,

36 *The political economy of Sambujat*

sometimes in large quantities; or steal his tools. For, during the height of the agricultural season, people leave their houses unattended from dawn to dusk. That more people do not steal someone else's crop or his tools is because they are afraid of what the shrines would do:

Silañibo tells me that there are many thieves in the village. *Bare pankuloli bakiin* ("but they will be afraid of the shrine"). Thus, he is not at all worried if someone tells him that he will steal his rice tonight. The shrine Enak, and also Sijak, will trap the thief and he or she will confess. I have noticed that he never locks the door to his granary, where he has many hundreds of kilograms of rice stored; as well as his cultivating tools. People go in and out of his house when he is away in the fields. But they never go near his granary. "Stealing is stealing," he added, "whether you take the rice in the fields or in the house."

A preoccupation with theft, reflected in the various spirits that safeguard against it, is only one aspect of the general concern with private property. Another aspect of the competitive nature of Sambujat, and indeed of all Esudadu society, is the pervasive belief in witchcraft (something concerning the *kummahl*, the *asay*). Beneath the apparent amiability of Sambujat social life there is a great deal of suspicion that witchcraft is being directed by envious persons at those individuals who are rich in resources, be these rice fields, cattle, palm groves, crops or children. Although such feelings are rarely expressed verbally, the fact remains that envy can kill. An envious person can begin by "eating" a person's children, poisoning his cattle, drying up his palms, and at the end killing the owner through witchcraft. Contrary to other African peoples, however, the Esudadu Jola do not have complex beliefs surrounding witchcraft, its expression and its cure. They do not engage in spectacular witch hunts nor in direct accusations. Instead, it is believed that a man's classificatory "brothers," with whom he co-resides in the same courtyard or *hank*, are often responsible for using witchcraft against him, and there is often not much that he can do, except be on the lookout:

Boisal lost his vision in one eye when an old musket exploded in his face at a funeral. "Someone put something in the gunpowder," he told me. When his gifted son went to pass his school exam, his pen refused to write. He finally borrowed a pen from his teacher and passed with flying colors. Both of the witches, Boisal revealed to me, were his "brothers," one of them living next-door. If you "have something" (i.e. if you are successful) you must always be on your guard.

The most effective remedy against witchcraft, however, resides again with the power of the spirit-shrines as it is mediated by their representatives. It is widely believed that the shrines were created in order to protect individuals against the witchcraft of others. Palm wine tappers, for example, are particularly vulnerable to all forms of mystical aggression since they must climb high and fast with only a hoop for support. When a tapper falls, which occurs rather frequently, someone back at home is immediately suspected of having used witchcraft against him. Young men are thus in dire need of protection when they go off during the dry season to tap palms in foreign lands:

> Ebetemai and Sumetelu are gathering palm wine in the Kalunay are this year. Like many of their cohorts, they go up into Muslim territory, where people are forbidden from drinking palm wine (though they often drink millet-beer, which lacks the association with the shrines) and obtain permission to tap the palms in exchange for gathering the fruit for the owners. Part of the essential gear they carry with them is the *bakiin* called Manga. As soon as they arrive at their collecting station, they sink a small carved stake into the ground. Around it they build a shrine of mounded earth, chicken feathers, and a small horn filled with medicines. Before they climb to "bleed" their first palm and put their collecting gourds in place, they kill a rooster and pour palm wine upon the shrine. Each day before they climb, they must pour additional palm wine on the shrine.

Economic pursuits are dangerous; wealth may be a blessing or a menace. In the task of protecting persons and things, the spirit-shrines can be highly effective. On the other hand, they can also fail miserably. If so, they may be reprimanded by an elder (Thomas, Luneau and Doneaux 1969: 66–67);

> Kuhuluŋ [the ancestor shrine] you have allowed the witch to eat [the soul of] X. Now his spirit is spoiled [he has gone insane]. He cannot work. He cannot honor you. He molests the children. He terrorizes the women of the concession. What good are you? What good did it do to offer you *bunuk* [i.e. palm wine]? One cannot trust you. Bad, bad, bad.

Thus, there is a direct link between the spirits and the protection of various resources. And spirit protection may continue even after death. For it sometimes comes to pass that a man, before dying, will go to a shrine and put a curse on his land, to ban his brothers from using his rice fields after he dies. He does this if he thinks that his brothers were more "powerful" than him, preventing him from having lots of children, or killing them through witchcraft. Or if he thinks they did not take good care of him in old age. The dying man usually places the curse in secret. This was described to me as follows: "If by chance his relatives did not take care of him, he goes to the *bakiin* during the night. He pours libations at the shrine while saying: I am old. Because I don't have an *acokoola* (someone to take care of him), if I die, anyone who cultivates my rich fields will also die." Since nobody saw the dying man place the curse, there is no way that it can be lifted by sacrificing an animal to the shrine. If his brothers want to lift the curse placed on the land, they will try to find out what shrine did it (i.e. where the curse was placed) and who is its officiant. If somehow they find out that it was the spirit called Enak, they will go to a man named Musabeli; if it was Kalem, they will go to the ritual elder (the *ai*). The brothers will be told what they have to pay; one or two bulls, a pig or several chicken. When they pay, they will be able to cultivate; if they don't, they won't:

> There were two brothers from the *hank* called Hojok who died, leaving behind no sons or obvious inheritors. There were several possible family branches that could inherit, however, but one family alone insisted that it should inherit all the deceased man's fields. The other side argued that the land should be equally distributed. The debate raged on and got so heated that both sides went to look for their spears. They were ready to fight when the elders of the village separated them.
>
> The only surviving descendant of the two brothers was an *ariimen* (a sister or female agnate). She took over the fields temporarily (women don't inherit land) and went to a *bakiin* to put a curse on them. Nobody saw her; perhaps she went to Enak, perhaps to Kalembekiin. Subsequently she died.
>
> To this day, nobody dares put a foot on the land. Even if one cultivates the fields next-door, one dares not cross the boundaries. For everyone knows that if he cultivates the disputed area without lifting the curse he would die.

Thus, through the elders who are charged with their "care," the spirit-shrines regulate land transactions, safeguard the cattle, guard against theft, punish mystical aggression. But spirits do not simply act as social deterrents. They can also be approached to ask for things: more cattle, more children, an abundant harvest. If after sacrificing to a spirit through its keeper you don't get what you want, the spirit will apologize and you will go to another shrine. In all this, elders play an essential role. By virtue of their association with powerful symbols, the elders help resolve the political and economic tensions that inevitably arise in the course of community life.

Waxing and waning powers: the "priest–king" or *ai* (*eii, oeyi*) and the chief (*aseefaw*)

Changes in a political economy often entail changes in power relationships. The inhabitants of Esudadu and neighboring communities speak of a time in the not so distant past when the role of elders was even more important than it is nowadays. One role in particular, that of *ai*, came to dominate the religious and economic life of the community. Described as "the king of the spirit-shrines" the *ai* was the main arbiter in matters having to do with land allocation and tenure.

The Esudadu Jola have always believed that rice fields belonged initially to Emit, the supreme but distant Jola deity, who immediately delegated their management to the spirit-shrines. These, in turn, transmitted their power to the local *ai* in each community (Thomas 1959: 274–275). It was the

The power of the spirit-shrines 39

ai who ultimately held the right of tenure, though only in a symbolic way. Periodically, he would "lease" usufructuary rights over unused land to members of his community "but reserved for himself the right to resolve all the conflicts [over land] which could arise between villages, families or individuals." "Historically then, the land-tenure system was entirely under the jurisdiction of the spirits, the *ukiin*" (Thomas 1959: 275).

In times past, the *ai* also helped to preserve the spiritual unity of the

Plate 4: A ritual elder (*ai*) with his peace-enforcing broom.

Esudadu people by mediating in disputes and preventing warfare.[15] When a fight broke out between two or more community members, the *ai* would call together the entire village and ask for witnesses to testify on either side. In the words of an informant: "Then he would decide who was the guilty party and tell him to stop." The guilty person would have to sacrifice to one of several shrines under the *ai*'s control. When I asked what would happen if the culprit refused to behave, the answer was "he wouldn't dare; the entire village would oblige him." The *ai* was also responsible for putting an end to warfare between villages: "in times past villages would fight over everything, but especially over rice fields. When two communities went to war, the *ai* would appear in the midst of the battlefield and raise his broom [his staff of office]. The fight would stop right there. Then people could talk." Conditions have changed at the present time. The Jola explain that all rice fields have been allocated to the families that work them. Hence the *ai* no longer holds tenurial rights to village lands. Moreover, warfare has ceased, so the *ai*'s peace-keeping role has diminished while other elders have now joined him in the task of settling land disputes.

Nonetheless, during the eighteenth century, when the trade in slaves was at an all-time high, the political role of *ai* is supposed to have been greatly expanded. Arguing from the verbal accounts he collected among the Banjal, a Jola sub-group in the Seleki region of Casamance, Snyder (1981: 15–19) suggests that the rain-priest or *ai* extended his control over the lucrative business of raiding for slaves. Together with other Banjal elders, the *ai* was able to enrich himself by accumulating cattle which he exchanged for slaves. During the subsequent century, the position of rain-priest of the Banjal grew even more important and became associated with the extraction of surplus labor from the congregation. Snyder concludes that nineteenth-century Banjal society exhibited "a tributary mode of production characterized by the development of two classes, namely shrine-holders and the rest of the population."

There are problems with Snyder's class-centered, economic analysis of Banjal society, however. As Snyder himself points out, even though the rain-priest of the Banjal peoples did extract labor from his congregation, it was mostly older men and women who worked for him. And even though some Banjal elders might have kept slaves for their own use, most captives seem to have been sold and exchanged for cattle – at least in the Esudadu area (Linares 1987).

A somewhat different, possibly more satisfactory, picture of the role of *ai* as it unfolded in the Esudadu Jola area has been presented by Baum (1987: 114–121). He emphasizes the numerous rules and prohibitions surrounding the *ai*'s activities over and above the wealth or privileges he enjoyed. "The *oeyi* offered sacrifices for the fertility of the land and of women, and he prayed for rain. However he was not supposed to involve himself in political disputes." Moreover, the *ai* was excluded from participation in the activities of *Huteendukay*, the shrine associated with the labor force of the community. This meant that he could not command at will the labor of others. "While the limitations on the mobility and political influence of the priest–king were said to ensure the purity of this powerful office, they were also designed to prevent the concentration of too much power in the hands of any individual." In short, Baum's analysis suggests that as many curbs may have been placed on the *ai*'s freedom of action during the nineteenth century as are placed now.

At the present time, the "ritual elder," or *ai*, symbolizes the power of the entire community. For he stands for collective peace, harmony and prosperity. But he can hardly be described as all-powerful, or unusually rich. The *ai* is constrained by too many prohibitions that ensure he does not use sacred power for private gain.

In 1985, the Sambujat *ai* was a man and an elder of the Hojok courtyard unit or *hank*. He was talked about as someone having a very "bad" or "mean" shrine (called *Kalembakiin*) which he must keep "in line" through constant rites of sacrifice and appeasement. *Kalembakiin* controls rain and is also associated with death. It is responsible for ensuring that the rice fields are productive, and that the work force reproduces itself. Yet despite the power it carries, the office of *ai* is not coveted; it is thrust upon a man by unavoidable circumstances. The *ai* refused time and again to accept the post after the previous incumbent had died. He even fled, together with his brother, to another village in order to escape this obligation. The shrine who "wanted him very much," proceeded to kill all his children (four of them), and seven of his brother's children. He was finally forced to accept the post of *ai* and its associated shrine. Thus, the most powerful shrines "seek" their owners as well as the reverse. And shrines can also make an elder poor.

Once a Sambujat person becomes an *ai*, he is condemned to eternal poverty. Although he cultivates like everyone else – for he does not have special fields allocated to his office like the *ai* of the neighboring village – he must give up climbing palms or the palms would die. By giving up palm-wine tapping, the *ai* gives up the chance to earn cash, for this is the principal dry-season remunerative occupation open to the Esudadu men.[16] His wife, it is said, will never have nice clothing. The *ai*'s actions are surrounded by other prohibitions: nobody can see where he bathes; he must wear a wraparound cloth, not the loincloth other men wear; he must at all times use a tall red bonnet so that women cannot see his head, for this is where his power lies. At the time a new incumbent becomes an *ai*, he receives a special name. This name cannot be mentioned by a woman, who must call him *ai*, or call him by the respectful term *man* (from the verb *kaman*, to be praised, to be glorified), which both sexes employ.

The post of *ai* rotates among three Sambujat courtyard units or *hank*, but in one direction only; from *hank* A to B to C, and back to A. When I asked the reason for this rotation the answer was that if the shrine were to stay in one *hank* only, that particular *hank* would become too powerful. Rotating offices, or transmitting them in zig-zag fashion, is part of a system that puts checks and balances on possible abuses of power. Thus, it is absolutely forbidden for an *ai* to be succeeded by his own son. As the *ai* gets older, a replacement is more or less lined up for him. If the designated person refuses to accept the post, the shrine will trap him and they will "finally put the hat on his head."

By 1986, the old *ai* of Sambujat had died and the post lay vacant. As late as 1990, it was still being temporarily filled by an elder of the Elufbajat *hank* until the time when the spirit-shrine would signal his choice. Meanwhile, the elder who was filling in was being allowed to tap palm wine. But if he were to become the new *ai* he would have to stop immediately.

Whereas the *ai* may be thought of as the "sacred leader of the shrines," the chief (*aseefaw*, from the French *chef*) may be thought of as a secular administrator. And whereas the *ai*'s power is waning under "modern" conditions, the chief's duties are waxing. In keeping the role of ritual elder apart from that of chief, the present-day Sambujat political systems enforces an effective separation of powers – ritual matters vs. secular affairs, external politics vs. internal struggles. By establishing a division of labor among the power holders themselves (on this point see Kertzer 1988) the system prevents the misuse of mystical power to gain worldly advantages.

The office of village chief was created by the French colonial authorities sometimes in the mid-nineteenth century, whenever they felt the need to secure permission for a trading station, or to "sign" a treaty giving them access to some particular resource (Baum 1987: 243–244). To this day, the chief serves as the link between community residents and representatives of the outside world. The present Sambujat chief deals with the Senegalese civil authorities. He passes on information, collects taxes and coordinates the occasional regional services provided by government agencies (such as the distribution of seed and fertilizer, the inoculation of cattle). He also sees to it that villagers inscribe their children in school. During the last decades, as the Senegalese State attempts to bring extension services into the countryside, government agents have relied upon the chief to help settle local disputes over land and cattle when these interfere with the government's mission. In addition, if there is a particularly violent fight in the community, the chief might call in the police. But by and large the chief is a civil servant and not a local authority in internal matters. As the present chief of Sambujat put it to me, he is mostly concerned with "affairs dealing with the *kululum*" (i.e. with Europeans, meaning outsiders). This concern extends to mediating in conflicts over land and cattle among other Senegalese groups living in the immediate area:

Today there was a gathering at the house of Janke, the Sambujat chief. Apparently, a man from Samsam [one of the Wolof "stranger" villages within the Esudadu territory] had some days ago come to complain to Janke that the Samsam cattle had entered his rice fields and eaten the crop. When I asked why a man from Samsam should come to him, Janke explained that all the land on the plateau that Samsam now occupies belongs to Sambujat. This particular man had in addition borrowed rice fields from a specific native-born Sambujat individual. Hence, the Samsam man had the right to come to the Sambujat chief for arbitration. At the gathering he had with the Samsam men Janke told them he would let it pass this time. But the next time it happened they would have to compensate the man for the damage their cattle had caused him.

In Sambujat, the post of chief is always passed down within one of the courtyard units or *hank*. As with most posts, it is transmitted in a zig-zag fashion: from a man to his brother or to his real or classificatory brother's son. Sometimes a mature man, whose relation to the previous incumbent is not altogether clear, is chosen for the post because he shows special qualities. Thus, succession to the office of chief is only partly hereditary; village elders and civil authorities have some say on who actually occupies the post.

Doubtless, the chief is respected and listened to. But, like everyone else, he cultivates his own fields; he neither extracts surplus labor from others, nor demands special services by virtue of his chiefly post. Moreover, a chief does not have a special spirit-shrine, or *bakiin*, associated with his post; though he may, through other channels, inherit one or more important shrines. The present chief controls the shrine connected with the boys' initiation (the *bukut*). But he was in line to take over responsibility for this shrine long before he became chief. As head of the most important rite of passage, he controls the activities taking place in the sacred forest. It is in this capacity, rather than in his capacity as chief, that he enjoys special authority. Thus, a social division of labor characterizes the Sambujat "political" system, with the *ai* as the sacred leader of the shrines, and the *aseefaw* as the civil authority. Both figures, however, regulate the economic life of the community, the first with respect to internal affairs and the latter with respect to the outside world.

Plate 5: The chief (center) and the men drinking palm-wine together after doing the *kawasen*.

Women's "strength": the *Sihuñ* shrines

The Esudadu women seem to contradict Friedl's (1975: 2–65) suggestion that in decentralized, egalitarian societies having patrilineal descent and virilocal residence women may be at a disadvantage because they have no hereditary political or ritual positions reserved for them. For it is clear that the in-married agnatic women of Sambujat "command" important spirit-shrines affecting both sexes. Despite there being no hereditary posts reserved for them (there are none for men either) women are charged with the important task of propitiating spirits that are essential to the survival of the entire community.

In fact, two out of the dozen or so functioning *ai* within the Jola area at the time Thomas (1959) did his study were actually women. Each was known as an *ai anaare* (female "queen–priest"). The scanty details provided by Thomas (1959: p. 649–654) seems to indicate that succession to the post of *ai anaare* followed slightly different rules from succession to the male post of *ai*. After being trapped directly by the royal shrine, the future *ai anaare* was to dream for two or three years. She was under the obligation to report these dreams to the elders. After sacrificing a pig at the royal shrine, she would finally take up the post with a simple ceremony resembling a funeral dance. Unlike the male *ai* the female *ai* had only the royal shrine at her disposal. Moreover, she not only had to be directly ratified by the male elders, but she could only sacrifice a pig and not a bull (Jola women do not own cattle), and her installment in office was very simple. All this suggests that the post of female *ai* was not the equivalent of the post of male *ai*. Even then, it is significant to note that women had access to the highest ritual post in the land.

The Esudadu women do not fit well the notion advanced by Meillassoux (1981: 75) that "women, despite their crucial role in reproduction, never appear as vectors of the social organization." For women enjoy a great deal of social recognition and respect. As sisters, women play a crucial role in their brothers' lives. They take care of them when ill, they help them with production if they lose their wives, and they bury them when they die.

Few occasions reveal the importance of the ceremonial and social roles that women play in the community better than funerals. If the deceased is a man, the agnatic females, among them his "real" sisters, help with the preparation of the body, accompany it throughout, demonstrate their grief outright, and question the deceased at the end. The in-married women of the *hank*, in turn, sing praise songs and also show their support, though in a more subdued way. During the proceedings, the widow is as prominent as

46   *The political economy of Sambujat*

the dead man's own sisters. Both types of women usually interrogate the corpse publicly, the same as do the male agnatic kin of the deceased. The songs and speeches women perform emphasize the dead man's accomplishments; how he was a great cultivator, powerful (like a bull), a good family provider. Women also help to bring out the heaps of rice that are displayed in front of the dead man's tent as a symbol of his productivity (the tools that the deceased used to cultivate with are also exhibited). The economic

Plate 6: The in-married women sing at an agnate's funeral.

prestations taking place at funerals also emphasize the importance of a man's uterine kin. The main flow of goods in the form of live cattle, rice and meat, go out from the members of the dead man's hank to his mother's brothers, who are part of the cognatic context in which he developed.[17]

At the death of a renowned female elder, the widower, his brothers and her sons, will sacrifice as many head of cattle on her behalf as if she had been a man. Her daughters' husbands will also each contribute a bull. If the deceased female elder was particularly respected – for example if she had been an officiant of one of the *Sihuñ* shrines – the married men will do the *ñiukul* spear dance for her. This dance, which is regularly performed at a man's funeral, is done to the sound of drumming by men arranged in age-groups (elders, mature men, married juniors).

As wives, women are also indispensable, not only as reproducers, but also as primary producers of rice and other essential products. Conversely, the crucial symbolic role that women play as guarantors of the fertility of the land, and of those who work it, ensures that their own work will not be appropriated without compensation. In this section, I will provide an outline of female ritual power as it is manifested through their shrines. In the following sections, I will trace the implications that female power has for the proper functioning of the rice-growing system.

The shrines controlled by women are called *Sihuñ* (pl.; *Ehuñ* (sing.). The name is probably derived from *huñ*, meaning "liver" or "heart," where feelings of anger are believed to be located. In order to join this shrine's congregation, a woman must be married and also have borne a child. At the time when she bears her first child, a woman becomes initiated into the particular *Ehuñ* shrine that resides in her husband's ward. The initiation ritual is very simple; it includes seclusion and a few days of instruction. An unmarried woman cannot participate in the rituals surrounding the *Ehuñ* shrine; childless women cannot be present either, unless they are having the shrine done on their behalf. This is because the shrines are concerned with insuring fertility, broadly defined.

In Sambujat, there are two *Sihuñ* shrines, bearing different names and having different histories.[18] The Sambujat *Ehuñ* called *Tengo* is a direct offspring of the *Ehuñ* shrine of the neighboring village of Kalomp, with which Sambujat's residents share numerous marriage ties. The incumbent of Kalomp's shrine often performs the propitiatory ritual (the *kawasen*) on behalf of a Sambujat child who has fallen ill. In case the child is being bewitched by close kin, the parents may take him/her to Kalomp rather than having the ritual performed at home. This often involves gathering and transporting large amounts of palm wine to that village. In 1981, the

Kalomp's officiant of the *Ehuñ* shrine had died. It fell upon Mari of Sambujat to continue "doing" Kalomp's shrine until a replacement was found for the previous incumbent.

To be considered for the post of officiant (*awasen*) of one of the *Ehuñ* shrines, or for the post of assistant, a woman must not only have given birth to a child but she also must have been born in Sambujat and married within it. Four different women, representing four different natal and married contexts, are in charge of Sambujat's two female shrines:

The first spirit, called *Jeketi*, always "resides" (has its shrine) in *hank* zz of ward 1; the woman in charge of it, the *awasen*, in this case a woman called Jagesa, must have been born in any of the *hank* of ward 2 but she must always be married into *hank* zz of ward 1. Jagesa "inherited" the shrine by getting trapped by *Jeketi*, after which time she consented to take it over. Jagesa's main assistant is born and married into a different *hank* from herself. The second shrine, *Tengo*, can "reside" in any of two *hank* of ward 2, for they were once a single unit. The present *awasen*, Mari, was born in *hank* yy but married into *hank* xx, where *Tengo* resides. Mari's assistant was born and married into different *hank* from herself.

Hence, as with the men's shrines, the female-controlled shrines cannot devolve from mother to daughter. This is indirect confirmation of the power that the *Sihuñ* command. Moreover, only married women can occupy the post of officiant or shrine-keeper (*awasen*) of either of the *Ehuñ* shrines, and a daughter never marries into the same courtyard unit as her mother.

It does not require much imagination to infer that the female shrines assert female power. They establish women's equality with men. For it is the case that the officiants of the *Sihuñ* shrines have been given a broad mandate. Like the shrine owned by the ritual elder, or *ai*, the *Sihuñ* are also concerned with rice production. At the beginning of the rains, women will bring wine and rice, and together they will oblate at one of the *Ehuñ* shrines, to ask it for a good season. If two consecutive years have been rainless, the women will sacrifice a pig, or one or more bulls, which they have bought with the proceeds earned from associative work. The prayer the shrine-keepers perform at this time has been described by Thomas (1959: 735–736) as follows:

When the rains have stopped suddenly in plain rainy season, great harm can befall the rice fields. The women of the ward gather at the *Ehuñ* shrine in secret. One morning, at dawn, one of the "priestesses" of the *Ehuñ* goes down to the rice fields and addresses Emit loudly: "Ata Emit, is it true that this year the rice is destined to dry out in the fields? The other year's famine was bad. But this time the distress will be so great that we will have no strength left to speak. Give us rain, give us life" ... etc., etc.

The other women hear the prayer and wail, as they do in funerals. All work stops and the women and children carrying jugs of water on their heads go first to the *Ehuñ* shrine, then to the houses of all the male elders who own important shrines, and put to them the case for asking Emit for rain. The elders agree on this necessity, and the women continue to pour water on the shrine every day during a week. If at the end of this time the rains have not fallen, the officiant of the *Ehuñ* shrine begins the prayer all over again.

The *Sihuñ* are also concerned with the fertility of the rice crop itself. Every year, when the first rains fall, the women must take a small amount of rice seed to the *Ehuñ* shrine to ask for abundant yields. And every year, after the rice bundles have dried in the fields and before the harvest can be brought home, the women gather around one of the *Sihuñ* shrines, where the officiants perform a first-fruits offering. Without these rites, neither the transplanting, nor the transporting of the crop to the granaries can take place. Thus, women's rites are not only essential for proper production to proceed, they are also essential for proper storage and distribution of the crop.

Moreover, the *Sihuñ* shrine-keepers also play a central role in the welfare and reproduction of the labor force. For they protect children, women and even men against the evils of witchcraft. The following case illustrates the point:

A woman from the neighboring community of Kalomp came to the *kawasen* which Mari was doing for the *Ehuñ* under her control. When the women finished eating, she tried to "steal a child in order to eat it" (i.e. to kill it because she was envious). Mari's *Ehuñ* promptly trapped her and forced her to confess. To this day, the woman had not recovered.

This story was told to me by an elderly and respected lady to show that Sambujat is a "dangerous" village where children are protected. But it isn't only children who are protected against witchcraft by the shrines. Baum (1987: 413) mentions in passing that in the village where he lived the *Ehuñ* shrine was often propitiated by the women in order to exorcize evil forces from communal grounds.

In addition, individual women can count on the *Sihuñ* to defend them against their husband's wrath, or to accompany them in their travels. For example, in the 1970s, an *Ehuñ* shrine was established in Dakar to protect women who had migrated there, and to safeguard their journey from Casamance (Baum, 1987: 164). This meant that they were safe in their quest for salaried employment. "Any woman, anywhere, even in France, can get the officiant of one of the shrines to help her; even if she was not born in Sambujat," I was repeatedly told. She can ask the shrine for more children, better health, more rice and so forth. Finally, on many occasions, men must also appeal to the *Sihuñ* shrines if they do not want to see a son who has fallen ill die. A man who is having difficulty getting a wife goes to one of the two *Sihuñ* shrines to ask for assistance.

The duties performed by the two women who are entrusted with the *Sihuñ* shrines are multiple, cover both sexes, reach far and wide. These duties revolve around redressing "things that are bad" in the village. The women also help their in-married "sisters" individually, by sacrificing on their behalf if they are ill, or want something special. They can, and often do, help men in distress. In all these cases, the ritual performed at the female *Ehuñ* shrine is similar to the ritual performed at the agnatic shrines (the *bakiin/ukiin*). The person for whom the *kawasen* is being performed (the supplicant) brings palm wine and an animal to be sacrificed. He or she sits on the periphery and speaks out on the subject of what he or she desires. The supplicant is forbidden from drinking or eating at the shrine.

It is repeatedly stated by men and women alike that the most distinctive feature of the Sambujat *Sihuñ* shrines is that the men cannot participate in their rituals, nor eat of the food, nor drink of the palm wine. In fact, a married man should not even touch, let alone eat, the meat from an animal sacrificed at the female shrines. Uninitiated boys, however, can eat at one of the two shrines, for they are in a real sense powerless.[19] As a woman said to me with obvious relish: "and we will kill his pig and they [the men] will not eat any of the meat." In fact, some women say their shrines are more important than the men's shrines, and there are those who believe them.

Each of the two *Sihuñ* shrines is said to be "an association of women, united under a common cause." As female friends repeatedly stressed, a woman cannot live alone; she must align herself with other women, to whom she can turn for moral support and, as we shall see, a great deal of actual assistance in agricultural labor. Thus, the shrines symbolize the corporation of all the women who have married within the village, placing them on an equal ritual footing with the corporation of resident agnatic men.

To summarize, among the Esudadu Jola both genders command important authoritative resources. They both have access to the religious life of the community. This is the main arena in which power and authority relationships are symbolically defined; in which gender relations are constructed. Thus, it is important that spirit-shrines can be female as well as male, can be introduced by men or by women, can be propitiated by both sexes. For particular shrines, the post of shrine keeper (*awasen*) must be occupied by a man, for others by a woman, or for still others by either gender indistinctly.

Who participates in what propitiatory ritual, when and how, depends on the nature and function of the particular spirit; but both sexes, on the same or different occasions, can be present. Illness, childlessness, and failure to produce are considered misfortunes that can strike anyone, regardless of gender or age. Women as well as men have a positive role to perform in life crisis and increase rituals that insure the continuity and reproduction of the present and future labor force of the community. In short, female as well as male ritual leaders guide the authoritative processes "through which labor and materials are commandeered for extraordinary occasions" (Friedl 1975: 9).

The same is also generally the case for allocative resources; both genders participate in its distribution and usage. It is true that Esudadu women do not own land, and as a consequence are not in a position to settle disputes concerning paddy-field ownership and transmission.[20] It is also true that they do not own cattle, though they own chickens, ducks, and pigs. Nevertheless, women have complete usufructuary rights over the rice fields they work, and they can also sell the rice from these fields, which are usually the best. And even though they do not own cattle, the prime symbol of wealth, many head may be sacrificed at the funeral of a distinguished female elder. Generally, women are more concerned with the problem of increase and reproduction – that is, with the rice crop they produce and the children they bear – and men are more concerned with securing the land and safeguarding the cattle. However, if some of the resources that women command are kept separate from the resources that men command, it is not because they are less important. It is "because male and female should be carefully separated in order to maximize the power of each" (Baum 1987: 140). A power which in both cases is directly implicated in the political economy of the community.

2

Rice fields and labor relationships

So far, I have tried to convey some idea of where the sources of power in Esudadu society reside, and how social control is exerted. Within general processes of resource allocation, elders play an important guardianship role. Men are generally more concerned with land and cattle, and women with crops and children. But shrine-keepers of either gender command important authoritative resources by virtue of the tacit support they receive from their congregations. In the present chapter, I will try to show how relations of control built around the spirit-shrines facilitate the flow of labor between individuals and groups. The shrines and their keepers help to keep in check the competitive relations that are built around property and people. In so doing, they mediate in social relations of production. For production to proceed, sanctioned forms of reciprocity are a social necessity. For it is the case that in Sambujat people do not automatically cooperate.

The cultural emphasis that is placed on working hard, producing great stores of rice, acquiring cattle and children, amassing wealth, has its obverse side. There is a great deal of secretiveness and competitive feeling surrounding resources. This competition shows up in many ways. We have seen that persons compete over rights to land. They also compete over cattle. A man will not say how many head he owns; he will keep his cattle far away in another village, to prevent their being stolen or "poisoned" by one of his classificatory agnates. A couple who loses many children will move to another *hank* for safety. Children are shipped out to the matrilateral kin, or placed as wards in another family, to avoid their being killed through witchcraft. The rice crop stored in the granary is not shown to outsiders lest "it flees." A man will rarely boast of his wealth for fear of being bewitched. The head of an important household expressed to me his intention to build up the crumbling wall around his house and backyard so that he could move his rice in and out unnoticed by his neighbors. And so on, for it is possible to multiply examples endlessly. The suspicion, that those who have much land, lots of kin, many children, have gained their wealth illicitly, lies just below the surface of Esudadu life. In the tight social space where community activities unfold, conflict is an ever-present threat. As we will see, neither overlapping membership in various kinships units, nor widespread affinal alliances, nor even enlightened self-interest suffice by themselves. There must be additional mechanisms for compelling people to engage in joint endeavors. "The necessity for cooperative work in herding animals, building dams, fencing the paddies, and roofing houses all remind the township [i.e. the community] of their independence and need for cooperation. There is a proverb that illustrates this point: 'With one straw one cannot cover a roof'" (Baum: 1987: 405–406). Thus, people must be compelled to give and receive assistance in the course of performing agricultural work.

Until recently, associative work – that is cooperative work performed by persons not closely related by kinship ties – was directly under the supervision of a spirit-shrine known as *Huteendukay*.

Huteendukay, the labor shrine

In neighboring Esudadu communities, *Huteendukay* is a major shrine, around which productive tasks are organized. Though Sambujat and its nearest neighboring community once did *Huteendukay*, the shrine has been inactive for quite some time. But, if the need arises, it will be re-activated again. Like many other shrines, *Huteendukay* was installed in the early eighteenth century, at a time when warfare was rampant and it "sapped the energy of the community to farm, hunt, and especially to maintain dams and fences that were essential to rice cultivation." Baum (1987: 132–133) has described how the council of elders who control the shrine accomplished these tasks:

At the Hutendookai [*Huteendukay*] shrine, problems concerning the whole township would be discussed. Work on the dams that regulated water levels in the rice paddies and on fences that protected the paddies from roaming livestock were coordinated through Hutendookai. Shrine elders also adopted regulations governing the hire of individual and collective labor. During most of the eighteenth century, these sessions were presided over by the priest king. His spiritual prestige and the power of the Hutendookai shrine reinforced the power of the town council's decisions. A group of younger men . . . served as the enforcement arm of the Hutendookai. Selected from each compound, they inspected fences and dams, seized stray livestock in the rice paddies and, together with shrine elders, they enforced unpopular decisions in their compounds.

The *Huteendukay* council also mediated in land disputes and heard accusations of theft and witchcraft. In especially severe instances, the council of elders would confiscate the guilty person's rice fields. "People in the community would buy these paddies with cattle which would then be sacrificed at Hutendookai" (Baum 1987: 133). In fact, all of the decisions taken by the council were consecrated with palm wine libations.

In former times, the *Huteendukay* council also discharged policing functions. When cattle were stolen, the shrine sought out the guilty person. Once he or she was found, members of *Huteendukay* congregation entered his home, plundered his belongings and set the fine in terms of the jugs of palm wine and the number of pigs, which the accused was supposed to turn over to the shrine. According to Thomas (1959: 232):

One cannot insist enough on the socio-political role of Hutendukay [*Huteendukay*]. Or on its economic functions. Thus, some years ago, the village of M'lomp [one of the large Esudadu villages] decided not to continue to procure cattle from one of the neighboring communities [this amounted to cutting off relations with that community]. Some of the inhabitants would have wished to ignore this decision but for the fines that the Hutendukay society imposed [upon them].

Even though in Sambujat the policing rule of *Huteendukay* is minor today, in the Esudadu community where Baum did his work the shrine still regulates labor, be it collective or individual. Baum (1987: 359) has described the labor-regulating functions of what he calls the township council or congregation, the body organized around the shrine, and including two representatives from each "extended family" (the *hank* unit?), as follows:

The Hutendookai [*Huteendukay*] establishes the wages for the various forms of individual labor for hire; enforces collective labor obligations such as work on a fence around the rice paddies that protect the crops from livestock; and provides a forum for complaints against employers who fail to meet their obligations.

Hence, within the Esudadu region, not only the forces of production (namely rain, land, tools, crops), but also the social relations of production (namely labor) may be under the religious sanction of the spirit-shrines and their representatives.

Marriage and the formation of the conjugal family unit
Despite the undeniable importance that associative labor plays in rice cultivation (pp. 64–70) the conjugal family unit (or CFU for short) still remains a basic unit of production. A conjugal family can only come into existence through the process of marriage. Hence it may be appropriate here to discuss the marriage process as it underscores the workings out of

the political economy of Sambujat. For the material goods that change hand during the marriage process have important political and symbolic connotations as well. As J. Comaroff (1980) has ably argued, marriage payments cannot be reduced, either to the economics of compensation, or to their social-cultural functions. Goods that are transacted in both directions during the marriage process, namely palm wine, rice and pigs, are at one and the same time comestibles, items that are central to the ritual system, and products that can be sold for cash. During the lengthy negotiations that go on, the girl's agnatic kin make palm wine libations to, and eat cooked rice together at the shrines. The groom, in turn, establishes a relationship between his own shrines and those of his new wife. All this puts an emphasis upon the future productive capacities of both partners, while at the same time counteracting the tendency for the new household to act in isolation, by structuring rites that facilitate wider networks of relationships. (See also Ray 1976: 17). By showing that he can actually accumulate enough "goods" to marry, the groom is also demonstrating that he will be a good provider.

Marriage is also an important occasion for transmitting property and goods from one generation to the next. During the *buposadu*, the prestations that initially flow from the groom or his family, to the bride's courtyard group or *hank*, qualify as bridewealth payments. That is, they are made from the groom or his kin to the bride's kin (see Goody 1973, 1976). In Sambujat, they consist mainly of palm wine (in large quantities) and animals (usually pig[s]). After the *buposadu* is concluded, prestations become more "dowry-like"; the bride's kin, through their own labor, endow her with property. "Brothers" of the girl, young men who were born in the same *hank* as herself, come together to furrow and ridge a large field which the bride, with the help of her real and classificatory sisters, transplant upon and later on harvest. The rice this field produces, plus contributions of rice from the bride's mother's brothers, adds up to several hundred kilograms. It is enough to feed the bride and her new husband for several years, until the product from their own fields fill up their granaries. Hence, this rice constitutes an important conjugal fund for the new couple. In this respect, it clearly qualifies as an "indirect dowry" in Goody's aforementioned classification. That is, as property that is produced and passed on by the bride's kin to her, and by extension to her new husband. The Sambujat residents think of it as being the equivalent of "bridewealth" payments; if the groom does not send the *bupos* wine,[1] the bride does not get the rice.

Another important conjugal fund for the new couple involves the transfer of usufructuary rights over land. For the new conjugal pair to survive, they must have rice fields that both partners can cultivate. It is expected of a new household that it be economically and socially independent.[2] A young man at the time of marriage receives a number of rice fields from his own father, or from other close members of his patriline or *buaju* if the father is dead. Almost immediately, the young man transfers usufructuary rights over half the fields to his new wife. The fields that are allotted to the wife are often the best yielding, for it is said that a woman feeds the family, though in reality both partners contribute their rice to the daily meal. In any case, the father of a newly married son keeps fewer fields for himself as he grows older. Every time a son marries, his father, alone or with his close kin, assess the land anew. Although some Jola groups allow female inheritance of land, among the Esudadu ownership of land by agnatic women is not customary. Nevertheless, women's usufructuary rights in their in-married context are secure, perhaps more secure in a *de facto* way, than the rights of their husbands. For the latter are under the constant obligation to redistribute fields to their descendants, while women are under no such constraint.

Where land has value, and labor is in short supply, it stands to reason that marriage is a strategy whose purpose, whether consciously formulated or not, is to keep property and people within the boundaries of the community. In Sambujat, marriage is definitely not a strategy for creating wide-ranging political alliances among the men by the physical "exchange" of women. In the other Jola communities we will be considering later it may be so, but in Sambujat there is no circulating connubiality (see also Linares 1988). The system, if indeed there is one, favors the constant reinforcement of existing community relationships through such practices as village in-marriage, late age of marriage, monogamy, widow re-marriage or women staying to live with a son. But just because marriage "rules" tend to confine strategic relationships within the community, they are no less "political" in nature. For in-marriage reinforces the moral authority of elders and facilitates the retention of the labor-power of women. The actual rules that express the inwardly directed nature of marriage preferences, and the importance of having a working pair (not necessarily a husband and wife), can be summarized briefly.

Although post-marital residence is virilocal – agnatic women move out and "affinal" women come into the *hank* (the co-resident group of agnates or semi-agnates to be described shortly) – the "movement" is more social than spatial: 42 percent of all women marry within Sambujat itself, and another 48 percent come from the village next door, barely two kilometers away. In fact, Sambujat residents aspire to marry someone as close as possible in space, though not too close in relation. Since exogamy rules are narrowly observed, there are only a few local categories of people or subgroups into which a person may *not* marry. Men who stand in the relation of fathers or brothers to each other tend to get wives from the same sources. Thus brothers from the same *hank* tend to marry women who are sisters. Put differently, sisters prefer to marry together, into the same *hank*. A man's son may marry a girl from the same *hank* as the one his father's sister was married into. That is, he may marry FZD. In short, marrying within the community, or nearby, is greatly preferred.

It may be appropriate here to ask why it is that the Esudadu Jola seem to limit community membership through mechanisms that discourage the incorporation of extra affines into the household? Is it because by maintaining village endogamy, and discouraging re-marriage or plural unions, a tightly knit, village-based, labor force made up of same-age male cohorts is created and maintained? The answer seems *not* to be because male in-laws will therefore be inclined to cooperate, but because related women, mainly real, or classificatory, sisters, and parents and children, can continue to do so. Men who stand in the relation of brothers-in-law to each other do not farm together on a regular basis, even though they do help each other occasionally; more so here than in the other areas we will be discussing later, where exogamy is the rule. However, their wives, if they happen to be sisters, will regularly cooperate. Moreover, if sons and daughters stay married within the community, or if they get married to a person from the nearby village, their parents can continue to benefit from their labor.

A related phenomenon is the age of marriage, which is relatively late: 22–24 years of age for women, 26–28 for men (these figures are higher in de Jonge *et al.* 1978: 98). As a result, young men and women stay around, to help their parents with the rice cultivation for an appreciable number of years after reaching adulthood.

In addition to being spatially circumscribed, marriage in Sambujat is almost exclusively monogamous. A few elders had two wives in the past, but this is unusual. "We only marry one woman at a time is the constantly made remark." Although a Sambujat resident might not explain it quite this way, monogamy seems to be one more example of the general distrust with which the accumulation by elders of "wealth" and privileges is generally regarded. For women can bring wealth; they have labor power which can be translated directly into rice production. And rice is convertible into food, cash, cattle (for men), clothes and so forth.

There are a surprising number of solitary men around in Sambujat. If the percentage of men who were divorced (13 percent in 1965 and 7 percent in 1981), or remained widowers (7 percent in '65, 9 percent in '81), are added together, the percentage of solitary men in Sambujat is quite high: 20 percent in 1965 and 16 percent in 1981. Men say they are hesitant to divorce a wife for fear they won't find another in time for the planting season.[3] In any case, re-marriage is not prompt: 6 out of 9, or 67 percent of all solitary persons alive in 1981 had been in that condition for at least five years. In fact, solitary men usually have trouble finding a wife. This is partly because solitary women are not always eager to re-marry.[4]

A woman whose husband dies may, if she wants to, re-marry by the widow remarriage (or *kataor*) convention to a real or classificatory brother of her deceased husband. But if she chooses not to do so, she may stay and live near her own son(s) while continuing to farm the same paddy fields she did before. Youngish widows with unmarried (*kukambani*) sons (from *kambad*, the state of not yet being circumcised) keep house for them and they both form a production unit by sharing agricultural tasks in the customary manner. Only when the son gets married will the mother go off and get married herself.[5] Although she might be past reproductive age at this point, it does not matter. As a Sambujat resident remarked, the new elderly couple "will still help each other with agricultural tasks." Clearly then, women have the choice to re-marry or not, and conjugal pairs are formed as a response to productive and not only to reproductive needs.

For this and other reasons, Sambujat's conjugal units replace themselves very slowly. This shows up in several ways. It is directly confirmed statistically. In the 16 years between the two complete village censuses I made, the number of conjugal family households (or *butoŋ*) had diminished, from 68 in 1965, to 57 in 1981. This is a reduction of 16 percent despite the constant trend towards the formation of new households.

The conjugal family and the gender division of labor

Not surprisingly, given the general equality that underlies much of Sambujat social life, the social division of labor within the conjugal family or *butoŋ* tends to be equitably divided between the genders and the generations. Nonetheless, like most societies everywhere (see Oboler 1985), some tasks are seen as more appropriate for one sex to perform than the other. The sexual division of labor is practice-specific in that most steps in the rice growing cycle, like land preparation or transplanting, are performed by only one sex (see Guyer 1984a). Other practices, however, like harvesting, are less sex-linked, and men participate in a casual and non-compulsory manner. In either case, the agricultural practices performed by both sexes

Rice fields and labor relationships 59

are closely interrelated in space, in time, as well as in total energy invested. Thus, husbands and grown-up sons prepare the land, broadcast the seed, tie-up the rice stalks and help carry the harvested crop home in baskets. Their wives and grown-up daughters transport the fertilizer, transplant and finally harvest. But these tasks are not perceived as being strictly gendered; men frequently help their wives to transplant or, more often, to harvest and carry the rice crop home. Solitary men sometimes perform all the agricultural tasks by themselves, plus doing the cooking and the drawing of water at the well. Otherwise, a widower may make an ad-hoc arrangement with a daughter or sister married nearby, or with another single woman, to have her transplant and/or harvest in exchange for having him prepare her land. And, as I have indicated, a widow (or solitary woman) can always rely on a married or unmarried son for his help. Significantly, both sexes generally work the same number of hours in the rice fields (Table Ib).

Except for the infirmed or the ill, everyone cultivates, beginning with children above the age of twelve. Elders who are still capable of work are expected to show up in the rice fields even though they cannot do as much as stronger members of the society. Parents are especially dependent upon their sons and daughters who are still unmarried, for they are the strongest and most able members of the family, to help with the heaviest work in the

Plate 7: A Sambujat man and his wife often work side by side.

Table Ib: *Labor inputs by gender for rice cultivation in Sambujat*

	Hrs/are[a]	Hrs/ha[b]	Work-days/ha[c]	Hrs/are	Hrs/ha	Work-days/ha
		Female			Male	
Nursery preparation	1.48	148	18.5	3.06	306	38.25
Land preparation				3.52	352	44.0
Pulling out plants and transplanting	2.31	231	29.0	6.4	64	8.0
Harvesting	4.56	456	57.0			
Tying bundles and taking home				1.4	140	17.5
Total			105.00			108.00

Note:
[a] An are is 100 square meters
[b] A ha is 10,000 square meters
[c] A work-day has been calculated as 8 hours

rice fields. Young men help their father with land preparation; young women help their mother with transplanting and harvesting.[6]

Thus, the conjugal family unit or the substitute pair commands important labor resources within it. In addition, it also commands the products of their labor. A man's granary feeds visitors and is also the source of the rice that is used on ceremonial occasions. A man may also exchange his rice for cattle. In principle, a woman's granary nourishes the family. But the husband must also contribute rice for domestic consumption, especially if his wife's stocks become depleted. More important, either partner can sell rice from his or her fields. Yet it is often the wife who sells the most, for her granary is usually fuller because she is given the best rice fields to work. Women prefer to sell rice unmilled, since they have little time during the rainy season to pound it. But if they sell it milled, which brings a better price, they can avail themselves of a machine in a nearby town. When short of time, a woman may pay for having the rice that feeds the family milled by machine. Payment for milling a basketfull weighing 40–50 kg. was less than one US dollar a few years ago, hardly an onerous amount, and as a by-product the women get the chaff to feed the pigs. A woman may use the earnings from the rice trade, or the money she earns from making and selling palm oil, salt, pottery and baskets, to purchase clothing for herself, to buy chickens, pigs and ducks, to have the female shrines propitiated on her behalf. But more often than not she uses part of the cash to pay for extra labor. Thus, women in Sambujat have an independent source of cash revenue which they can re-invest for profit, to produce more rice for consumption, for sale, or for use in everyday rituals. Decidedly, therefore, the Sambujat women do not fit comfortably the generalization made by Rogers (1980: 126) that: "women's rights to dispose of crops by home consumption, retention as an emergency reserve, exchange, and gift-giving are all unlikely to be recognized in economic terms; particularly as they do not involve cash."

Cooperative patterns: the "extended" family or *buaju* unit

Despite the pivotal role played by the nuclear household in matters of production, it is not the only, nor even perhaps the primary, unit of agricultural labor in Sambujat society. This statement seems to run contrary to what some Jola experts affirm (e.g. Pélissier 1966: 683–87; Marzouk-Schmitz 1981: 38). In fact, it also contradicts what the Sambujat inhabitants themselves have reported to me. In 1981, there were exactly 60 conjugal family units in Sambujat. Thirty-seven (37) reported that they habitually worked alone; twenty-three (23) said they regularly worked with another conjugal family unit (F, B, FBS). In other words, 62 percent, or slightly more than half of the Sambujat conjugal or nuclear family units, reported that they regularly worked alone.[7] However, this information, abstracted from interviews of what people said they did, was not corroborated by my observations of actual work groups out in the rice fields. Out of 31 conjugal family units I followed systematically for the entire 1981 season, 17, or 55 percent, worked with another closely related conjugal family unit, while 14, or 45 percent, habitually worked alone. Hence, the ratio was close to 50–50. In other words, despite the claim to self-sufficiency, in reality only half of all conjugal families regularly cultivate alone; the rest regularly co-produce in association with one or more closely related households.

The primary form of inter-household cooperation involves parents and their married son(s). After marrying and building his own house, a young man and his new wife often continue to cultivate with his parents in what I have called a "multiple" co-producing (but not co-residing) household (Linares 1984; see also table Ic). Notably, parents work in their son's (and daughter-in-law's) fields as well as the reverse. Even though Esudadu elders obviously work less hours and perform easier tasks than the younger team, it is significant that they work in the fields of the younger generation at all. In the other Jola villages I will be discussing parents *never* work for their children.

In Sambujat, not only fathers and sons, but also two married brothers and their respective wives may pool their labor; but, again, not always:

Jisalo and Hujége are full brothers. They and their respective wives regularly cultivate together. Yanke and Boisal are also full brothers. They and their wives always work apart. It is said that "there is bad blood" between these brothers.

In any case, even though nuclear families may cooperate in production, when it comes time to harvest, each conjugal household takes home the rice from its own fields, to store it in its own granaries. There is nothing like an "extended family" granary. In fact, there isn't even a nuclear family granary; wives and husbands either have their separate granaries or, if they are forced to share the same granary, each partner will store his or her rice in a separate corner. Moreover, when it comes to cooking and eating the rice, each conjugal family also acts alone.

Because sharing close kin ties is still a significant factor in labor recruitment and mobilization (if not in co-residence or co-consumption) it seems necessary to gain some idea of how kin ties are conceptualized and how they work out in social practice.

Table Ic: *Sambujat: household "types"[a] according to two criteria*

	Solitary	Elementary	Multiple	Fraternal	Grand	
Co-residence	0 (10)	30 (30)	0 (0)	0 (0)	0 (0)	CFUs 60
Co-production	0 (10)	27 (27)	8 (14)[b]	3 (6)	1 (3)	CFUs 60

Note:
[a] Household types are described as follows: solitary households are composed of a divorced man or a widower, elementary households have only one CFU in them, multiple households include a married father and a married son, fraternal households are composed of two married brothers and grand households have a married father, at least two married sons, and often the son of a deceased brother of the household head.
[b] Number of CFUs (conjugal family units) is given in parenthesis. Extended or "complex" households involve more than one CFU (hence are multiple, fraternal and grand).

For all Jola regardless of place, agnatic filiation is the primary principle of kinship recruitment to be recognized. Children "belong" to the father's group. They get their patronym from him, and if they are sons they get their land as well. However, agnation is not an elaborated system of belief which classifies, let alone incorporates, a wide range of kin with reference to some apical patrilineal ancestor. Unusually so (Kopytoff 1971), ancestors are not very important in Jola society. Rather, in the Sambujat context, agnatic descent (as contrasted with agnatic filiation) is a weakly developed ideology.[8] It is not appealed to as a "morally evaluated principle of belief" (Barnes 1962: 6), but as a way of defining where one lives, and where one's close kin are also to be found. And it is not the only principle to be recognized in actual practice.[9]

The small group of kin who can trace descent to the same forefather, or to two brothers, all living no further back than three generations, belong to the same *buaju* unit. For this reason, I have glossed the term as patriline. A *buaju* may include paternal brothers, their out-married sisters, their fathers and grandparents. Male members of a *buaju* unit or patriline hold residual rights to land in common, and also cultivate together. In 1981, there were 23 such units in Sambujat, scattered among 9 courtyard units (*hank*) to be described later on. The following example may serve to clarify the composition of, and the activities engaged in, by members of sundry patrilines or *buaju*:

The Bajatelup courtyard unit (or *hank*) is physically made up of six house structures, tightly clustered around a courtyard area surrounded by a fence. Socially, it is made up of two patronyms, the Bassen and the Jaata. (1) Within the Bassen patronym there is only one *buaju*. In 1965, it consisted of three brothers: Jafogo and Panding, who had the same father and mother, and Hufila, who had the same father only. Their paternal grandfather was supposed to have moved to Bajatelup from the Habinkun *hank*. Panding had two sons, Jisalo and Hujége, by the same wife; they were married and had children of both sexes. Jafogo had had only daughters, and Hufila had two daughters and a young son. Each of the brothers lived in their own house, together with their own children. By 1981, Jafogo had died, Panding was too old to cultivate, Jisalo and Hujége cultivated together with their respective wives and children and Hufila, who was a widower and a solitary, cultivated alone, with the help of his in-married daughter and the remittances sent by the town-dwelling son. (2) Within the Jaata patronym there were several Jaata patrilines or *buaju*: (a) In 1965, the elder, Assimbajat was alive, but his brother, Asawahin, had died some time before. Assimbajat's son, Siina, had built a large house for himself and his father. The two halves were completely separate. By 1976, Assimbajat had died and Siina had opened up a connection between the two halves of the house. In 1981, he cultivated with his two unmarried sons and their mother; two of his other sons, and his daughters were away. (b) The second Jaata *buaju* was made up in 1965 by Sambujati, the old chief, his son Seku and his deceased brother's son, Jonsal. By 1976, the old chief had died and his son had taken over the house. By 1981 Seku had gone off to Gambia, his mother had returned to her village and the house was abandoned. By 1981, Jonsal had died in an accident, and his widow, Humankilen, lived in the house that her married son, who worked in Ziguinchor, built for her after his father died. Her other unmarried son lived with her, and together they formed a working team.

(c) Sisimañ was the elder of the *hank*. His married son, Basil, built a new house for his father and one for himself and his family next to it. In 1981, both households, Sisimañ's and Basil's, cultivated together regularly. By 1984, disaster had struck. Basil had died first, then his father and mother. The only one left was Basil's young brother. (d) Boisal and Yanke were brothers by the same father only. They lived separately and cultivated separately. (e) Sentu, the chief, had a new house. He cultivated with his two unmarried sons and his second wife. One of his sons was a schoolteacher, the other a student, in Ziguinchor. They both came regularly to Sambujat during the rainy season, to help their father with land preparation; so did his daughter, who worked as a domestic in Dakar; she came to help her stepmother transplant.

Clearly, the *buaju* or patriline is one of the basic units of production in Sambujat society. It is also the land-holding corporation. However, a person's loyalties to his or her *buaju* are in direct conflict with his loyalties to members of his own courtyard group or *hank*, among whom he lives in a tight residential arrangement. The ideal that all men residing together around the same courtyard should cooperate as a group in agricultural tasks is strongly held but not always easy to enforce. When, after much insistence on my part, a Sambujat household head offered the term *buaju* for the group composed of two brothers and their children he quickly added that the *buaju* were unimportant: "all men are really one, together, acting as brothers living in the same *hank*." In fact, the *hank* is the focus of most associative work, as well as of many other economic activities.

Associative work: the *hank*, the elders and the village
What needs to be emphasized at the start is that the immediate family, whether we are talking about the conjugal family or *butoŋ*, or the extended family or patriline (the *buaju*), is not self-sufficient in labor requirements. Additional labor is absolutely necessary at some crucial junctures in the cultivation cycle. There is a seasonal profile to labor needs in different Jola regions (see Sall, Posner *et al.* 1985: 48–50). Among the Esudadu Jola, labor demands are up in August and September, when fields have to be ridged and furrowed and then transplanted upon. Another peak is reached in November and December, when the rice harvest begins. At both these times, persons who are not in the same *buaju* unit, but who reside together, are compelled by necessity to cultivate in groups. For, as Swindell (1985: 135) observes, the flow, not just the stock of labor, is of primary importance to African farmers (for that matter to all farmers): "Co-operative labour groups allow the use of irregular labour inputs, often on a massive scale, which means the delays in the farming cycle can be made good."

The most prominent male-constituted work groups providing extra labor are recruited on the basis of common residence around the same courtyard or *hank* (Plate 8). *Hank* is a polysemic word referring to an open area or courtyard as a physical space bearing a proper name (Elufbajat, Kékeniin, Hujok etc), to all the men and their unmarried sisters residing around this space, or only to the male household heads occupying tightly clustered buildings surrounded by a common wall or fence (for detailed genealogies and illustrations see Linares 1983, 1984). Here I will refer to those individuals who reside in the same *hank* as "semi-agnates" because they themselves use a fraternal idiom when they refer to each other. As I have indicated, in 1981 the 23 *buaju* units present were distributed into 9 courtyard units. These varied markedly in size: the largest courtyard group or *hank* comprised 12 resident male household heads, the smallest 3. A continuous shift in personnel characterizes life in the 9 *hank* units we find in Sambujat. If a particular household living within a particular *hank* loses many children, or if its members are constantly ill so that witchcraft is suspected, it will move to another *hank* for safety. A household that moves from one *hank* to another will not, however, be absorbed into one of the existing patrilines or *buaju* units.[10]

As a residential corporation, and not an ancestor-based descent unit like the ones described for other African peoples, the *hank* is structured through the reproductive rituals and productive routines that people perform by virtue of living in close proximity. Cooperation among "semi-agnates" does not come automatically, however. A dynamic tension underlies a person's relationship to his "real" brothers and his own father, all of who are members of his more restricted patriline (the *buaju*), and his relationship to his classificatory brothers and their fathers, who are his "semi-agnates" (his *hank* unit). This tension frames much of Sambujat's material activity. The effort to build wider networks of cooperation in subsistence endeavors is constantly being undermined by the obligations to contribute labor to closely related members of one's patriline or *buaju*. "Semi-agnates" living in the same *hank* are supposed to cultivate together on frequent occasions, yet the bulk of the day-to-day inter-household cooperation takes place within the *buaju* unit. And though rights to land are vested on the *hank*, rights of disposition over productive resources lie within the *buaju* unit. The absence of an all-encompassing ideology of descent, binding members of particular *buaju* units into more inclusive groups, thus creates problems for the practical organization of productive tasks.

These problems are overcome by framing cooperative labor in terms of fulfilling socio-ritual obligations. Within the two Sambujat wards, for example, certain courtyard groups regularly work together. They may be

Plate 8: Elders and junior men in Sambujat cultivate together in the same work-group.

described, following Swindell (1985: 146), as "corporate wage earning organizations, rather than a means of providing *individual* wages for members." *Hank* A and B of ward yy, for instance, always band together to form an association called *Sapoti*, centered on a shrine called *Jilamba*. In 1981, *Sapoti* worked for whoever of its members had 3,500 CFA francs (about US $22.00) to pay it. It also worked for several elders.

When *Sapoti* works for an elder, the most common form of payment is a pig. On some occasions, an elder may contribute a bull for a sacrifice to be staged at one of the principal shrines. But any agnate, not just elders, can use *Sapoti*, even twice in a season. If the group works for an outsider, say a man from the neighboring village of Kalomp, however, it may demand to be paid 6,500 CFA francs or more.

Now, the money that members of the *Sapoti* association earn by laboring in each other's fields is not distributed among the members. It is usually put aside until the end of the dry season, before the rains begin. A six-day ceremony takes place then, during which the whole village stays home and performs the propitiatory rite for the shrine *Jilamba*, and sometimes also for *Kasira*, which brings rain. Hence, *Sapoti* functions as a ritual corporation. The profits that are made by its members are reinvested in ceremonies that benefit the entire community.

Given the reality that "semi-agnates" living in the same *hank* are not always related by traceable kinship ties, and besides which compete over all sorts of "allocative" and some "authoritative" resources, what brings them together to work in each other's fields in the first place? Certainly, it is not simply a feeling of *communitas*. For, if anything, "semi-agnates" often distrust each other. It is also doubtful if enlightened self-interest alone would do the trick. A man who has received help from a "semi-agnate" may refuse to give help when his turn comes up:

The men of X *hank* have decided to remove the cattle from the central courtyard, where they have been tied up at night, to a place outside. The reason for the move is because dung-beetles have been making sizeable holes through which rainwater seeps and is ruining the house foundations. When the dung is scraped off and taken to the rice fields by the women to serve as fertilizer, the courtyard looks like a colander. Twice, all the men of the *hank* have been engaged in day-long efforts to build a fence around the new enclosure. Twice Hujége has not shown up. He first went to visit his son in town, then went off fishing. For a while, nobody was able to force him to work on the enclosure. Yet Hujége did not refuse indefinitely to cooperate.

If a person refuses to participate in associative work without giving a legitimate excuse, the elders will first try to shame him. Other members of the village "will also try to force him" to cooperate. But if the individual goes on refusing, the council of elders of the ward will "pull him out" of the work-association in which he was a member, and which is structured around an important shrine. In this condition, the individual in question cannot share in any of the group's sacrifices to the shrine. This amounts to being socially ostracized; he doesn't eat meat, drink palm wine, benefit from communal prayers and, most important, will not get help from the group in preparing his fields:

There was a man from Ñalu (a particular *hank*) who refused to cultivate with other members of the Sapoti work-association. He was talked to by the elders once, then twice, but he still refused. The elders then took him out of the *Jilamba* shrine – *let a rin to* (he will not get there, i.e. be present) – and the man could not eat pork, drink wine or get *Sapoti* to work for him. He was given the option to re-join Sapoti by sacrificing a large pig and contributing significant amounts of *bunuk*. But he died without being able to do so. To this day, the man's children cannot even approach the Jilamba shrine. "*Jilamba* enforces discipline," I was reminded.

Besides Sapoti, all other work-groups in Sambujat are structured around specific shrines. *Hank* C, D and F of ward xx form a permanent work-group which takes its name from a powerful shrine called *Enak*. Another association takes its name from a shrine in the neighboring community of Kalomp. Still another group which was more common in the past (*Kanabo*) involved several of the *hank* located in both wards, and sometimes even the entire male membership of the community. All these groups spend the money they earn on buying food supplies (tomato paste, some oil, onions and generous amounts of palm wine) for village-wide, annual ceremonies.

Regardless of the form payment takes, whether in cash or in kind, male constituted work-groups, involving one or more courtyard units or *hank*, and working for one of its members, are seen as mutual-aid societies that give assistance to an individual while at the same time benefiting the collectivity by virtue of their ceremonial overtones. That an agnate must pay for this extra labor does not mean that Sambujat is permeated by "commodity relations" or "monetized labor" as Snyder (1981) suggests for the Banjal Jola. The Esudadu Jola are not, at least not yet, enmeshed in impersonal, contractual arrangements. Rather, paying out for services is a fundamental aspect of all transactions, from "doing" the shrines, to arranging for marriage, to complying with funeral obligations. That an individual who is rich in land, and moreover has earned enough money in the palm-wine trade, or has received substantial remittances from urban relatives, is able to engage more work-groups and produce more rice than many other individuals is an undeniable fact of life. But this sort of payment is culturally construed as cooperative labor, often aimed at fulfilling religious obligations. The purpose is to earn enough money with which to buy rice, sacrificial animals, condiments and palm wine in order to propitiate the community shrines. On these occasions, members of the association with their guests will feast amply.

Unlike wage labor that is performed in the city, associative labor is directly under the supervision of the spirit-shrine *Huteendukay*. As indicated, this shrine ensure(s) that the terms of agreement between the work societies and the person they are working for "are upheld" (Baum 1987: 360).

Female associations
Like the men's associations, the women's work-groups are an essential part of the rice-growing system. Female cooparative labor is most widely used at harvest time, when the crop must be gathered before it lodges or gets eaten up by birds. It is also used for transplanting, however, even though the pace is more relaxed. The women's associations are drawn along the same lines, as are the corporations surrounding the *Sihuñ* shrines – for women also appeal to common symbols and rituals to organize their endeavors.

The women's work-groups are called *etondiŋ* and are composed of all women married into a particular *hank*. Hence they are referred to as the

Plate 9: In Sambujat, women of all ages often transplant together.

etondiŋ of *hank* A, or the *etondiŋ* of *hank* B. Any woman belonging to the group, or even a woman from another village, can engage an *etondiŋ*, but outsiders pay more than the 2,500 CFA francs that in 1989 was charged to members.

Unlike the men's associations, however, the women's groups do not regularly work for the elders as a social category. They may, however, work for an elder's wife, but only in her capacity of in-married female. Rather, women tend to work for each other, or for another woman from a nearby community who can pay them. The money earned by members of a female work-association, or *etondiŋ*, is spent at the beginning of the rains, when the women stage a ceremony to propitiate one of the two female *Sihuñ* shrines, the one located in a small forest patch next to the rice fields. Each woman takes part of the rice seed she will use that year, as well as some palm wine, to the shrine for an oblation. One or more pigs, or a bull purchased with the proceeds from their labor, is also sacrificed, to make sure that the rice fields will produce next year. Hence, as is the case with the men's workgroups, the in-married women's *etondi* is a mutal-aid society whose ultimate aim is to maintain proper relations with the shrines. The association has practical, as well as symbolic, functions. Profits made from corporate activities are re-invested in rituals that ensure every person's productive, and hence reproductive, success.

In an important discussion of the power relations underlying the social division of labor by sex among the Beti of Cameroon, Guyer (1984a) argues convincingly that women have no recourse to outside labor. Her model certainly fits the situation that I will be describing for two other Jola communities I studied, in which women are largely dependent upon their husbands for cash, clothing and most everything else costing money. Among the Esudadu of Sambujat, however, the situation is quite different. As I have repeatedly mentioned, women have real access to cash. They can sell any extra rice they produce and with the proceedings hire outside labor. They can go up to Dakar for a few years and earn real money. And they are equal partners in the palm-wine trade (see below). In fact, Sambujat women have power, not because power struggles among sexual lines are absent from the Sambujat social fabric at large, as Burnham (1980) describes for the Gbaya of Cameroon. Or because without women production could not proceed. In many West African societies, women are the sole, or at least the main, agricultural producers, and yet they have little or no power (political, ritual or otherwise). Esudadu women make their presence felt in the community because they control mystical forces that affect the present health and future success of the labor force. Women's power is taken seriously. This becomes evident when one witnesses men carefully staying indoors while the women come together, to collect money with which to propitiate the *Sihuñ* shrines, by themselves and for themselves.

Obviously, I am not arguing that religion is "responsible" for the secure position that Esudadu women enjoy. There is no single "cause," no utilitarian explanation for the ways in which particular peoples build up their gender relations. Cultural notions make sense in terms of their own logic, their own logistics. But the fact that women have ritual power doubtless helps them to gain a measure of control over other resources. The influence (or power) they exercise as ritual agents serves to protect them against abuse. It is also intimately connected with, a constitutive part of, the state of equality that characterizes relations between men and women, male and female elders, parents and children. Relations that are translated into an egalitarian division of labor whereby both sexes and all generations work side by side. This is as true for rice production as for more commercial endeavors like the palm-produce trade.

The role of religion in the palm-produce trade

The Esudadu Jola carry on an active trade gathering and selling palm wine. In addition to being a central symbol of their religion, an essential item in the propitiation of the spirit-shrines, palm wine has also become an important commercial item. It is the main source of cash for the Esudadu Jola who do not grow groundnuts as a cash crop. In the palm-wine trade both sexes participate.

Palms of the African oil palm species *Elaeis guineensis* begin producing at 4 years of age and continue producing until they are 50 or 60 years of age. Several bunches of fruit, weighing from 1 to 20 kilograms, and bearing as few as 100 fruits, or as many as 1,000, ripen on a plant at the same time. Whereas the Muslim Jola we will be describing later collect the fruit to make cooking oil, the Esudadu Jola mainly climb the palm and tap the stems to collect the sap.[11] Left to ferment, the sap turns into *bunuk* or palm wine.

At home, palm-wine tapping takes place the year-round. But less so in the rainy season, when the sap is diluted and work in the rice fields is demanding, than in the dry season. In all the Esudadu villages, including Sambujat, each ward has its own grove or *bujal*. Each section of the grove is owned and tapped collectively, by all the male agnates of a particular ward. As a friend put it: "the *bujal* are not like the rice fields, where everyone has his plots; here they work the groves together." Palms that are scattered between the village compounds, however, cannot be tapped without the owner's permission.

The palm wine that is gathered at home is consumed by men and women as the mid-day meal, or is drunk at group gatherings. Most important, *bunuk* or palm wine is an essential ingredient in the *kawasen* rituals performed to propitiate the spirit-shrines. Occasionally, when an individual, man or woman, needs to purchase a large quantity of wine to sponsor a libation ritual at one of the shrines, he or she must purchase it locally, at the cost of 25 to 35 CFA francs ($0.10 to $0.15) the litre. This is considerably less than the 50 CFA francs ($0.20) a litre paid in town.

Palm-wine tapping has become a major commercial endeavor, the principal source of seasonal cash revenue other than working for wages in the city. After the rains have stopped and the harvest is put in the granaries, young and middle-aged men from the Esudadu and other southern Casamance communities leave their villages to go on the palm-wine tapping trip (the *kawaw*). They travel alone or in pairs, some going down south to the Guiné Bissau, others heading north to Muslim areas. Because of its symbolic association with the shrines, plus the Islamic interdiction against drinking alcoholic beverages, Jola Muslims do not drink palm wine (though they drink millet beer). Thus Muslim men have lost the ability to climb; as a result, their palms are full of fruit and sap. For this reason, they allow non-Muslims like the Esudadu Jola to tap their palms in exchange for trimming the palms and gathering the fruit for them. They do so by enforcing regulations aimed at conserving the palms and the fruit.[12] Hence non-Muslims and Muslims partition palm-tree resources, with the former tapping the sap to make wine (*bunuk*), and the latter using the fruit to make oil (*miit*).

While on their trip, Jola tappers spend 3 to 4 months of arduous climbing and collecting palm products. They sell the wine to Catholics and townspeople who can, and do, drink. There are reports of Esudadu tappers who can climb 40 palms between 6:00 a.m. and 10:00 a.m., or an average of 10 palms an hour. However, a more realistic estimate is probably 20 palms, each of which must be climbed twice daily. In any case, it is hard work; tappers loose a great deal of weight while on the *kawaw*. The following example, taken from one of my interviews of tappers, may illustrate the particular way the collecting trip is conducted:

Buli Sembu and Lui Jeju are from the Esudadu. This year (1985) they are collecting palm wine in the Muslim community of Tangori (near Fatiya, described in the next chapter). Their host is the chief. Some months previously they had paid him a visit, and advanced a small sum against the right to tap the palms. When they arrived, they had to contribute an additional sum (about 15,000 CFA francs, or US $60.00) to the village coffers, to be allowed to tap in the village grove. In addition to the family shrine *Hupila* which they bring with them, Buli and Lui bring enough rice for 3 months. Once daily, they buy a kilogram of fish, costing 50 CFA francs to add to the rice. Otherwise, they have few expenses.

In the first days of tapping, the boys gathered 30 litres a day, considered a good start. After a week, Lui was taking in 46 litres a day, Buli 42. After tapping the same palms for 3 days, the boys would move on to another group.

To transport the wine every day to the Bignona market to sell, the boys have hired two young girls. In gourds cushioned by wet straw inside a basket, the girls run to town to sell the wine. Occasionally, they help the boys by boiling the sap to accelerate fermentation. During four days, the girls carry the wine for the boys. On the fifth day, they carry the wine for themselves.

While in Tangori, the boys keep the earnings they make with the mission priest. In previous years, they had kept their money hidden in one of the many gourds they had placed on top of one of the many palms they were tapping. But this is still a risky procedure. With the money they earn, the boys will buy a young heifer, perhaps a pig or two, and possibly a nice indigo-dyed cloth to give away in funerals. Hence, most of the purchases they make are with an eye to the sorts of ritual practices they participate in back home.

Profits from the palm-wine trade vary somewhat from year to year. The two young tappers mentioned above made close to 100,000 CFA francs (about US $400.00) in 1985. This is considered excellent. However, average earnings are lower, between US $250.00 and $300.00 a season. Nonetheless, this sum compares quite favorably with the earnings from the groundnut trade made by Jola Muslims living north of the river.

Conclusions to Part I

"The study of human life, Marx emphasises, is the study of definite social practices, geared into human needs" (Giddens 1979: 151). Surely, however, the study of human life is more than this. It is also the analysis of cultural symbols and ideologies through which members of a specific society perceive their surroundings and organize themselves to act upon it. These are as much a part of the forces of production equation as are tools and know-how, for they mobilize people to perform essential tasks.

Sambujat's rice-growing system is both labor-intensive and highly routinized. Once the appropriate strategy is chosen to accommodate particular weather conditions, the same tasks are repeated day after day until a stage in the cycle, say field preparation or transplanting, is completed. Not surprising, the inhabitants take their work very seriously. In itself, work is socially meaningful. It labels a person as being an *aroka* (a "hard," "real" worker). Someone who is *puteput* (rotted, decomposed) is lazy. The Jola have a proverb: "To be sitting is never to one's advantage" (from Thomas 1959: 423; quoted in Baum 1987: 405). What Bourdieu (1977: 175) says of the Kabyle is also true of the Jola of Sambujat: "Activity is as much a duty of communal life as an economic necessity." However, it is not activity *per se* but the cultural constructs through which social control is exerted, the corporate tasks through which the labor process unfolds, the collective symbols through which it is organized, the mystical forces through which it is maintained, that gives the Sambujat system its very particular cast.

Not only within community boundaries, but also in capitalist production as well, religious beliefs and ritual practices have played an essential role in the conduct of economic life. Both, the non-Islamicized Esudadu Jola living south of the Casamance river, and the Muslim Jola living north of the river,

Conclusions to Part I   75

meet their cash demands in religiously appropriate, symbolically sanctioned sorts of ways. For palm-wine tapping and groundnut growing are not "neutral" endeavors. They are both embedded in "wider orders of material, ideological and moral relations" (J. Comaroff 1985: 154). Palm wine is a mediating symbol in the indigenous *kawasen* religion, and for that reason it has been forbidden for Muslims to drink it. Groundnuts have been historically linked with Islam and the world of the marabout, and for that reason neither non-Islamized nor Jola Catholics grow it.

Thus, the spirit-shrines and their representatives play an essential role in the productive process. For they command important "allocative" and authoritative resources. Shrines oversee production and protect private property. They supervise the labor force and compel cooperation among "semi-agnates," persons who live around the same courtyard or *hank*, but who do not always share close kin ties. Their power enters into the constitution of productive relations in at least two ways: directly, by deflecting conflict, safeguarding the health, and insuring the reproduction of the labor force, and indirectly, by imposing sanctions upon the ways in which resources are distributed and controlled at the local level. Answers to such questions as who controls the shrines, why do the spirits attack, what categories of persons can be present at certain rites, when should the shrines be propitiated, have political as well as economic implications. They have to do with the management of social tensions and conflicts arising between individuals or interest groups during the process of production or other social endeavors.

To gain an additional perspective on how the Sambujat elders and sundry shrine-keepers do social work, how they proceed in their specific social arenas, it may be helpful to contrast the Sambujat notions about the spirit-shrines with the equivalent notions among the Lugbara of Uganda (Middleton 1960; 1977: 80). Like the Sambujat Jola, the Lugbara are "singularly lacking in any effective sanctions for the maintenance of proper authority within the field of social relations of man or family" (Middleton 1960: 18). Unlike Jola religion, however, Lugbara religion is focused almost exclusively on ancestor cults, which in turn re-affirm the authority of lineage elders. This authority is extensive: it is the Lugbara elder's duty "to allocate land"; he "holds automatic authority over all members of the family cluster"; he "act(s) as (a) representative of the minor or major lineage," and so forth. The lineage includes the living elders and the dead ancestors. Together they maintain their authority by the rite of sacrifice. For sickness is thought of as punishment brought by the ghosts of the ancestors on persons who have flouted the authority of lineage elders. Thus, the Lugbara elder enjoys an independent basis of political power: "as the holder of lineage authority he can appeal to the genealogical experience of the lineage to buttress the network of relations that are dependent upon his authority" (Middleton 1960: 265).

In contrast, Esudadu elders do not acquire their authority by virtue of their genealogic position, for neither ancestors nor corporate lineages play an important role in Jola society. Instead, elders must compete for the "job" of shrine-keeper or *awasen*; and, once they have it, they must do what they can to intercede with the spirit-shrines on behalf of anyone in the community. Although some of the Sambujat elders, like the *ai* discussed at some length, enjoy a special mandate, there are strict limitations to what they can do. In the practical arena of daily politics, a Sambujat elder must tread a thin line. He does not automatically command respect, but must "earn" it, in a very Jola sort of way, by making sure that he can impose his will on the volatile will of the spirit-shrines. In the process of mediating in spirit attacks, elders must try to channel the ambitions of community members in socially non-disruptive and cooperative ways.

The direction taken by the flow of labor among Sambujat households is also revealing of authority relationships. Both J.V.D. Lewis (1981) and Donham (1981) described systems in which elders, who have a low consumer to worker ratio (C/W), channel extra labor down to junior households, which have high C/W ratios, in exchange for political patronage. The Sambujat data suggests, on the other hand, that if labor tends to flow, it is upwards, towards the older generation, and not in the reverse direction. Sons, whether married or not, continue to help their parents cultivate. Work-groups made up of unmarried youth charge less when they work for a mature or elderly villager than when they work for a youngish adult man. Old men who are poor, like the paramount ritual elder (the *ai*), quite often receive a great deal of unsolicited help. In some neighboring Esudadu villages, there are fields set aside for the *ai* which the entire community must cultivate. If a man has a number of unmarried sons in his family, he often asks them, at the end of the day, to go over and give a helping hand to an elder who is short of labor. Women have their own work associations. Widows and elderly ladies can count on the labor of their sons and daughters. Elders of both sexes depend upon voluntary, *ad hoc* labor contributions from relatives and/or younger members of the community in order to survive.

Through their constant appeasement of the spirit-shrines, elders contribute to the health and welfare of all village members. They insure the future reproduction of the labor force by propitiating the increase family shrine

(*Hupila*), as well as by safeguarding pregnant mothers and small children from witchcraft attacks. But they are powerless when it comes to expecting help from other than family members unless they are also custodians of important shrines. Elders who do not reciprocate by providing ritual services find themselves cultivating alone.

It was first suggested by Meillassoux (1964), with specific reference to the Gouro of the Ivory Coast, that one of the ways in which African elders control the labor of junior men was by withholding bridewealth payments. A Gouro elder controls the granary of the entire lineage sub-segment. "Because of his position at the apex of the community, the elder is logically appointed to store and centralise its produce. He is also in a good position to manage it" (Meillassoux, 1981: 42). Since first formulated, Meillassoux's theory has gained wide acceptance. His model has served as an explanation for such dependency prolonging mechanisms as late marriage and/or late male initiation (see Muller 1985).

Unlike the Gouro elders, however, and probably many other African elders as well, the Sambujat elders do not have rights of disposition over matrimonial goods. They neither direct joint activities, nor control a joint family granary, nor play a decisive role in amassing bridewealth payments for their sons. Because a "junior" man must raise his own bridewealth payments, he often marries late. And because Sambujat's mature men and elders must amass great stores before their sons can be circumcised, the age of initiation is often very late. It is these factors, rather than the problem of bridewealth payments, that explains why in Sambujat there are many grownup youths around who are uncircumcised, and so many eligible bachelors.

Be that as it may, it is clear that Sambujat's elders are both, similar to, and different from, those elders who have become the focus of much anthropological theorizing. "La différenciation entre aînés et cadets, la gradation des générations tendent à introduire une opposition entre ceux qui travaillent et ceux qui contrôlent les moyens de production" (Abélès and Collard 1985: 13). A simple opposition between those who do the work (the juniors) and those who own the means of production and/or reproduction (the elders) hides and confuses the complex relations of dominance and dependence, but also of equality and complementarity that characterize relations, not only among the generations but also between the sexes. It also hides the fact that these differences may be socially constructed in entirely dissimilar ways, and do social work in an unlike manner, among various groups and in diverse contexts (Donham 1985). In Sambujat, an elderly man may own more land or cattle, but these are not constitutive of his authority. An elder of either sex cannot "buy" more help in an open, competitive market. Although labor is sometimes paid for in cash, an elder must be able to cajole and convince other persons, who are as busy as himself, or herself, to lend him/her a helping hand. An elder cannot appropriate "surplus labor," for there is none, cannot withhold marriage payments, for these can be raised by the groom himself, cannot exploit a ritual office, for shrines can make him poor, cannot dispose of the products of other household members since women "own" their crop and young men have potential rights in land. To get help, an elder must earn respect. By interceding with the spirit-shrines he helps to mend strained relations and create some anew, he entreats the spirits to punish and give out favors. Above all, he looks after the health of the inhabitants and guarantees the reproduction of the work-force through the production of children. But an elder may be simply an aged person; he may be poor or wealthy depending upon circumstances, and he may or may not be respected. Only if he has an important shrine in his custody can an elder be said to wield "power." But this is the "power" to appease a-social forces: for "Mais, de toute façon, c'est toujours l'autorité religieuse qui excerce la justice" (Thomas 1959, vol. 1: 292). It is through this authority that the "weaker" members of society, like the elderly, the women (and their children), the handicapped,[1] not only survive, but in some cases do rather well.

Throughout this chapter I have emphasized that the Sambujat labor process cannot be appropriated by one age category, or by a powerful person. It remains to be emphasized that it cannot be monopolized by one gender alone. For, like men, women can defend their own rights and economic interests by using the considerable symbolic powers they have at their disposal. Women perform socio-symbolic services by restoring the working capacity of those who are ill, and by reducing deaths, increasing yields, assuring reproduction, "exorcizing" things that are "bad in the village." But they have ritual power, not only because they can "pray," but because they can "pay." They have access to outside sources of cash with which they can propitiate the spirits and sacrifice to them. For women can sell rice, the items which they make, and, above all, their labor-power. The latter they can "sell" inside their communities, mainly through their work associations, but also outside their communities, by participating in the palm-wine trade and through wage-labor migrations.

Starting with Boserup (1970), numerous authors have argued that cash crops and wage-labor migration, both male monopolies, have contributed to a decline in women's status under colonial and post-colonial conditions. Although doubtless true in some cases, this generalization does not quite apply to the Sambujat situation. To begin with, the Esudadu Jola do not *grow* cash crops. However, as I have indicated, they collect and sell palm products for cash, a task in which both sexes participate and profit from. For though women do not tap palms, nor collect palm kernels, for they do not "climb," they process the wine and kernels, and they also carry the product to market for sale. This is culturally expected of them. For women do most of the food preparation at home, and also much of the heavy carrying (they carry children on their backs, water from wells, fertilizer to the fields, and rice harvested home to the granaries). In fact, women are reputed for their ability to carry heavy loads on their heads. So much so that at the turn of the century they began to be hired by French commercial firms to unload ships in the port of Ziguinchor.

Hence, Jola women, including those from the Esudadu area, have been steadily involved in seasonal wage-labor migration since the end of the nineteenth century (Journet 1976; Hamer 1983).[2] Women were first employed by a French company to carry groundnuts and rubber (i.e. latex from the vine *Landolphia*) to steamships cruising the Casamance River, or docked in Ziguinchor; in 1905, they were also employed by another company to unload oil and bricks coming from Europe. In these jobs, they were the equal of men and received the same (low) pay for the same type of work (10 hours a day carrying sacks weighing 25 to 40 kg). Journet (1976: 197) calculates that as many as 1,500 to 2,000 Jola women from south-shore communities (including those of the Esudadu region) may have been engaged in seasonal wage-labor migrations. Although, as Hamer (1983: 244) observes, one does not know how many men were similarly engaged, "there is conclusive evidence that such labor was essentially a female endeavor by 1911."

As an active force shaping political relations within and beyond the domestic economy, changes in religious ideologies can set off major historical changes in the economy. They do so by changing the balance of power through symbols that invest new tasks and relations of production with new practical meanings. How power, labor, and production have become re-combined after the introduction of a new ideology and a novel technology will hopefully be clarified as we explore the impact of Islam and cash cropping on the political economy of the Jola living north of the Casamance River.

PART II:

AT THE CROSSROADS: THE KUJAMAAT JOLA OF JIPALOM

3

Islamization and the introduction of a cash crop

All Jola communities without exception are the product of centuries, if not millennia, of social transformation (Linares 1971). However, the inhabitants of the Kajamutay region north of the Casamance River seem to have experienced change in particularly disruptive and discontinuous ways. From the sixteenth to the end of the nineteenth centuries, Kujamaat social relations were largely subverted by their own territorial expansion, and by threats from slave raiders, European traders and zealous religious clerics. At first, the violent attacks of their neighbors seem to have had little effect on Kujamaat political and economic relations. For these incursions were too infrequent and disorganized to have caused lasting damage. But they did open up the area to the eventual penetration of ideological forces of an entirely different nature and scale from what had gone on before. Features of Islam as a universalistic religion, elements of European colonial government and African State formations, aspects of the world economy, were eventually to transform the political economy of the Kajamutay.

Much has already been written in general about conversion to Islam; and even more about the penetration of capitalist relations of production into the African countryside. But there is still a glaring need to explore the contradictory effects that these processes have had on particular social and economic developments. In the Kajamutay, in some periods and some areas, new ideologies and economic forces worked in mutually reinforcing ways, whereas in other periods, and in other areas, they did not, eventually leading to major contradictions in the social fabric. Among the Kujamaat Jola of Jipalom productive units have become atomized along territorial, generational, gender, and kinship lines. Usufructuary rights to land have become more conflictive. Associative work has greatly diminished. Inequalities in the access to land and labor have increased. At the same time, there is yet to appear a fresh synthesis between old rituals and new ideas. The religious authority of elders, which in the Esudadu area defined and delimited the boundaries of practical, productive action, are no longer effective. And the penetration of Islam as a clearcut moral charter, capable of guiding the political and economic decisions of community members, has yet to be completed. As indirectly related to productive activities as religious beliefs may seem to be, there is a crisis of authority when they are absent. When institutionalized belief fails to sanction property relations and conflicts flare up. Or when the ideological and political vacuum that is created with the erosion of the old moral order leads to the dissolution of cooperative patterns of labor.

In the community of Jipalom under discussion, Islamization has paved the way for the acceptance of new subsistence systems and new social relationships. And these have in turn ushered in profound changes in the political economy. But neither Islam nor commercial agriculture have provided sufficient conditions for the emergence of new structures of production. The social disorganization that has resulted is the by-product of ideological contradictions. Until very recently (see Epilogue), the inhabitants appeared to have been caught between a crumbling old belief system and the failure of religiously sanctioned structures of power relations to emerge. And yet, in the absence of more encompassing forms of secular government, local religion seemed to be the only alternative way, capable of providing meaning and structure to changes set in motion with references to a wide range of new material forces.

In the two chapters that follow I will be dealing with the processes of confrontation and change in Jipalom society. Chapter 3 will be an essentially historical discussion of Kujamaat Jola territorial expansion, the trade in forest products, their exposure to Muslim proselytizers and colonial administrators, their adoption of Islam and the introduction of groundnuts as a cash crop. I will be arguing that these processes often worked in contradictory and disruptive ways. Chapter 4 traces the impact of new ideologies and novel technologies on present-day political and economic relations. I will be arguing that the actual state of the Jipalom economy is largely a by-product of the slow and incomplete manner in which a new moral order is being forged.

Bañuñ history and Jola territorial expansion
Despite their relative geographical isolation, the Jola's strong sense of identity has been constantly challenged by external encounters and internal migrations along time–space edges as defined by Giddens (1984: 245). By

this Giddens means interactions that are framed along continuously changing territorial boundaries, among societies of different structural types. At some undetermined point in the past, but probably beginning some time before the fifteenth century and lasting for several centuries, the Jola began to expand from areas south of the Casamance River, to areas north of the Casamance River stretching from the ocean to the Soungrougrou River and up to the border with Gambia. Many of their social institutions at the present time are both the cause and the consequence of their uneasy relations of conflict, avoidance and partial symbiosis with their new neighbors.

One of these neighbors, the Bañuñ, played a crucial role in the history of Jola migrations. The Bañuñ (also referred to as Banjuk, Bañuun, Bagnun, Banhun, Bainounk etc.), speak a language belonging to a different branch (Teenda-Ñuuñ) from the branch (Bak) to which Jola belongs (Sapir 1971, Doneaux 1975). Nowadays, the Bañuñ are confined to some 30 small villages surrounding the city of Ziguinchor and the town of Bignona. They are also found in a few areas in Guiné Bissau. Yet several centuries ago they occupied a vast area. In the sixteenth century, Bañuñ lands stretched from the Cacheu River in Guiné Bissau, north to the Bintang (Vintang, Vintain) *marigot* and east to the Soungrougrou River dividing Lower from Middle Casamance. In the same century (1594), the Jola – at the time known as Fulup (Floup, Fulup, Falupos) – were still largely confined to a coastal strip running from the Casamance River entrance, south to the Cacheu River in Guiné Bissau, according to the chronicler Almada (in Brásio, ed. 1964). From this narrow coastal belt, which included the Esudadu homeland discussed in Part I, the Jola expanded dramatically to the northeast, into Bañuñ occupied lands. A great part of what is now the Jola Foñi (Fogny) region north of the Casamance River, with its Kajamutay and Kalunay subdivisions, was once Bañuñ territory. Although the Bañuñ lost most of their lands, much of their population and certainly a great deal of their cultural identity at the hands of the Jola, both groups were not strangers to each other. They had coexisted in Lower Casamance long before the Europeans had made their presence felt in the region. In 1510, V. Fernandes (in Monod *et al.* 1951: 71–73) had described a Bañuñ ritual bearing close resemblance to present-day Jola indigenous religious rituals.[1]

Bañuñ hegemony was expressed commercially, in the important south to north trade route which they controlled, linking the lower Cacheu, Casamance and Gambia Rivers via the Soungrougrou River and the Bintang *marigot*. According to Brooks (1980a, 1980b), the Bañuñ trading network was probably established much before the Portuguese appeared on the

Figure 2: Map indicating the present-day distribution of neigboring ethnic groups, including remnant Bañuñ communities.

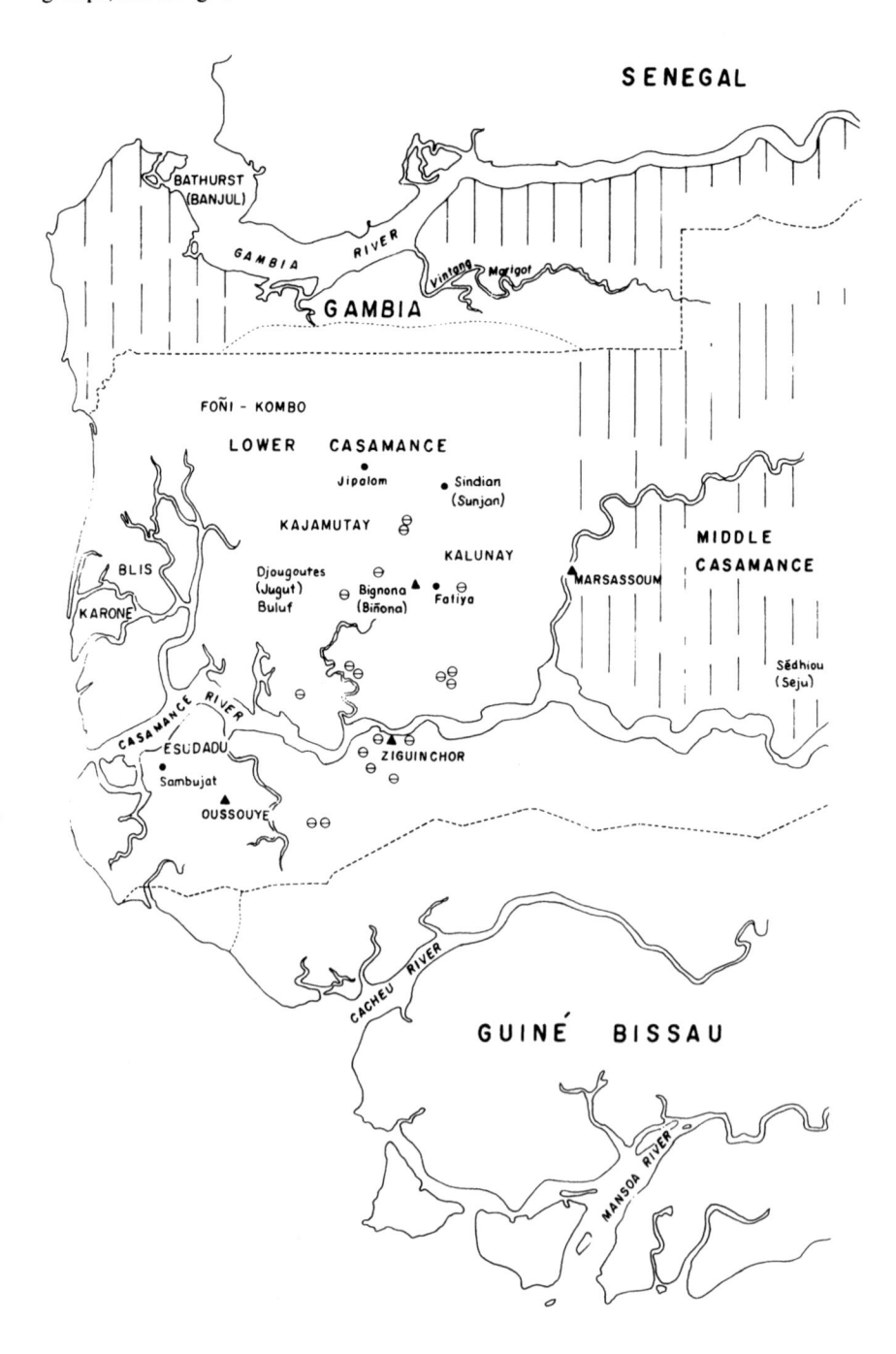

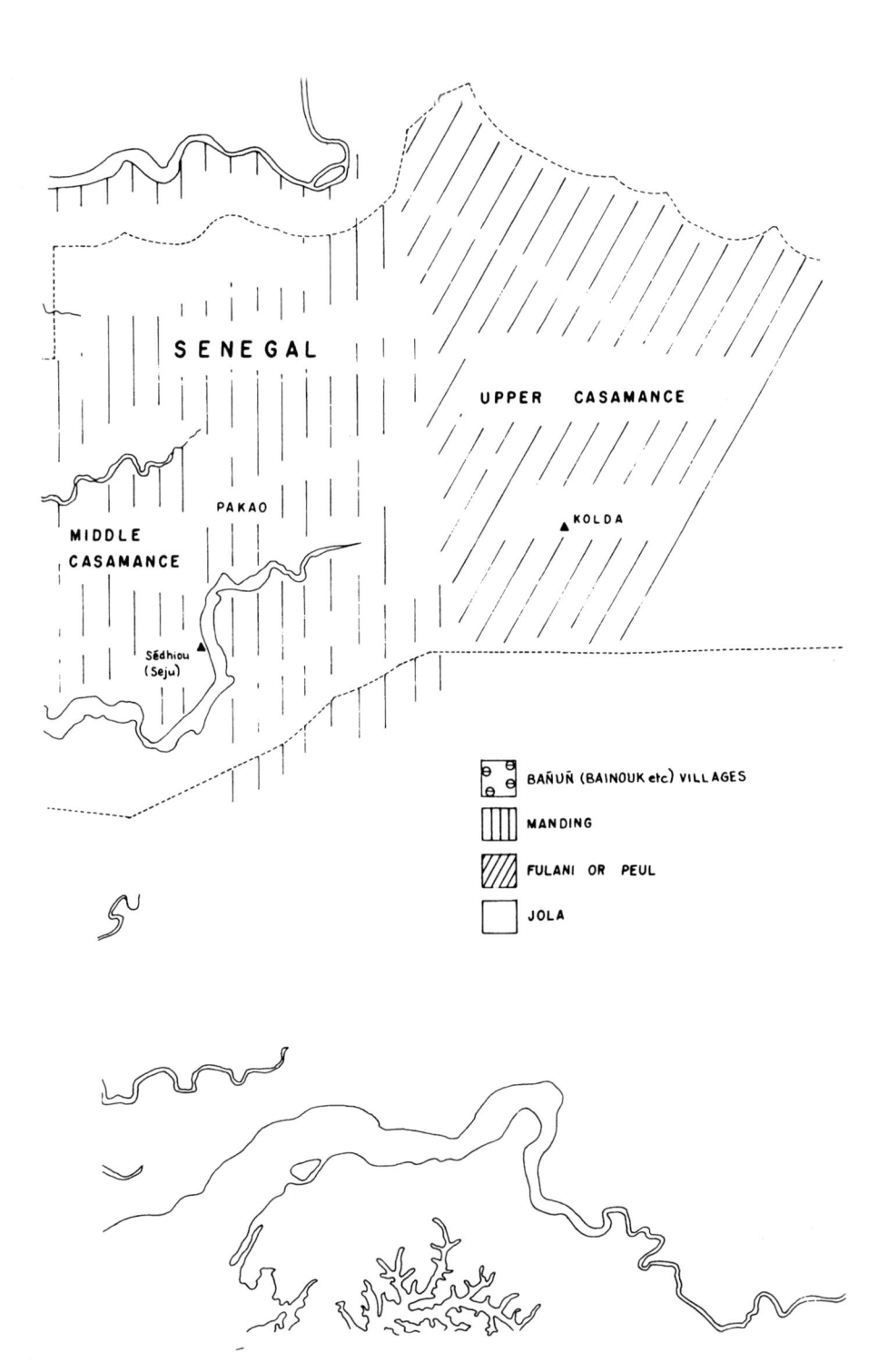

Islamization and the introduction of a cash crop 87

scene during the fifteenth century. In pre-European times, trade items included cloth, kola nuts, indigo, malaguetta pepper and other foodstuffs such as grain and dried fish; in post-European times beeswax and captives were added to the list (Brooks 1980b: 22). The Jola themselves may have been indirectly involved in the beeswax trade. In 1685, la Courbe (in Cultru 1913: 203-205) mentions that Africans from Gueregue (Heregues, one of the Bañuñ states), working for the Portuguese ("negres qui sont a leur gages"), would travel from village to village buying beeswax. Mark (1985: 24) is of the opinion that they were Bañuñ, purchasing beeswax from the Jola. To this day, the Jola keep beehives in large numbers.

Besides making good traveling merchants and middlemen, the Bañuñ were also gifted market-place salesmen. This emerges from Fernandes' 1506-1510 description of Bañuñ "fairs," which took place every 8 days and attracted some 7,000 visitors from various ethnic groups (Monod *et al.*, eds. 1951: 69-71). In contrast, the Jola were often described by the first European travelers as bellicose because they refused to trade. They were thus very different from *some* Bañuñ groups who were said to be very "civilized" – people "who loved commerce and strangers" and were therefore ill-prepared to wage constant war. To these elusive characterizations may be added the Jola's superior productive capacity and their independent economic base. One observer remarked that the Bañuñ, once upon a time great cultivators, had become lazy and self-indulgent. This also made them less secure, more vulnerable than the Jola to the incursions of other peoples present in the area.

The new commercial opportunities that were opened up by the presence of European and Euro-African traders aggravated competitive relations among local groups. Thus, for example, the Bañuñ and their close linguistic relatives, the Kassangas (Casangas, a "Mandingized" Bañuñ group; Roche 1985: 25), were constantly at odds with each other. Some time prior to 1545, the Bañuñ of Bichangor (Ziguinchor) "in alliance with the Jabundo group of Diola [Jola] on the north bank of the river had closed the mouth of the Casamance River to trading craft" (Brooks 1980b: 21). In the trips he made to Casamance between 1570 and 1585, Donelha (1625; see Teixeira da Mota *et al.*, 1977: 167) reports that the Kassangas had recently conquered the Bañuñ, disrupting trade along the Soungrougrou.

The Portuguese themselves, as well as the *lançados* and Luso-Africans who settled in the land, contributed to the general climate of competition and chaos. Until the end of the sixteenth century, the Bañuñ had allowed Portuguese and Luso-African traders to settle within their territory and increasingly monopolize trade.[2] Permission for these groups to travel and trade among the Bañuñ continued on and off throughout the seventeenth century (Brooks 1980a). In contrast, the Jola (and also the Balanta and Bijago) "generally excluded Portuguese and Luso-African traders from their territories and restricted commercial exchange to places and arrangements of their choosing . . ." (Brooks 1980a: 5). From the eighteenth century onwards, the Portuguese trade declined as the activities of Europeans and Euro-Africans were mostly confined to Ziguinchor and Cacheu.[3] But the cumulative effect of many decades of European and local African participation in the slave trade had a disruptive effect on Bañuñ society, as well as on Jola society (Linares 1987).

While the various Bañuñ sub-groups warred among themselves, and also with other groups, Foñi-speaking Kujamaat Jola were steadily moving up the Diouloulou creek, into the fertile lands bordering on the upper Baila *marigot* basin surrounding the town of Bignona (Lauer 1969: 58–59). It is not possible to determine exactly when this movement actually began. Probably, it was some time before the second half of the seventeenth century, when Coehlo (1669) found the Jola (i.e. the Fulup) well to the north of the entrance to the Casamance River. In all likelihood, the Jola pattern of movement involved conjugal family units migrating separately from various villages, coming together at their places of destination for mutual defense and support. By the middle of the nineteenth century, the Jola had pushed the Bañuñ well over to the eastern side of the Soungrougrou River. According to Lauer (1969: 59), "the uncoordinated but incessant raids of the Jola deprived them of much of their best land."

The Bañun [Bañuñ], who controlled much of the territory west of the sixteenth meridian in 1500, controlled very little in 1850 and even less in 1900. Most of the reverses came at the hands of the Jola, rather than from the more powerful Malinke [i.e. Manding]. (Lauer 1969: 56–57)

During the nineteenth century, however, the Manding also contributed significantly to the Bañuñ's demise. The westward expansion of Manding state rule halted the eastward movement of Jola families and groups (Lauer 1969: 59). This meant that the Bañuñ were caught in the middle. At the end, they were eliminated as a buffer State between two very different but similarly outreaching peoples.

Lauer (1969) has argued convincingly that the acephalous nature of Jola society contributed to the difficulties that the north shore Bañuñ, who were more centralized, experienced in retaliating against them. The hit and run tactics of small groups of Jola, who were following no higher order than those of their local spirit-shrines and village elders, proved difficult to counteract. Later on, European colonizers were to meet with the same problem; they continually complained that the unruly and "savage" Fulup were impossible to subjugate. When one group surrendered another one would take up arms. Lacking designated leaders, persons who could be captured so that their followers would give up fighting, the Jola proved impossible to conquer by force. As we will see, the same tactics also served them in good stead when resisting forced conversion to Islam.

It has been asserted of Senegambian societies that "the question of land was largely *not* involved in conflicts between communities and states" (Barry 1981: 34). The same has been said of other West African groups such as the Gouro (Guro) of the Ivory Coast, of whom Meillassoux (1964: 39) remarks: "on ne faisait jamais la guerre dans le but de conquérir la terre." The Jola, however, are clearly an exception. For them, conflict over land was, and to some extent still is, widespread. Even without experiencing major population growth, the Jola may have still wanted to increase the amount of good alluvial lands at their disposal. Whatever the causes, their settlement of the north-shore lands – starting some time before the fifteenth century and continuing until the nineteenth century – represented a spectacular territorial expansion. At the end, the defeat of the Bañuñ, who until then had formed a barrier between the Jola and the Manding, brought the Jola closer to the trade networks located within Gambia and to the influence of Manding-style Islam.

The trade in forest products

Doubtless the expansion of the Jola to the lands north of the Casamance River had a big impact on productive relations. For it brought an enormous territory under their control and it permitted the extension of their rice-growing techniques.[4] Moreover, what in the sixteenth to eighteenth centuries had been a sporadic pattern of indirect trading with the Europeans through intermediaries and middlemen, shifted to more direct commercial relations by the end of the nineteenth century. But, contrary to what other authors have argued, the consequences of this trade were indirect. It did not convert the Jola into a nation of traders, for what they did then, and still do now, is mostly exchange natural products from the land against manufactured items.

During the nineteenth century, the Jola turned to gathering forest products for profit. After its inception in the 1850s, the palm-kernel trade increased rapidly.[5] Exports from Casamance rose from 198 tons in 1869–1877, to 287 tons in 1884–1886 (Hamer 1983: 70). Almost the entire Lower Casamance crop was exported to Hamburg for processing into cattle feed and machine oil (Mark 1985: 71). The Jola also produced some palm oil for the market, but in smaller quantities. Palm oil requires a great deal of effort to process. The fruit must be boiled, then pounded; the pulp must be put into water and the oil must be skimmed off the top. Then, as now, the processing was most likely done by women, whereas the actual gathering of the fruit was done by men.

The European Depression of 1893 brought the palm-oil trade, if not to a halt, certainly to diminished proportions. However, the Jola continued to trade in palm kernels, which in times of scarcity they exchanged for rice (Mark 1985: 71). At this point, they were also engaged in the extraction of latex from the vine *Landolphia* which grew wild in the forest (Mark 1977, 1985: 72–74, 93–97; Harms 1975; Roche 1976: 193–198). The nascent industries of Europe had created a surging demand for rubber products, things like hoses, tires, fittings and so forth. After the trade began in earnest in 1879–1880, it expanded rapidly: from 59 metric tons produced in 1883, to nearly 400 tons produced in 1893 (Hamer 1983: 70). The gathering of rubber was done mostly in the dry season and was largely the work of men, whereas the preparation of the latex was done mostly by women and children who boiled down the liquid, rolled it into balls, and sold it, either to middlemen, or directly to buyers in Kombo and Bathurst. An added "stimulus" for extracting rubber came from the French administration. For a while, the French allowed the Jola to pay for their taxes in latex rather than in cash, then turned around and raised the head-tax at the time when the Jola were getting cash for their rubber (Mark 1985: 95).

After the turn of the century, however, the same story had repeated itself. This time it was rubber grown in Indo-Chinese plantations which began supplanting the Casamance trade in wild rubber. By the First World War, the Casamance rubber trade had all but disappeared. An added factor in its demise had been the poor quality of Casamance rubber in comparison with Gambian rubber. Here, rubber extraction had been developed by the English, who brought Kru speakers from Sierra Leone to the Gambia to teach the inhabitants how to prepare the vine and process the latex.

The unstable character of the trade in foreign products militated against it having a lasting effect upon Jola productive relations. As Hamer (1983: 63) has correctly observed, the nineteenth-century trade was modest in scale. Local Jola communities remained largely self-sufficient, only sporadically involved with other groups in market-place exchanges. To this day, the Jola have remained primarily an agricultural people. Thus, their society is quite different from Manding Dyula society, for example, or from the Bañuñ in times past. Of course the Jola did engage in commerce – they still do – but in a casual way and not as a full-time occupation. Very few Jola, then or now, earn their livelihood as middlemen.

A good case has also been made by Hamer (1983: 72–73) that neither the trade in red rubber, nor in palm products altered significantly the Jola gender division of labor. Both partners were equally involved in production and trade. Men collected the latex from the rubber vine; women boiled it down until it coagulated. Men climbed the palm trees to harvest the kernels; their wives extracted the oil from the fruit. When it came time to sell the products, both spouses had an equal share in the profits. It was also customary for the Jola conjugal family to migrate as a unit, and either reside in their host's house, or build a temporary hut nearby. In the odd chance that a man migrated alone, he was provided cooked meals; if the single migrant was a woman, she cooked for herself (Hamer 1983: 237).

The rubber and palm-product trade did have a profound effect upon Jola society by encouraging patterns of migration towards the Gambia that have become amplified in recent times. Some Jola made the trip to Bathurst and other Gambian towns to sell wild rubber, then to gather palm oil and palm kernels. In Gambia, they received better payment for their products than they did in Senegal, and they also could choose from a wider and less expensive selection of consumer goods (Mark 1977: 351). In addition, some Jola actually gathered palm products within Gambia itself by leaving shortly after the rice harvest and staying with an *ajawáati* (host, literally "one who does not go"). The host was usually a Manding of the Muslim faith. The Jola reciprocated for the right to use the palms by giving part of the harvest to their *ajawáati*. Before returning at the beginning of the rains, the Jola would sell their palm oil in Bathurst, then buy cattle, clothing and other items to take home (Mark 1977: 352). To this day, the Jola Foñi of the Baila *marigot* continue to migrate north, to the region called Kombo, and also to the Gambia, in search for better remuneration for their cash crops.

Hence, the rubber and palm kernel trade brought the north-shore Jola into closer contact with their Muslim Manding neighbors discussed in Part III. But relations between them continued to be hampered by the pillaging and slave raiding that went on under the banner of Islam.[6] The *jihads*, or holy wars of conversion unleashed by the Manding, were to have a delaying effect upon the Jola's acceptance of Islam.

Threats to Jola autonomy: the Holy Wars and colonial administration
Like their experience with new commercial endeavors, the Jola's exposure, first to Islamic clerics and proselytizers, then to French colonial administrators, did not change their society overnight. But, unlike the peaceful nature of trade and barter, their violent clashes with marabouts and colonizers had the opposite effect from that intended. The Jola's readiness to react aggressively to displays of force meant that the Manding incursions, often

carried out with the tacit support of the French, often met with little success. The Holy Wars retarded the Jola's acceptance of Islam (Leary 1970). Their armed conflicts with the French increased their suspicion of centralized government, postponed their acceptance of new economic endeavors and delayed their incorporation into the nation-state.

The holy wars of conversion began around the 1860s when a group of Muslim Manding and Fula proselytizers marched into Casamance determined to make war upon the "pagans." These "pagans" included not only Fula, Jola and Bañuñ groups, but also the Soninke. The Soninke were a group of Mande who were either "animists," or lapsed Muslims living on the edge of Manding territory, in the regions of Foñi and Kombo (Leary 1971: 232). Some Manding immigrants had actually been forced to settle among the Soninke, and pay tribute to them. It was they who finally revolted and in 1864 began a series of holy wars of conversion against their Soninke overlords; as well as against surrounding "pagan" tribes.

One of the principal figures to emerge as a *jihad* leader among the Manding groups of the Casamance was Fodé Kaba, a Jakhanke of the Tijaniyya (Tijani) sect. The Jakhanke were a specialized caste of Mande-speaking Muslim clerics and educators (Sanneh 1979). Fodé Kaba's devastating wars of conquest and conversion of the Jola living in the Kombo and Foñi regions are remembered to this day with a mixture of fear and admiration. In 1878, Fodé Kaba invades the Foñi and with the aid of 400 Manding horsemen pillages three Jola villages near the Soungrougrou (Roche 1976: 136-138). In 1880, he is defeated by a united front of Jola from Tionk-Essil (Thionk Essil, Conk-Esil). In 1893, he attacks the Jola of Sindian with the help of a contingent of French soldiers, only to be rebuffed. Many Jola were forced to flee south to escape death or enslavement at his hands. Yet, in the end, Fodé Kaba could not muster enough support among the Casamance Manding, who were tired of fighting the French, the "pagans" and also the Fulani (Fula, Peul), to conquer Lower Casamance. But many of those who had joined his ranks from a genuine desire to convert the Jola, settled in the region and eventually contributed to the spread of Islam.[7]

A crucial point to be emphasized here is that, since the 1830s, the Manding had oriented their economy to the production of groundnuts for export using slave labor (Weil 1984). In the Manding kingdom of Wuli, far up the reaches of the Gambia River, for example, large tracts of land previously used in bush-fallow cultivation of millet were put into cash-crop production of groundnuts. Agricultural slaves worked on official lands, as well as on lands assigned to them, to grow groundnuts and food. The prior existence of forms of internal slavery among the Manding had created antecedent conditions for the development of a large-scale, slave-based, production of cash crops. Not surprisingly, as some of the Jola captives had actually worked as slaves on their estates, it was the Manding who introduced groundnuts to the Jola of the Kajamutay.

The Islamization of the north-shore Jola

The maraboutic wars had an adverse impact upon the Jola: "The *jihads* which formed part of these troubled years accomplished few conversions and actually encouraged the conception of Islam as a militaristic and slave-raiding phenomenon in the eyes of the French and of the affected Diola and Foula" (Leary 1971: 236). Moreover, as Leary (1970: 142) makes amply clear, the marabout-warriors were really out to make immediate converts or lucrative slaves. Basically, they were uninterested in establishing an Islamic state governed by the Koran, so they made little effort to enforce a more rigorous form of Islam among the believers. Eventually, however, "French pacification opened new roads to the Mandinka for proselytization and conversion of peoples they had been unable to conquer militarily" (Leary 1971: 242).

Slowly at first, then in great numbers, the Jola north of the Casamance River converted to Islam after the turn of the century (Linares 1987). The expression he or she was converted – *natubitub* – comes from *tubi*, the Manding (i.e. Mande) word for repentance (*tubi*, in turn, is derived from the Arabic *tawba*; Trimingham 1959: 48). Conversion itself was (and still is) a fairly simple procedure. A marabout shaves the convert's hair (a forelock if it is a woman) at a baptismal ceremony, bathes the head, whispers Koranic verses into the ears, and gives advice. Previous to the ceremony, the marabout teaches the new convert how "to Koran" (verb, *kakaraŋ*); this means teaching him or her by rote a few verses of the Koran, enough so that the individual can pray (*kaséli*) alone. Conversion occurred in groups or, more rarely, alone. In either case, the convert's kin then distributes rice flour with sugar and kola nuts to the guests, and the ceremony is over.

Conversion did not follow a geographically even progression. Thus, while a village like Tiobon in the Buluf had a small community of Muslims living in it by 1894, other villages like Tionk-Essil had no permanent followers until 1916 (Mark 1985: 100–101). For at least two decades, Islamization proceeded very slowly. The period of most rapid Islamization covered the 1930s, at a time when the Jola were undergoing particularly severe hardships in the form of a drought, grasshopper plagues and the collapse of the palm-product trade.

It has been suggested that conversion naturally occurs when a "traditional" and "insular" peoples (like the Jola) see their chances for economic advancement increase with new commercial opportunities (Horton 1971, 1975a, 1975b). Mark (1976) endorses this point of view, arguing that there was a close relationship between trade and the Islamization of the Jola of Buluf. In a later publication, however, Mark (1985) criticizes Horton for not explaining why Jola women did not always convert to Islam despite being among the earliest migrants to the Gambia. This makes the point that trade was only one of several interrelated processes contributing to the spread of Islam.

A considerable number of Jola who converted to Islam had indeed, at some point, traveled to the Gambia to trade in forest products: "many of the earliest Diola adherents to Islam were young men who had spent time living in the Gambia" (Mark 1985: 100). Doubtless, Islam offered them "a viable personal and universalistic group identity when socioeconomic changes are [were] expanding social and experiential horizons" (Lewis 1986: 97). But religious conversion did not take place in a vacuum. Relations of control and prestige among local Jola "notables," and between them and Manding proselytizers or French colonial officers, played an important part in determining who converted to Islam, and why. Elsewhere (Linares 1987) I have recounted the experiences of a particularly influential man in order to illustrate how these power relations worked at the local level.

The political alliance (or conspiracy) that French administrators forged with the marabouts was crucial in hastening Jola conversion to Islam. Some instances of political manipulation were rather blatant, as when the military commanders (*résidents*) of Bignona in 1913 put Manding chiefs at the head of villages in the Sindian–Balandine area, within the Kajamutay. The new Manding chiefs promptly brought in numerous marabouts to carry on with the peaceful task of converting the Jola to Islam. The Manding were put in charge of censusing the Jola population, of establishing a kind of registrar office, of collecting taxes and, of all things, of administering justice (Trincaz 1981: 54). Marty (1916: 465), himself a colonial officer, remarked in retrospect upon the consequence of this policy:

It is under those circumstances, and with our complicity, that the Manding infiltrated the [very] country from where they had just been chased. They knew the people and the villages, their practices and customs, the roads, the *marigots* and the forests, the crops and the natural resources. They would volunteer their good offices. Being that it was impossible to approach the Diolas (directly), one utilizes these Manding. They were put in charge of censuses, of statistics on crops, of administering justice, of arresting [people]. One good day, the "animist" Diola country woke up to find itself split up into somewhat artificial cantons, ruled over by Muslim Manding chiefs.

On the eve of French forced recruitment into the army in 1915, numerous Jola of the Foñi took the occasion to rebel against the imposed Manding chiefs (Roche 1976: 336–354). The revolt was successful in that the Manding *chefs de canton* were shortly after removed and the Jola went back to being under the authority of their village chiefs, who reported directly to the French commander of the Bignona post. The deposition of the foreign chiefs did not end Manding efforts to extend their influence over the Jola, however. The Manding insinuated themselves in all sorts of ways, prompting Marty (1916: 468) again to remark that "Manding Islam should remain in Manding country."

The alliance forged between the French colonial authorities and the marabouts was not unconditional but, in Trincaz's words (1981: 45), "largely conjunctional," and it was politically decisive in promoting Islam. In asking, rhetorically, why Islam was gaining ground, a Catholic missionary remarked: "Perhaps it is because the local Administration seems often to reserve all their favors and honors for Muslims. Thus, at this moment, the Président du Tribunal Indigène is a Muslim; the two interpreters for the Administrator are Muslims, all the Chefs de Canton are Muslims. Jola animists see this and quickly conclude that, to become a great chief, one must become a Muslim" (*Bull. Congr. de St-Esprit*, t. XXX, 1921–1922: 426).

Mark correctly emphasizes the important *de facto* role played by the French colonial administration in promoting Islam. He is of the opinion that "the French had no explicit policy to foster or approve the spread of Islam among the Diola" (Mark 1985: 103). However, it is also clear that the French informally voiced support for the spread of Islam – at least among some Jola groups – as a politically useful tool. Dr. Maclaud, in his monograph of 1911 describing the Casamance *cercle* (quoted in Roche 1976: 312), seems to confirm this:

Islam in Casamance does not represent any danger for us ... we can only wish for its acceptance and progress as a means of peacefully penetrating the animist populations of the lower river to impose upon them some discipline. The marabouts of a comfortable age and position have well understood the interest that there is in their important role of maintaining the closest and most devoted of relations with the administration [my translation].

The Foñi Jola living in the region north of the river became rapidly Islamicized after the turn of the century. According to Roche (1976: 153), this occurred "thanks to the zeal of numerous peaceful marabouts introduced into the villages by Muslim *chefs de canton*, very often Malinké [Manding] and put in place by the French administration."

For the Jola north of the river, embracing Islam meant giving up palm wine and the raising of pigs, or (for some reason) ducks. It also meant adopting a host of practices such as praying five times a day, fasting during Ramadan, washing constantly, changing one's name, and so forth. Structural changes in notions of descent, marriage payments, relations with strangers and in life-crisis rituals have also come about, but they have been more profound in some regions than others. However, they are not an immediate by-product of the Jola's acceptance of Islam, or of groundnut farming *per se*. Rather, they are the result of the adoption of a particular Manding style of religious comportment by a segment of the Jola population. Only in those areas like the Kalunay, where the Jola and the Manding live side by side, have Manding religious and social practices been adopted wholesale.

In fact, though Islam is the country's dominant religion, Senegalese Islam has very little to do with "l'Islam légaliste et rigide" of the *ulamas*, or those trained in legal studies (Coulon 1981: 6). Instead, Senegalese Islam is organized into brotherhoods centered upon the cult of saints. As Hesseling (1985: 90) observes, "Senegal is the sole African country where Islam is completely organized in terms of brotherhoods." These are modelled along the lines of traditional Wolof and Manding social structures, a fact that, according to Coulon (1981), explains the pronounced hierarchical nature of the Senegalese brotherhoods; especially when compared with those of North Africa or other Islamic states. However, as Coulon rightly points out, the relationship between marabout (or Muslim leader) and his *talibés* (or disciples) may be inegalitarian, but it is neither arbitrary nor unjust. The marabout comes under the code of patronage, which entails some redistribution of resources. In becoming institutionalized, the brotherhoods accommodated themselves to the realities of power.

The two Muslim congregations or brotherhoods (*tariqas*) which predominate in Lower Casamance are the Qadiriyya, which is the oldest, being founded in the thirteenth century, and the Tijaniyya (Tijani) which was founded at the end of the eighteenth century and spread to Senegal in the nineteenth century. The Qadiriyya brotherhood appears rarely in the forefront of current events. "Its rituals are simple, calm and non-ecstatic" (Hesseling 1985: 93).[8] Tijanism, on the other hand, is more formal and intellectual in its beliefs. Tijanism draws its congregation from the educated urban elite, and also from the most well-off peasants.

The official Senegalese census of 1970 for the whole country (Gellar 1982: 106, note 2) lists the population of Senegal as being 52 percent Tijaniyya, but only 13.5 percent Qadiriyya. Hesseling (1985: 93) talks about 16 percent to 17 percent of the country being Qadiriyya. In any case, this brotherhood has a minority overall representation among the Senegalese population. Yet the overwhelming majority of Jola are Qadiriyya, for the obvious reason that most of them were converted by the Manding, who are prominent members of this particular brotherhood. Not surprisingly, however, some educated Jola youths from Ziguinchor have recently shifted to Tijanism (Trincaz 1981: 50). And there are some communities in the Buluf–Jugut area, including Tionk-Essil and Tiobon, where the Tijaniyya brotherhood had a large following by the 1930s thanks to the activity of a famous Tukulor (Toucouler) merchant-marabout (Mark 1985: 121).

Very few Jola, on the other hand, have joined the Muridiyya (Murid, Mouride) brotherhood, a locally based Senegalese order that in the nineteenth century broke away from the Qadiriyya. In 1970, its million or so adepts (29 percent of the population) were mostly Wolof peasants from Cap Vert and the groundnut basin to the east, around Diourbel. The Murids are tightly and hierarchically organized under a supreme officer (the *khalifa*), and a ruling group of marabouts with their *talibés* or peasant dependants (see Cruise O'Brien 1971, 1975; Copans 1980). Although Muridism seems to be rapidly gaining ground, and by the 1980s may be rivaling Tijanism in importance (Coulon 1981: 9), it has gained few adepts among the Jola, who dislike the authoritarian aspects of its leadership and the abject condition of the *talibés* or disciples.

Adopting groundnuts as a cash crop

The increasing monetization of the economy taking place during the second half of the nineteenth century finally encouraged the north-shore Jola to shift to a cash crop by the turn of the century. Accustomed to seasonal migration, and needing regular cash earnings to pay taxes, the Foñi Jola began cultivating groundnuts on a large scale after the trade in wild rubber finally collapsed around 1910.

However, trade in itself does not suffice as an explanation. A more profound understanding of why the Jola adopted groundnuts at about the same time as they converted to Islam must take into account the actual way in which these processes are linked in people's minds. Among the Jola, symbols associated with the old and the new religions have played an important role in conversion. For, in their minds, Islam and groundnut cultivation are intimately related. In Lower Casamance, many non-

Muslims do not grow groundnuts. This is as true of those who practice the "traditional" shrine-centered indigenous religion as of those who have converted to Catholicism. On the other hand, palm wine is one of the central Jola symbols, associated with the indigenous "traditional" religion and to some extent also with Catholicism. In fact, palm-wine libations define what a shrine is, who commands it and how it is to be enlisted in a person's favor. For that reason, a non-Muslim is described as an *aranaao* (from the verb *raan*, to drink), a person who drinks palm wine. The reason why the Jola gave up palm wine and took up groundnuts was not simply because Islam prohibits the drinking of alcoholic beverages, for Muslim Jola can and do drink millet beer. It was also because Muslim marabouts were bent on stamping out "pagan" symbols and practices. In so doing, they also stamped out one of the principal sources of cash revenue open at the time to the Jola, namely the tapping and selling for cash of palm wine, and/or exchanging it for other products. This sparked off the need to adopt groundnuts as a substitute cash crop.[9]

The Manding themselves, through the legacy of the French, played a key role in the introduction of cash-cropping to the Jola north of the river. Within the Casamance, groundnuts were first cultivated in the Middle Casamance, in what is essentially Manding territory. The French had encouraged groundnut production among the Manding marabouts through free donations of seed, of money to build mosques and travel to Mecca, and by bestowing upon them honors of all kinds. By the 1850s, the town of Sedhiou in Middle Casamance, which had been a French *comptoir* since 1838, had become a major exporter of groundnuts under French commercial control. "Just to this year, in the Casamance, one had cultivated groundnuts only at Sedhiou. This crop has greatly developed in a very short time" (Bertrand-Bocandé 1856: 411).[10] Apparently, small amounts were also grown early on in the island of Karabane (Mark 1985: 103–4).

Unlike most Senegalese groups the great majority of the north-shore Jola, did not, however, take up groundnut cultivation until later, in the first decades of the twentieth century. In the Buluf-Jugut (Djougoute) area, some villages like Tionk-Essil and Tiobon were growing it in small amounts by 1910 (Mark 1978: 4). The inhabitants of Tionk reported that they had learned to do so from Manding traders. The Jipalom elders I used to talk with twenty years ago still remembered when groundnuts were first cultivated in their community:

When Mamanding (age 55–60) was about eight years old, she witnessed when groundnuts were first cultivated in the region. All of the men of the *eluup* (the compound) cultivated together in a small plot they owned in common, in the midst of the forest. They did not grow much. People did not know what to do with the crop, so they would pull up the plant and bring it home, in bunches, to pull off the nuts, crack them and winnow them in a flat basket, like rice. [Today, all operations, from beating the peanuts to separate the nuts, to bagging them and taking them off for sale, takes place in the fields].

During the First World War, when the French administration was preoccupied with forceful recruitment, little had been done to improve the groundnut trade. But as soon as the end of the war was in sight, France turned its eye to the economic condition of its African colonies. The French administration had also correctly surmised early on that the "pacification" of Lower Casamance could be hastened if the Jola were incorporated into the European export economy. The colonial administration also wanted Casamance to be self-supporting, and local merchants agitated for new markets. These were standard arguments for pushing cash crops. To make sure groundnut cultivation developed rapidly, the French colonial administration increased taxation. "Between 1918 and 1920 the head tax was doubled from five to ten francs and collection was enforced with increased vigor" (Mark 1985: 105). French policy involved creating needs for new goods, providing actual support in the form of advances of seed, storage facilities and loans, and backing the whole thing by taxation enforced through military force (Roche 1976).

Transportation problems were so serious that groundnut cultivation advanced very slowly at first. Casamance was isolated from the rest of Senegal. It was difficult to sell all the groundnuts produced within the region thus it served as a seed reservoir for the entire country (*Serv. de l'Agric.*, *Rapp.* 1905). Roads were built by conscripted labor in order to connect trading and administrative centers like Bignona and Ziguinchor. Forced labor was imposed by the French through the *indigènat*, the colonial system of native "justice" (1921–1946) involving administrative sanctions and the penal code. It gave the *commandant* the right to jail anyone who refused to comply with forced labor, to pay the head tax, to show proper respect for French authorities and so forth (Gellar 1982: 10). Not surprisingly, the Jola abhorred the system. In 1925, for example, the Jola of the Bignona *cercle* were convoked to contribute their labor for the construction of the Baila–Belai causeway, near the village of Jipalom. The inhabitants of the villages of "Diougol" (Diagon, Jagon?) and "Djiboudie" (Djigoudie?), who had never been visited by an administrator, not even by the *chef de canton*, refused formally to comply with the orders. When the French administrator or *résident* of Diouloulou went to check, he found "Diougol" abandoned by its inhabitants and "Djiboudie" armed to its teeth. Although only one *tirailleur* was wounded, the Administrateur Superieur de la Casamance simply moved in by force and made the natives give up their guns. The methods he actually used against the villagers were carefully not specified in the *Rapp. Pol. Ann.* for 1925.

Despite the initial slowness of the groundnut trade, French authorities were confident that it would eventually succeed. This was certainly the case, for groundnut production increased steadily. In 1920, the Casamance (mostly Middle and Upper) was producing 18–20,000 tons of groundnuts; by 1925, this production had climbed to 42–45,000 tons (*Serv. de l'Agricult., Rapps.* for 1920 and 1925). The share contributed by Lower Casamance had augmented significantly, so that by 1930 statistics on yields were reported by sub-region: 2,600 tons for Ziguinchor, 12,000 tons for Bignona (still low when compared with 22,000 for Sedhiou in Middle Casamance, and 196,000 tons for the groundnut basin in Kaolack); (*Serv. de l'Agricult., Rapp.* 1930). From there on, the story is well known; groundnut production by the north-shore Jola continued to increase, even throughout the Depression years, despite the fact that the revenues the Jola received for the groundnut crop did not increase proportionally. The Depression caused a steep decline in price, to less than half the price in pre-1930s days (Mark 1985: 108). This situation continued, and was aggravated by drought, a locust plague and a cattle epidemic. By the time conditions improved in 1935, the Jola north of the river were now dependent upon the groundnut for cash revenues. Centuries of relative economic independence had gradually drawn to a close.

It should go without saying that none of these historical developments can be considered in isolation. Islamization, cash cropping, and colonialism were all interrelated processes, acting in complex ways. Their cumulative impact upon Jola society north of the Casamance River was doubtless enormous. Yet these processes did not always work in mutually reinforcing ways. Often, they created internal contradictions, retarding or even impeding the emergence of coherent new systems of production and new labor relationships.

The religious wars certainly delayed the Jola's acceptance of Islam. But Muslim religious teachers and traders accelerated the Jola's adoption of groundnuts. Trade in forest products facilitated access to manufactured products. But contacts with the Gambia also encouraged a drain on human and material resources. Armed confrontations with French authorities increased the Jola's determination to remain independent. But the economic policies of the colonial states drew the Jola into dependent relations with the emergent nation-state. Forced labor and conscription encouraged the exodus from the countryside. But new roads also facilitated local commercial initiatives.

In short, the impact of exogenous forces, rooted in colonialism and the world economy, have had a very uneven effect upon local political processes in the countryside. Despite causing considerable disruption and disarray, they have neither eliminated, nor completely replaced in all areas, old power structures and productive relationships. True, that in some regions like the Kalunay the Jola have re-structured their own productive arrangements to conform to those of their Manding neighbors. However, in other areas, like the Kajamutay described in this chapter, the Jola have not. The causes and consequences of this strategy will be examined in more detail in the next chapter.

4

The impact on social and productive relations

The Kujamaat Jola have finally embraced Islam and embarked upon commercial agriculture. But the chaotic experiences of the previous century have left their mark. The Jipalom inhabitants seem to be at a crossroads: they are socially atomized, politically marginalized, and economically dependent upon the nation-state. As a result of past upheavals and population displacements, Kujamaat communities have become little more than aggregations of largely independent wards and courtyard units. Internal contradictions in the social fabric have emerged between the genders and the generations. Production has been channeled into two conflictive, task-specific agricultural systems that compete for labor and land. A coherent new ideology relating "traditional" beliefs to new Islamic rituals has yet to be forged, one that can negotiate the gap that now exists between old practices and new relationships. For Islam does not participate in a highly articulated structure of power relations. And it also lacks the direct association that once existed between the spirit-shrines, their keepers, and the forces and relations of production. Only in those areas like the Kalunay, where Islam has been associated with a clearcut and prior Manding model of social relations, has the transition to a new economic order been negotiated.

The present chapter begins by placing the Jipalom community in its proper historical context. It then deals with three spheres of present-day community relations: social, religious, and productive relations. The focus is on the causes and consequences of the lack of viable linkages between these dimensions. In analyzing society as a "nexus of economic, political, and ideological relationships," rather than "as a totality of bounded relationships" (Morris 1987: 139), the negative or disruptive effects of the new religion come to the fore, as well as its more positive, integrative aspects.

The history of a community: Jipalom in the Kajamutay

The Kajamutay is the name given by the Jola north of the Casamance River to the region bordering the upper reaches of the Baila *marigot*, itself a branch of the larger *marigot* of Bignona. On valley floors and swamps, the inhabitants grow rice. On slightly higher, better-drained upland areas, they grow groundnuts for cash. Both men and women work both types of land. While new productive practices have been introduced, old productive relationships have remained generally the same. The Kujamaat Jola speak Foñi, a dialect variant of Jola that is mutually intelligible with Kasa, the variant spoken south of the river by peoples such as the Esudadu. This is added confirmation of the fact that the migration of the Jola, up the Baila *marigot* from the immediate regions to the south, was a relatively recent phenomenon.

The general turbulence and population disruptions that characterized Lower Casamance history in the nineteenth century did not fail to leave their imprint upon the manner in which their village was initially founded. How villages were founded in turn affected the social and economic structures that emerged.

In the oral accounts I gathered concerning the founding of Jipalom, each of the five wards (*ulol* pl., *kalol* sing.) making up the village had its own unique version of the past. The wards had been founded by different families, originating in separate villages within the Foñi territory:

Informants from the present-day Bojas ward, for example, say that initially they came from the village of Meijeij (Medieg), located behind the town of Sindian. From there, they first went to Telum (Talloum), where they joined the Jiba house within the ward called Baruk. As a result of Manding-instigated attacks, several of Telum's Baruk families, including the original Meijeij group, fled to separate villages. One of these villages was Jipalom. At that time, Jipalom had a ward called Bekei, which had previously been settled by peoples bearing the Koli patronym and originating in the village of Baralir (Baranlir). The group coming from Telum, Baruk, settled down near to, but not within, the Bekei ward; they adopted the Bojas name for their ward and changed their patronym from Jiba to Koli. Changing patronyms was a very common practice in the past. It was the first step in the partial absorption of strangers into local fictional descent categories.

The next step in the history of the Bojas ward came when they went to war with a people of obscure origins, living in another neighboring ward called Bunen, whose ricefields the Bojas group coveted. As a present-day resident put it: "in the old days, the *biit* (rice fields) was insufficient, not like nowadays with groundnuts and Dakar." Anyhow, the Bojas people continually taunted the Bunen into war, raiding their rice crops and selling those they captured to the Manding. Finally, when the Bunen were too few to defend themselves, the Bojas people descended upon them, taking over their ricefields.

Other Jipalom wards similarly trace their recent origin to villages like Mambiñé (Mambigne), Baralir and Katuje (Katoudie), from where they fled during the Manding wars. They changed their patronymic ascription and, eventually, fought to gain rice lands in the alluvium. Oral accounts repeat the same themes: how a group rich in land was killed off, except for those individuals who managed to hide out with their uterine kin; how they recovered the land by activating matrilateral ties; why some ended up as losers; why others gained ground, and so forth.

Besides marking a distinction between agnatic and matrilateral relatives, oral traditions reveal the piecemeal fashion in which Jola villages were settled. The religious wars, and the constant fusion and fission of groups taking place at historic junctures, meant that villages ended up being conglomerates of families with heterogeneous origins. The contradictory nature of this experience is reflected in the conflictive nature of social relationships.

Agnatic filiation versus uterine ties
The Kujamaat social system is based on a dual structure of opposing principles of recruitment to social groups, namely patrifiliation and matrifiliation or uterine ties. These work in different ways within a community. Although Jipalom is a fairly small place of approximately 600 persons – only twice the size of Sambujat – it is considerably less coherent as a social unit.[1] This "incoherence" is a by-product of historical circumstances. It is also the outcome of a partial and incomplete shift in the kind of ideologies that reinforce kinship ties, political processes, and productive practices.

As is the case with the Esudadu Jola, the Kujamaat Jola do not build elaborate notions around the concept of descent. Two heads of household living in close proximity to each other seldom feel compelled to claim an agnatic ancestor in common, someone who lived at some point in the remote past. Beyond three generations of ascendants, everything fades into vague notions of brotherhood. "Their fathers were brothers" (*sipay siraferore*, literally their forefathers nursed one after the other) is the usual answer to questions concerning how two co-residing men are related (i.e. how they "touch" each other). However, as a practical and useful "fiction" that lends a measure of legitimacy to a residential unit forged on an *ad-hoc* basis, agnatic filiation (as contrasted with agnatic descent) is a useful construct.

The co-resident unit made up of male household heads is known by the polysemic term *eluup*, which I have glossed elsewhere as compound (Linares 1983, 1984), but which could just as well be rendered by its literal

106 *At the crossroads: the Kujamaat Jola of Jipalom*

translation as House, which better reflects the fact that it refers not to a descent unit but to a residential corporation. Members of the same House often (though not always) share the same patronym and are also forbidden by rules of residential exogamy from marrying each other's daughters. They also hold residual rights to land in common. The out-married female agnates (*the kuriimen*) also have rights to shelter and protection within the House.

Plate 10: The entrance to an *eluup* or House unit. Rice granaries are on the right. The open hut on the left is where women pound the daily rice.

In turn, the House or *eluup* unit is made up of a number of semi-independent, extended patrifilial families which, at least in principle, have common interests to defend. A patrifilial family can include any of the following persons: a father, his brothers, their unmarried children, their married sons, their grandchildren and so forth. Within this group, descent is indeed traced to a known elder who lived in the not so distant past. In principle also, conjugal families within the patrifilial unit reside in separate structures arranged around a common courtyard or *fank*.

It is not always the case, however, that within the same *fank* genealogically close agnates, say two brothers, or a man and his dead brother's son, actually live around the same space. Often, they are found living in separate courtyards, though not too far apart. Like all such co-residential agnatic units, the courtyard group or *fank* has the internal potential for conflict over land and cattle. Moreover, there are also married individuals, unrelated to any member of any House unit, who are living with sundry kinds of hosts. These men are referred to as "strangers" and as such do not enjoy full rights of membership in the various Houses where they reside. Other, loosely attached men, can claim matrilateral ties to a household head and as such have more security of residence. In both cases, these "outsiders" have received loans of rice fields from several residents, and for that reason they are pleased to stay. Though not obligatory, it is expected of outsiders that they will occasionally cultivate for their hosts. Determining how often they are supposed to do so, and which host is served first, may often cause problems.

Feelings of solidarity and cooperation should, and often do, underlie relations between members of the *eluup* unit. But there is also a great deal of competition and friction among them. The same is true to a lesser extent of patrifilial families; they, also, have the in-built potential for discord, or at least for less than perfect unity. This is related to the fact that marriage often separates particular sub-sets of descendants who share exclusive networks of matrilateral ties. Whereas, in Sambujat, uterine and agnatic kin tend to be merged conceptually into some sort of cognatic principle by virtue of the practice of close in-marriage, in Jipalom these constructs are in large measure kept apart. A social contradiction or disjunction exists at the very heart of the patrifilial family unit, between the structural principles that underlie agnatic descent and those that underlie the formation of ego-centered uterine groups. Uterine ties are crucial for the creation and reproduction of dyadic relations of production, but they are also potentially divisive at higher levels of organization.

The men of Jipalom give sisters and daughters, and receive wives and mothers, from 17 different villages. Numerous individuals, belonging to

108 *At the crossroads: the Kujamaat Jola of Jipalom*

several *fank* or courtyard groups, are involved in these marriage exchanges. This, then, is Jipalom's matrimonial area, broadly defined. Narrowly defined, however, the effective matrimonial unit consists of 6 communities, including Jipalom, whose members regularly intermarry. These communities are 7 kilometers from each other, well within walking distances. Females married into Jipalom are known by the Foñi term *kuseek*, meaning "women"; 128 out of 154 *kuseek*, or 83 percent of the total number of wives in 1981 came from the 6 villages, including Jipalom. Together, the 6 villages form a marrying community within which women move around, though not in any pre-determined or unidirectional manner.

Marriage with a real or classificatory uterine relative is surrounded by the same exogamy prohibitions that apply to marriage within the *eluup* unit. Marriage with a woman or a man who was born in the same House as one's mother is strictly forbidden. Marriage with someone from father's mother's House, or mother's mother's House, was also considered bad form until recently. Such marriages, however, are not unheard of nowadays. The most common type is patrilateral cross-cousin marriage: a young man marrying a classificatory father's sister's daughter. (She, of course, marries her MBS, a uterine relative). Patrilateral cross-cousin marriage is, as we will see, common in Fatiya, the "Mandingized" village discussed in the next chapter. It is still uncommon and frowned upon in Jipalom, but there is a term for it, *kabaajor* (from *baajor*, to be in conflict).

The marriage of an agnate of the ascending generation to a woman from one of the villages within Jipalom's matrimonial area brings into existence for their descendants several potentially important categories of uterine kin: mother's agnates, father's mother's agnates, mother's mother's agnates. These persons constitute his personal kindred; they do not in any sense form a resident group with jural continuity, but are instead scattered among several villages. The uterine kin seldom come together as a group; they do so only when a sister's son dies, or when they arbitrate in disputes among two local agnates, or when they help with the initiation of their brothers' sons. A man obtains from his *sipaay*, or collectivity of male uterine kin, usage rights to extra rice fields, and to seed and equipment when he needs it. In the old days, he also obtained defense from slave raids and support in personal feuds. From his *siñaay* or female uterine kin a man gets protection from witchcraft and advice and support in times of marital trouble. At his initiation, or at his funeral, all his matrilateral relatives are there to bury him and contribute prestatory gifts of rice and meat. Thus, rules excluding uterine kin from marriageable categories amount to a mandatory extension of valuable matrilateral ties; but only for the men.

Women live out their lives in two largely contradictory contexts: their own agnatic environment and their place of marriage. A woman's first loyalties are those to her parents and brothers. The collectivity of out-married females is known by the term *kuriimen* (pl.; *ariimen* sing.); the collectivity of in-married women by the term *kuseek* (pl.; *aseek* sing.), which means "woman" and can be glossed as "wife." Every married woman is both, an *ariimen* in her natal House, and an *aseek* in her husband's House. In the role of female agnate, a woman exercises a great deal of influence. Female agnates care for, and, when necessary, bury their male kin. They protect their "brothers" from witchcraft. They play an important role in agnatic rituals like initiation. And they also have some say in their brothers' domestic lives and productive practices. But the *kuriimen* are scattered; their "political" influence can only be exerted by activating agnatic ties. In her other capacity as wife (*aseek*), a woman is, nominally at least, quite powerless. She can only rally her "sisters" – women agnates married with her into the same context – to her support. But these women, also, are mostly in-married affines, not locally born agnates.

To summarize, Jipalom's system of kinship relations is riddled with contradictions. A man should first and foremost rely upon his "brothers" and "fathers" for assistance in times of need. In point of fact, however, a man's compound brothers may also be his worse enemies. For it is they who are most often responsible for using witchcraft against him. They do so usually by "killing" his children. A man who is being bewitched by an agnate cannot retaliate directly; rather, he often moves in with his own uterine kin, or sends his children to live with theirs. For a particular male individual the uterine kin represent an individual resource, a counter force. But it is a resource that only a man and his full siblings share. In a way, then, uterine ties divide rather than unite the resident male population. The female population is also divided with respect to kinship roles. Every woman is torn between the duties she owes to her own agnates and having to adapt to her own affines. Moreover, as an agnate, she enjoys a real measure of influence and even power. As an in-married affine, however, she is entirely dependent upon her husband and his kin for practically everything.

The girls' excision rite
Much ambiguity surrounds the position of an in-married wife (*aseek*) in Jipalom. This is clearly reflected in the recently introduced, foreign (Manding and Fulani) practice of female circumcision (the *eñakey*, from the verb *eñak*, to pull). The "sacred" patch in the forest where girls are

excised is called *ebiir*, from the Manding word *biiree* for the same place. The spot is also the location of a shrine (*ejilai*), which women occasionally propitiate on behalf of other women, children, and men. On these occasions, the pouring of libations – referred to by the word *duei*, which is probably derived from the Arabic *da'wa*, meaning incantation – consists of water and rice flour. The few old "animist" ladies that are left cannot participate; only Muslim women can. Among the Kujamaat, the rite is of very recent introduction; it was not performed two generations ago. When I was first in Jipalom in 1964–1966, most of the elderly women had not been excised.[2] The women's excision rite must be put on by the "wives" on behalf of their daughters who, unlike themselves, are female agnates (*kuriimen*) of the ward. Everyone is quite aware that it is not only "pagans" like the Esudadu Jola who refuse to circumcise their girls, but also people like the Wolof, who have been practicing Muslims for a long time. Though Wolof society is in many ways more hierarchical than Jola society (Diop 1981), female status is not subordinated, as it is to a large extent among the Manding. It is from the latter that the Jola of Jipalom adopted the practice of excising girls.

Female circumcision has been interpreted in the anthropological literature in rather confusing terms. It is claimed that girls favor the practice because it brings them into equality with boys, who are circumcised. But there is enough variation in the performance of female initiation to make us beware of such assertions. Whereas the girls' excision ceremony is accepted with some reluctance in Jipalom, in the more "Mandingized" village of Fatiya considered later, the girls' circumcision is much more important. In Sambujat, on the other hand, it is seen with horror.

In Jipalom, the girls' circumcision is not equivalent in social importance to the boys' initiation. Whereas the boys' initiation marks the transition from childhood and dependency to adulthood and independence, the girls' initiation does the reverse; it makes her available to become a dependent wife. A girl eventually leaves her natal environment to become a "stranger" at her husband's place. Until she becomes incorporated into the mature community of in-married wives somewhere, she goes through a difficult period. The idea proposed by La Fontaine (1985), that what the girls' initiation is communicating is the mutual loyalty and authority that women derive from long-term residence in their respective husbands' compounds, finds full expression in the third community I will be discussing in the next chapter. In Jipalom, however, attitudes towards it are still ambivalent. Some men slough it off as "play"; others have confessed to me: "the Manding have ruined our women." And the women themselves are not completely convinced that it is effective, or worth the cost and the suffering.

The affair is rationalized by men and elderly women as something needing to be done before a woman can pray to Allah. A non-excised woman is considered unclean. A female friend explained to me "when you wash before praying and then ask God for something, it will 'take'; but if you haven't been circumcised your prayer will not 'take'; it will not be good before God." Then she added "maybe true, maybe not true; all of us, we don't know and this is why we do it to our children." Her statement reveals the feelings of doubt and ambiguity surrounding this recently introduced rite.

The demise of the *sináati*
It has been argued before that the system of shrines and shrine-keepers that underlies the Sambujat, and by extension the whole of Esudadu religious life, is both a symbolic projection of social dynamics and a mediating force in the constant competition over allocative and authoritative resources. With reference to women and elders, the shrines guarantee that they also play an important role in community affairs. In Jipalom, by contrast, religious processes have followed disjunctive directions. Rituals that were once associated with the spirit-shrines – called *sináati* pl., *enáati* sing. in Jola Kujamutay – have become separated from the rituals surrounding Islam. Because they tend to pull in opposite directions, the two sets of rituals form a poor basis upon which to focus productive and reproductive activities.

Relatively few of the spirits or *sináati* (pl.) of the Kujamaat Jola still remain, and these tend to be negatively defined. The *sináati* have been classified by Sapir (1970) into two large categories: those that are "attached" and have a shrine (that have a "head" according to the Foñi metaphor), and those that are "unattached" or "headless." "Unattached" spirits have to do with life processes (female vs. male, elders vs. younger men). They are free agents, unconnected to any specific social grouping.

The "head" or shrine of an "attached" spirit (an *enáati*) is usually located in a specific compound or ward and is generally associated with a particular social group. Let us take as an example *Kaneewak* or "rope," the agnatic, extended family shrine. It should be kept inside the House or *eluup*, where it once looked after the total welfare of resident agnates, assuring their increase in wealth, cattle and children. In principle, *Kaneewak* has to do with the process described by a particularly sophisticated man as "the rural economy." In the very recent past, before a monetary economy took hold, *Kaneewak* also supervised exchanges, making sure that equivalences were justly worked out. When rice was exchanged against a bull, for example, the person getting the bull should have given back a chicken; the person getting the rice should have given back kola nuts or tobacco. When the exchange was of a bull against a young cow, the one getting the cow gave back the chicken. When the bull was destined to be sacrificed at a funeral, or at the propitiation of a spirit-shrine, however, nothing needed to be given back. The idea behind these exchanges was that when someone gets something that will increase, something that will reproduce, he or she must give something back that also increases, a chicken for example. Something that does not increase, for example tobacco or kola nuts, cannot be given back for an animal. Thus, *Kaneewak* regulates a large segment of economic life.

Interestingly enough, *Kaneewak* is also concerned with theft, for this is an obvious case of "increase" gone rampant, of outright greed. Thieves run in the family. When a famous thief dies, a man who is reputed to have stolen lots of cattle, his friends will propitiate the *Kaneewak* shrine on behalf of his son. They will get palm wine and do the *kawasen* ritual. Henceforth, the son will be afraid to steal. This is what friends recommended for the son of one of my assistants, who had the uncommon Jola habit of stealing money (mostly from me).

Twenty years ago, *Kaneewak* occupied a central place in Jipalom's *sináati* system. Nowadays (1981), *Kaneewak* is still propitiated, but in a casual, almost desultory way, as the following extract from my field-notes shows:

Today, *Kaneewak* was propitiated on behalf of a girl called Sire, who must take her school exams next week. Abas, who inherited *Kaneewak* from his father, took out the shrine, a forked stick with two pieces of rope hanging from the stake, from behind a door in the old family house. The floor on which the shrine rested was so dirty it had to be swept first. While Sire sat on the floor facing the shrine, a calabash full of water (in the pre-Islamic days it would have been palm wine) was twirled around her head. Abas then blew twice into Sire's ears, while asking the shrine to *katiña ajaŋa* (leave the girl alone, do not to "grab" her). When *Kaneewak* grabs a person, it renders him or her deaf. To end the ritual, Abas poured some of the calabash water on the shrine. The whole thing had taken less than ten minutes.

Another important male agnatic shrine of the "attached" variety is the one associated with the sacred forest (*kareŋ*), where boys are initiated. Initiation (the *futamp*) is still a huge affair, ideally taking place every fifteen or twenty years, but in reality often postponed, especially in years of drought. The symbols and prestations employed in the *futamp* are also used in "traditional" funerals. Emphasis is placed on agnatic solidarity in the face of possible symbolic aggression. Two categories of relatives give and receive prestations at this time: persons having uterine ties at an initiate's House (the *kusámpul* or nephews), who are supposed to be mainly on the giving end, and his *sipaay* and *siñaay*, or matrilateral kin of an initiate, who should be mainly on the receiving end. Again, these two groups represent the principal lines of cleavage in Jipalom society.

Transmission of the *sináati* or shrines should take place, as in Sambujat, in a zig-zag fashion: from father, to eldest son, then through FB down to the next generation. Actually, however, in Jipalom the whole transmission apparatus has fallen into disuse. "There is precious little authority left to the 'owners' of the shrines, except when the latter are really needed" (Sapir, pers. remark).

With the coming of Islam, the negative or sanctioning properties of all the shrines have also surfaced over their more socio-symbolic and beneficial roles (Sapir 1970). A spirit (*enáati*) that has been neglected, or whose interdictions have been violated, seeks retribution by inflicting disease on the transgressor. It does so by "catching" or "trapping" (*esof*) the violator. However, unlike the Sambujat shrines who can trap anyone, a Jipalom spirit traps only those persons connected to it by agnatic or matrilateral ties. That is, it sanctions close kin only, and in so doing displays its weakened control over larger, more inclusive groups. A person trapped by a spirit goes to a native curer (an *alaak*), who must be Muslim. The latter will "mince medicinal plants, cool them with rice and give them to the ill person to eat." In this procedure, the spirit is only indirectly appealed to. If anything, the *alaak* is viewed as a second-order Islamic cleric who cures through prayer, not as someone who is powerful because he commands an important spirit.

The female shrines: contrasts with Sambujat

The demise or declining importance of the old spirit-shrines or *sináati* is particularly noticeable when it comes to the shrines that are under women's control. For, like the women of Sambujat, the women of Jipalom also "own" shrines. The collectivity of out-married female agnates of a specific ward (the *kuriimen*), who are married out and dispersed, have a shrine called *Ebune*. In principle, the shrine only "traps" female or male agnates; it never "traps" the in-married women.

In times past, the *kuriimen* of Jipalom staged a village-wide ceremony in which the *Ebune* shrine of each ward was propitiated a week apart. This ceremony took place regularly, every few years, and brought a large number of visitors together. By 1965, the *kuriimen* of only one Jipalom ward were performing this village-wide ceremony, and even then it had not been held for many years. By 1981, the *Ebune* shrines were only being propitiated privately, by small groups of *kuriimen*, in some wards but not others, and only once in a while. *Ebune* is still being celebrated in some

114 *At the crossroads: the Kujamaat Jola of Jipalom*

places in the Kajamutay with a spectacular village-wide festival lasting several months. At this time, the otherwise dispersed female agnates of a particular ward assemble at their natal wards, accompanied by their sons. Sapir (ms. 1983) has interpreted this event as symbolizing the female agnates becoming "single" again, under the protection of their own agnatic "brothers." However, other social processes are also at work (Linares ms. 1990). In any case, nowadays the festival is more secular than religious in tone.

Ebune is the linguistic, as well as the functional cognate of *Ehuñ*, the female-controlled shrine I have described for the village of Sambujat. But there are important differences between them. In Sambujat, the female shrines are propitiated by women who are, at one and the same time, in-married and agnatic females. This underlies the symmetry and status equivalence of both categories of women. It underscores the fact that female ritual power in Sambujat resides in making an endogamous marriage. In stark contrast, the Jipalom *Ebune* ritual marks the separation of female roles; it underscores the fact that only as a female agnate, within her own natal House, does a woman have some measure of ritual power.

Moreover, the Sambujat female shrines can bring serious illness or death, but they can also bring children and rain. In contrast, the Jipalom *Ebune*

Plate 11: In some Kajamutay areas, the *kurimen* come together every few years to perform the village-wide *Ebune* festival.

The impact on social and productive relations 115

can only bring pain. Further, the *Ehuñ* of Sambujat must always be propitiated by a woman, never a man, even when the propitiatory ceremony is being performed on behalf of a male agnate. On the other hand, in 1981, the *Ebune* shrines belonging to some Jipalom Houses were being propitiated by men. Finally, the *Sihuñ* of Sambujat are not activated only occasionally as in Jipalom, but must be exorcized continually on behalf of everyone, village agnates, in-married women, and even "outsiders" from other Esudadu villages. The aforementioned traits that distinguish the female *Ehuñ* shrines of Sambujat from the female *Ebune* shrine of Jipalom point to the fact that Sambujat women retain more independence, and a broader political base, than do Jipalom women.

So far, I have mentioned the female agnatic shrine. In principle, Jipalom in-married women (the *kuseek*) also "own" a shrine. Called *Furámban*, it has a woman in its charge (the officiant), who is elected to her post on the basis of her seniority. While propitiating the spirit, she must be flanked by older women. Younger women must sit apart. The performance itself highlights status distinctions between senior women and younger wives. It is conceived of as a service performed by the "wives" on behalf of their husbands and co-wives. But the shrine has not been propitiated for a long time.

Other female shrines besides *Furámban* also highlight social or gender distinctions, between the in-married *kuseek* themselves, or between them and other categories of people. In contrast to Sambujat's female-controlled shrines, however, those of Jipalom have to do with female functions exclusively. They have little to do with problems facing the entire community. Thus, for example, *Kanamak* belongs to the old, in-married women. It can only be propitiated by elderly ladies on behalf of a young, pregnant woman who is experiencing difficulties. Another shrine has to do with too much fertility; it is controlled by persons who had given birth to twins. The shrine called *Kuboos*, the word for afterbirth, keeps men and virginal girls away from birth functions. The shrine called *Ujujaw* ("postherds") is located outside the compound, where all Jipalom women used to give birth. Men should never approach it.

The minimal Muslim
In the preceding sections I have described pre-Islamic beliefs that are still extant in Jipalom, showing how they are expressed in rites performed at the spirit-shrines. I have also indicated that the system is changing as a result of the (relatively) recent introduction of Islam. At present, we can learn more about who has the respect and prestige of the community from seeing

116   At the crossroads: the Kujamaat Jola of Jipalom

who officiates at the mosque, than from knowing what elders still "own" shrines. Finally, I alluded to the way beliefs and practices surrounding the traditional shrines are kept separate from beliefs and practices surrounding Islam. This is an important point worth pursuing.

In the Jipalom I first knew (1964–1966), Islam was not what I would have called a deeply felt faith. In watching an elder perform his daily prayers only once, while greeting his friends, and in noticing how few people actually fasted during Ramadan, I was convinced that Jipalom's residents were at best minimal Muslims. The fact was that they had converted very recently:

The first man who converted to Islam in the village was Afaru, an elder of the Bojas ward, who was still alive in 1971. He was converted by a Kounta marabout, a member of the great maraboutic family which brought the Qadiriyya brotherhood to Senegal. Afaru converted late, when he was already an adult with children. The other elder of Bojas ward, a man called Landing, converted even later, when a Manding marabout from the region of Tobor came to live in Jipalom. The marabout stayed in Jipalom for 10 years, and died there. He seemed to have exerted considerable personal influence on Landing, who unlike Afaru was unusually pious and ceremonious.

When I was first in Jipalom, an *atalibao* (Koranic instructor; from Arabic *talaba*, disciple), a man called Saja, was residing in the same ward as I did (Bojas). But he was accorded little respect. While instructing the children to memorize verses of the Koran, he also would "make" prayer by the usual procedure of writing on a wooden tablet certain passages of the Koran, washing the ink off with water and drinking it. Part of the reason for the low esteem in which Saja was held was that he came from a nearby village and was therefore a "local," yet he refused to cultivate. But a more important reason was that he thought everyone should stop propitiating the local shrines. This did not sit well with the Bojas people. They resented the confusion that Islam and its practitioners had created between Satan and the spirit-shrines or *sinàati*. What was difficult in those days was that both were on the scene so that a person "could be touched" (i.e. made ill) *qua* Muslim or *qua* Jola, without there being appropriate diagnosticians around to identify the exact source of the malady and its cure. As a result, people who were ill would go around, from one marabout (Islamic cleric) to another, spending money with little success. For it was the case that the marabouts knew little about the shrines.

Yet most Jipalom residents considered themselves to be good Muslims. In fact, 1966 marked an important symbolic milestone in the Islamization of the community. It was the year when the members of the Bojas ward got together and built the first prayer house (little mosque, *miserey* from the

Manding *misiro*), a modest structure of wattle and daub. The prayers that broke up the fasting at sundown during Ramadan were said in the little *miserey*, with men praying inside and women praying outside.

Twenty-five-years later (1990), Islam had gained considerably more acceptance in Jipalom, more so certainly than when I was first there. Many more persons seemed to be observing the daily prayer and the yearly fasts. Every ward had now an *awadani* (Manding for a local man who calls to prayer). The only requirements for the post are that he knows the Koran well and has a clear and strong voice. However, there was still no *imam* in the community, no *ejamon* – from Manding *jamango*, the big mosque where Friday prayers can be said – nor anyone who had been to Mecca. In fact, no one person has "control" over each of the small mosques that are found in every ward of the village. For the Qadiriyya brotherhood to which the Kujamaat Jola belong stress individual communication with God. As a friend explained to me: "If you are not tired, you can go to the mosque to pray. When it comes time to do one of the daily prayers you go to the *miserey* and find someone to pray with, for that which is best is to gather and pray together. But if you are tired, you will pray home. In any case do not fail to pray, *jakut* (not good)."

Interestingly, much before 1990 the Arabic school had ceased to exist. The few students who received Koranic instruction had to go elsewhere. At least 3 boys from the Bojas ward were studying with a marabout from the

Plate 12: A visiting marabout.

village of Kaken, 4 kilometers east of Sindian, in the border with the Kalunay. On the other hand, the secular school taught in French had become one of the largest in the Kajamutay, with 6 grades, 6 instructors, and students coming from all the neighboring villages. By supporting a secular, as opposed to a religious, education, the Jipalom residents have chosen a somewhat ambiguous path: they have chosen the road to "modernity" while at the same time upholding a conservative version of Islam and not quite abandoning their "traditional" shrines.

In what has become a classical (if somewhat controversial) series of articles, the historian H. J. Fisher (1973; 1985) has suggested that in Black Africa Islam has undergone three stages. In the "quarantine" stage, the faith is dominated by strangers and immigrants; in the "mixing" stage, local converts combine pagan practices with Islamic tenets; in the final stage of "reform," a purer faith is achieved through the establishment of the rule of saints. Fisher's model raises important questions concerning how Jipalom's residents have reacted to the penetration of Islam. Indeed, Islam had become a more accepted way of life among Jipalom's inhabitants in the twenty years between my first and last lengthy visits. But it has become so without ushering in the rule of saints as Fisher's model would predict. Rather, Islam has indirectly aggravated tensions inherent in Kujamaat Jola society by eliminating the sources of ritual control and reciprocity that structured productive relations around the propitiation of spirit-shrines. In so doing, they have left exposed the lines of cleavage and conflict that characterize much of Jipalom's ownership of land, and the relations that have grown around it.

Productive forces: land "ownership" and "usufructuary" rights

As a construct that legitimizes rights to residence and land, agnation is an important force working towards social cohesion. As actual practice, however, agnatic co-residence has the built-in potential for competition over land and other property. There is a great deal of conflict over paddy-field ownership in the Kajamutay; even in those communities like Jipalom where there is a land surplus. To understand the process of land ownership, and of gaining usufructuary rights to paddies and contesting claims, it is first necessary to gain some idea of the layout of the fields.

The rice fields (*biit*) cultivated by the members of the Jipalom ward called Bojas comprise more than 1,200 separate parcels, each surrounded by a low bund. A person may own up to 65 or 70 different parcels, located in separate parts of the *biit*. Some parcels are small, 20 square meters; some are large, 3,300 square meters. Each parcel, singly or in clusters is owned, worked, and transferred individually.

Table IIa: *Area, exclusive of nurseries,[a] cultivated by six Jipalom conjugal households.[b]*

Agnates	m²	has
A	11,125	1.13
B	10,460	1.05
C	8,525	0.853
D	7,435	0.744
E	7,175	0.718
F	6,051	0.605

Note:
[a] The number of individual paddy fields cultivated by each household is 30–80.
[b] The households are roughly the same size: 2 adults and 3 children.

Considerable differences exist in the total amount of land owned by particular individuals. In Table IIa I have given the paddy area, exclusive of nurseries, that is cultivated by 6 Jipalom households of roughly the same size. As we can see, household A cultivates twice as much land as household F, while the rest fall in-between. But, just as important as the amount of land an individual works, is the kind of land he or she works. For it is crucial to work parcels in each of the several rice-fields categories that community members recognize (Linares 1970, 1981). There were years during the 1970s when only the fields drained by rainwater runoff (the *kuyelen*) could be counted on to yield a decent crop. Hence, the Jipalom inhabitants must scramble in order to balance land needs against available parcels in different sectors of the rice fields.

It is often asserted that the Jola practice "lineage ownership of land" (Thomas 1963; Pélissier 1966; Marzouk-Schmitz 1981). But this confuses a local and limited pattern existing among Mandingized Jola, discussed later, with realities everywhere else. As I have explained, the Jola are not organized in terms of lineages *sensu stricto*. Each head of a conjugal household has full control over his land. He is free to pledge it, lend it, transfer it permanently to his kin, or leave it uncultivated if he so desires. While a person is alive, his rights over his land, even over unused parcels, are inviolable; a co-resident "brother" who needs more rice land has no claims over the former's paddy fields, no matter how desperate he may be.

A young man is given land by his father at the time he marries. If a man dies when his sons are young, which is often the case, his land is entrusted to

SIBAAF

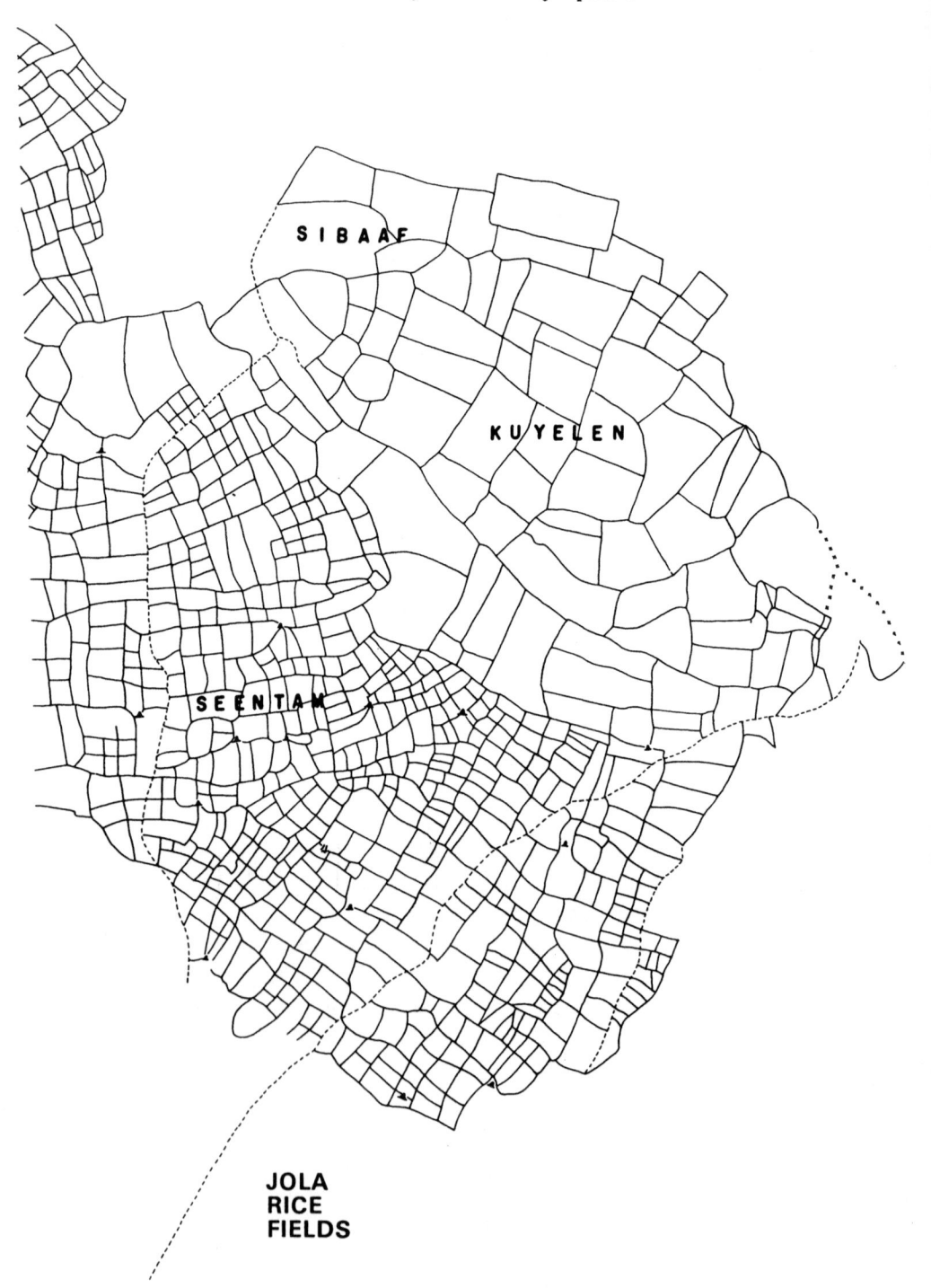

KUYELEN

SEENTAM

JOLA
RICE
FIELDS

his oldest brother in the interim. This often builds up friction between a young man and his paternal uncle, especially when the latter refuses to give him his full share. Only when a man dies without leaving brothers or sons behind does his land revert automatically to the agnatic members of his patrigroup or House (the *eluup*). Also, if the last member of the House disappears, then the agnates of the *kalol* or ward will inherit the land. But, again, who gets what parcels may be up for a great deal of litigation, as indicated below.

Another structural contradiction that underlies ownership of land is built into the marital institution. Unlike the Esudadu Jola, the Jipalom Jola are polygynous and also practice *per stirpes* inheritance. This means that parcels allocated by a husband to each wife for her use will pass down to her own sons when she dies, and not to her co-wives' sons. Thus, three sons from one mother could get the same amount of land as one son from another mother. On the other hand, an in-married woman (a *kuseek*) can request from her own brother land that her son can use. For it is usually through his mother's kin (his uterine or matrilateral relatives) that a married man who is experiencing a land deficit can gain usufructuary rights to extra rice fields. This is not the only way to get extra land, but it is one of the most common. The majority of the men have, at one point or another in their lives, borrowed fields by activating uterine "rights." These "rights" can be "stretched" quite far, as the following example shows:

Brama Baji came to live in the Jinebél House of Bojas because he was always sick in the village of Baralir, where he was born. He was lent land by the elder called Landing, with whom he claimed a relationship by virtue of the fact that Brama's father's mother, and Landing's mother, both came from the same *eluup* or House in the village of Katuje.

Uterine "rights" are not automatically extended, however. Although a maternal "uncle" who has a great deal of land is under strong pressure to

Figure 3: Section of the *biit*, or rainfed rice fields, in Jipalom. Each parcel is permanently surrounded by a low bund or dike. Clusters of parcels in different parts of the *biit* are owned individually. A gentle gradient goes from the *seentam*, which have sandy soils and are fairly shallow, to the *kuyelen* which have clayey soils that retain the water runoff. The *sibaaf* can no longer be cultivated because salts accumulated in them after the drought of the 1970s. Not shown are the *kuyolen* or nursery area behind the *seentam* and the *weng* or deep fields near the *marigot* which have been abandoned. An even more complex pattern of rice field categories exist in Sambujat (Part I), whereas the rice fields in Fatiya (Part III) are little differentiated.

lend some to his sister's son, he may refuse to do so in actual practice. He may argue that he does not have enough land for his own sons; or that his sister neglected to carry out her agnatic obligations.

The in-married women (the *kuseek*) themselves enjoy substantial usage rights to paddies, but they do not have security of tenure; they do not "own" land. Neither do the women of Sambujat, of course, even though some women in the non-Islamized areas south of the Casamance River do own land. But Sambujat women have more security of tenure than Jipalom women for several reasons: because they are monogamously married and their respective husbands depend entirely upon them for help; because they are married within the village or nearby so they have kin to defend them; because they can always stay to live with a son after being widowed; and, last but not least, because they command important ritual resources. In contrast, if a Jipalom widow who is of marriageable age does not become re-married via the widow re-marriage convention (*bulaañ*, from the verb *laañ*, to return) to one of her deceased husband's real or classificatory "brothers" she loses her usufructuary rights to paddy land. She can sometimes keep these if she is fairly elderly and in addition has a son, or a father's brother's son, living there. But only under those conditions.

When a Jipalom woman who has no sons divorces or becomes widowed and goes home to live, she will try to find a substitute: "*anare abajut añiil anine panañes fujúnk*" (a woman who has no male son, will search for a support, a cane):

Ajen does not have a son. When she divorced some years ago, she returned to live with her own brothers in the Jinébél House (*eluup*) of the Bojas ward. She then "adopted" Musaba, her older brother's son, whose mother had died some years before. Ajen shares a granary with Musaba, treats him as a son, and feeds him from it. She also buys him clothes, has the *Ebune* shrine done on his behalf, and sends him to school. Musaba's father does not object. In fact, he gave Ajen a goat for bringing up his son. If he objected, and forbade Ajen to live with Musaba when she grew old, she would curse him. And the rest of the *fank* members would side with her.

A woman who has been a good *ariimen* (i.e. a good agnatic female) can go home and have fields lent to her for her to work, either temporarily, or in a more or less permanent basis. The lending, however, is not usually done by her close male agnates. In order to avoid the possibility of future conflict, lending is done by a more distant agnate, by uterine kin, or even by affines:

Ajen has had no trouble borrowing fields, for she is a respected *ariimen*. The fields she works have been lent to her by the following persons: an agnate of the Kúrúnkúla House of the Bojas ward, not the Jinébél House because this is the one to which Ajen and her "real" brothers belong; Jancuba of Baruk, the ward with which

Bojas shares fictive kinship ties; her own mother's brothers, who live in another neighboring village; her sister's husband, who also lives in the nearby community; her daughter's husband, who lives in another ward of Jipalom.

Hence, an agnatic woman of Jipalom who is widowed or divorced has the option to borrow land back home, where she was born. Unlike her brothers, however, she does not have automatic rights to use agnatic land. For unlike them, she does not inherit land; that is she has no inviolable rights of use and disposition over "family-owned" paddy fields. Whether she is successful in making some sort of arrangement depends on how well she is thought of, and whether there is actually someone around with extra parcels to lend her.

Conflicts over borrowed land

So far, we have been considering the problems of land "ownership" and transmission. However, in Jipalom, not all men "own" enough land (at least a hectare) to feed a "normal"-sized household. Hence, there must be other jurally prescribed ways of gaining usage rights to extra rice fields besides inheriting them. One of the most common ways is to pledge a bull against a particular parcel of land owned by someone living in one's own House, or in another *eluup* in the community, with the proviso that when the animal is returned, the land is returned also. Actually, many cases of pledging become permanent by default. Before Islam and legal courts came came in, people say that a specific *enáati* was in charge of punishing people who attempted to keep borrowed land. Who this *enáati* was, and which particular elder controlled it, has been lost from living memory. Elders no longer command important shrines. Hence, they are unable to pressure individuals into returning land they pledged or borrowed so long ago that there is no one around who witnessed the original transaction:

There is a large and fertile area (7 to 10 ares), that includes a great number of separate paddy fields, which Afansu and his brother Brama, both of who live in the Bojas ward, cultivate more or less permanently. Their father, a respected elder called Arafan, told me in 1965, when I was living with them, that he had many years earlier "paid" three cows to Acuse, a man from the neighboring ward of Baruk who had gone off to Kombo (i.e. Gambia) to live, for the right to have his sons use the land. The Bojas and Baruk wards share the "fiction" of being descended from the same ward in the neighboring community of Telum. This helps when it comes to having to "pledge" land, as does the fact that Arafan's mother was from Telum. For it was the case that Arafan had suffered from a land shortage all his life. His own father had died when he was very young, and his father's brothers had kept most of the land for themselves, giving him very little. Because Arafan grew up to become rich and renowned through his partnership with a French merchant, he was able to marry many women (he had more than 20 wives in succession). They gave birth to many sons, who in turn needed land when they married. Anyhow, when I was back in Bojas in 1970, 1976, and again in 1981, I observed that Afansu and Brama were still cultivating Acuse's land. I finally asked Afansu about it and he responded to the effect that the land was very good. If Acuse's descendants asked for it back, he added, he would never return it. For his father, Arafan, who had done the original transaction, was long dead: "maybe in the old days they would get it back, but not now, for the State is here" he concluded.

As the person in the example given above readily admitted, the presence of the State, in the form of legal courts, has to a large extent "frozen" the land-tenure pattern. The shrine(s) that once upon a time, through the agency of elders, punished persons who attempted to keep borrowed land have largely disappeared with the coming of Islam. Unlike the situation in Sambujat, in Jipalom there are presently no elders who have enough ritual power at their disposal to make certain that verbal contracts made long ago are upheld by individuals out of fear of being "trapped" and made ill by the spirit-shrines. Muslim elders do not have the authority to mediate in disputes unless they were witnesses to the original transactions. And neither do those who officiate at the mosques, for they have little punitive power and no jurisdiction over civil matters. For Senegal is a secular, not a religious, state; there are no Muslim courts of justice to enforce Koranic law. And with no elders around to control production through their control of shrines, conflicts over land can go on for years. Disputes over land now follow the same general course: the "wronged" party goes to the village elders, and if they cannot do anything, he goes to the matrilateral kin of his House. As the last resort, he goes to the *chef d'arrondissement*, then the *préfet* of the department, the police, the tribunal in Ziguinchor and, finally, the first tribunal of Dakar, in that order. The following are just a few examples of the cases I recorded involving conflicts over land. They are meant to illustrate some of the complex sorts of alignments that may go on in these occasions:

In 1966, a murder was committed over the issue of rice-field ownership in the community of Butolab. It had involved two Catholics. The first, Michel Koli, was an *ancien combatant*, now retired, who had lived in Dakar, then Bignona, for many years. But he still kept his lands in Butolab. The second person involved was Prospere; he was a Diola herdsman from Kañaru (Kagnarou), who decided to settle down, and to that effect borrowed land from the Koli in Butolab, including some of Michel's fields. After many years, rumors came to Michel to the effect that Prospere was saying the fields he borrowed belonged to him. Michel came back to Butolab and decided to get his fields back. When Prospere refused, he took him to the Ziguinchor tribunal. Unfortunately, not all of Michel's brothers within his own *eluup* sided with him. If they had done so, the matter would have probably rested there. But because they had co-resided with Prospere, who was always helpful, they had grown to like him and therefore took his part. They argued to the effect that Michel had neglected his obligation to come back to participate in associative work, or in its place, to send remittances to his relatives. The tribunal agreed and gave the land to Prospere. Michel wrote a warning letter to Prospere: if he found him cultivating his fields, he would kill him. That same year Michel came back to Butolab and took up his *kajandu* (the metal-capped fulcrum shovel men use to cultivate) to straighten out the boundaries of his fields. He found Prospere in the midst of preparing his (Michel's) fields. When Prospere saw him, he wanted to leave; but his wife urged him on. Michel cut Prospere's throat with the *kajandu*, then went straight to the *gendarmerie* in Bignona (where he resided) to declare. He was in prison for only nine months (he had a good lawyer). Though Michel still resides in Bignona, his sons go back every year to cultivate his fields in Butolab. The affair is now closed. But it might some day erupt again. For Prospere's children are fast growing up.

A second example of conflict over land involved members of two villages, Ñankit (Niankit) and Kañaru (Kagnarou), over rice fields located near their common boundary.

Each village claimed that the area was theirs. The dispute went on year after year. It moved through the tribunals of Sindian, Bignona and Ziguinchor, until the latter finally ruled in favor of Ñankit. Kañaru's people did not abide by the court's ruling, however. They secretly met and decided to attack and get their fields back by force. It turned out, however, that several Kañaru men had mothers who came from Ñankit. That is, they had uterine ties in the other community. So they did what they had to do, namely let the Ñankit people know Kañaru's plans to attack them. The Ñankit community members rounded up their muskets and spears and prepared to defend themselves. This time, those Ñankit persons who had matrilateral ties in Kañaru did the reverse and let the other side know. As the two sides marched on to the rice fields, bearing their guns and getting ready to shoot, the police, who had been warned by the chief of a third village, arrived and disarmed everyone. The Dakar tribunal was uneasy about deciding on whose favor to settle, fearing that the conflict would begin all over again, so it ruled that neither side could cultivate the land. To my knowledge, the land remains uncultivated to this day.

A third instance of conflict over rice fields involved members of the villages of Baila and Jatang (Diatang). Their fight had started roughly fifty years before, and was still going on in the 1960s.

The father [probably grandfather] of Ibreima Koli (ex *chef de canton*) and his brother Kamara (ex chief of Jatang) once lived in the lands that formed the boundary line between the two communities. But they were forced to move to Jatang when they could no longer take the constant harassment of the Baila people, who attacked them because an isolated family cannot defend itself. Ibreima and Kamara went on cultivating the rice fields. Eventually, however, Ibreima died and the Baila people immediately claimed his rice fields as their own. By this time, the house walls of their father's original residence had collapsed, leaving few traces.

Kamara took the matter to the "tribunal of the Europeans" (which some *metise* headed), where he swore over the Koran that he owned the contested lands. If he had lied, he and his family would have died. The tribunal accepted his word, and gave him the "papers." But the Baila people refused to comply. Years later, they reopened the affair when a Baila person was elected deputy. He got the *Préfet* to say that the land was Baila's. The matter went all the way to the secretary general for the Casamance, who said he couldn't do anything (which was true enough). So, in desperation, Jatang's people prepared for war, and so did Baila's people. Just as they got ready to march into the rice fields, ten truckloads of police arrived. Jatang's men had barely enough time to hide their arms. But Baila's men got their guns taken away, and had to pay 250,000 CFA francs (about $1,000 US dollars) to get them back. In the 1960s, Baila had three lawyers, Jatang two, and the case continued. It was the unanimous opinion of my informants that Baila had a land surplus, while the rice fields were essential to the survival of Jatang's inhabitants, including Kamara.

A final example of conflicts over land involved a dispute over groundnut fields. The litigants were classificatory "brothers," living in the same ward but in two separate Houses:

Nahu Baji had "borrowed" groundnut fields from Sane Baji's father some forty years ago. Now (1970), Sane wanted them back, because his family had increased. But Nahu refused to return the fields, saying they were his. [At this point of the story one of the men who were listening asked: "but who cleared the land initially?" apparently no-one knew.] But though the elders of the village had not witnessed the land being cleared, they did remember when Sane's father had built his house next to the contested fields. So they settled the dispute by giving the lands back to Sane, who cultivates them now.

The particular cases presented above suffice to show that the Kujamaat Jola land-tenure system is in flux. In three of the four cases cited the conflict continues. In the last case there was a witness still alive. With the passing of time it is to be expected that conflicts over land will get progressively more severe – especially if the 1964 *Loi sur le Domaine National* is ever invoked in a specific instance by the Senegalese government.

At the level of the community, the main problem still resides in the absence of mediating structures through which disputes over land can be resolved before they go on to State authorities. Since obligations on the part of lenders to transfer extra parcels to another person for temporary use are not binding, much depends on good feelings. These feelings were regularly maintained in the past by constant participation in propitiatory rituals for the spirit-shrines, and by discharging social obligations to the matrilateral kin at life-crisis transitions. Ritual practices made prestatory transactions hold. The elders who "commanded" the *enáati* charged with the supervision of land transactions made sure that borrowers did not turn into keepers. Nowadays, under Islam and the State, many of these practices are falling into disuse; their effectiveness is obviously diminishing. Certain conditions are required for another system to replace the old moral order and re-structure the rules that govern ownership of the productive forces. In the meantime, practices change, improvisations occur, problems have to be solved on an *ad hoc* basis. This is essentially what has happened with access to plateau lands that are used in cultivation of groundnuts and millet.

Gaining access to land on the plateau
Certain technical characteristics inherent to the groundnut system – a shortage of land in some areas and an abundance of land in other areas, the need for rotation and so forth – has encouraged an opportunistic pattern of land ownership and usufruct that is also potentially conflictive. If we recall, groundnuts are a relatively recent introduction into Lower Casamance. They came in essentially as a cash crop, at the same times as, and in association with, Islam. In 1964, I was able to interview Jipalom elders who still remembered when groundnuts were first planted around the turn of the century. Soon after their introduction, groundnuts became an important cash crop.

The general term for groundnut field is *karamba*, the same term used for "bush." Within a village, a man owns 2 to 4 sizeable *karamba* fields. One or 2 fields he inherited agnatically, from his father. The rest he cleared himself. Inherited fields are owned in common by 2 or more brothers, who rotate them and cultivate them together. This allows some fields to rest while others are being used. It takes about 20 days of very hard work to clear (*kalibut*) a new field. After a few years of usage, the field is invaded by a special grass, a sure sign that it must be fallowed (Pélissier 1966: 786). Thus, considerably more work is required to clear a new plot in the forest, than to borrow a field that has been lying fallow elsewhere.

Men who have a land-deficit, or who want to increase cash-crop production, are forced to scramble, borrowing extra groundnut and millet fields wherever they can. The general pattern is to cultivate one's fields at home until these have to be rested, then to look elsewhere for a good field to borrow from friends and acquaintances in other villages. Younger, adult married men often go far north, to villages like Kanao (Kona?), Jira (Djiral), etc., in the heart of the old Islamized Jola area, to cultivate groundnuts for several months each year. These villages were once decimated by the Manding. Nowadays they are lightly populated and as a consequence have a surplus of land.

Upland fields used for groundnut cultivation are not rented. Extra fields on the plateau can only be borrowed by relying upon individual ties of

128 *At the crossroads: the Kujamaat Jola of Jipalom*

Figure 4: Map of a region in the Northern Kajamutay surrounding Jipalom. Since the 1960s, when the map was done, the surface cultivated in groundnuts has increased while that in paddy rice has shrunk.

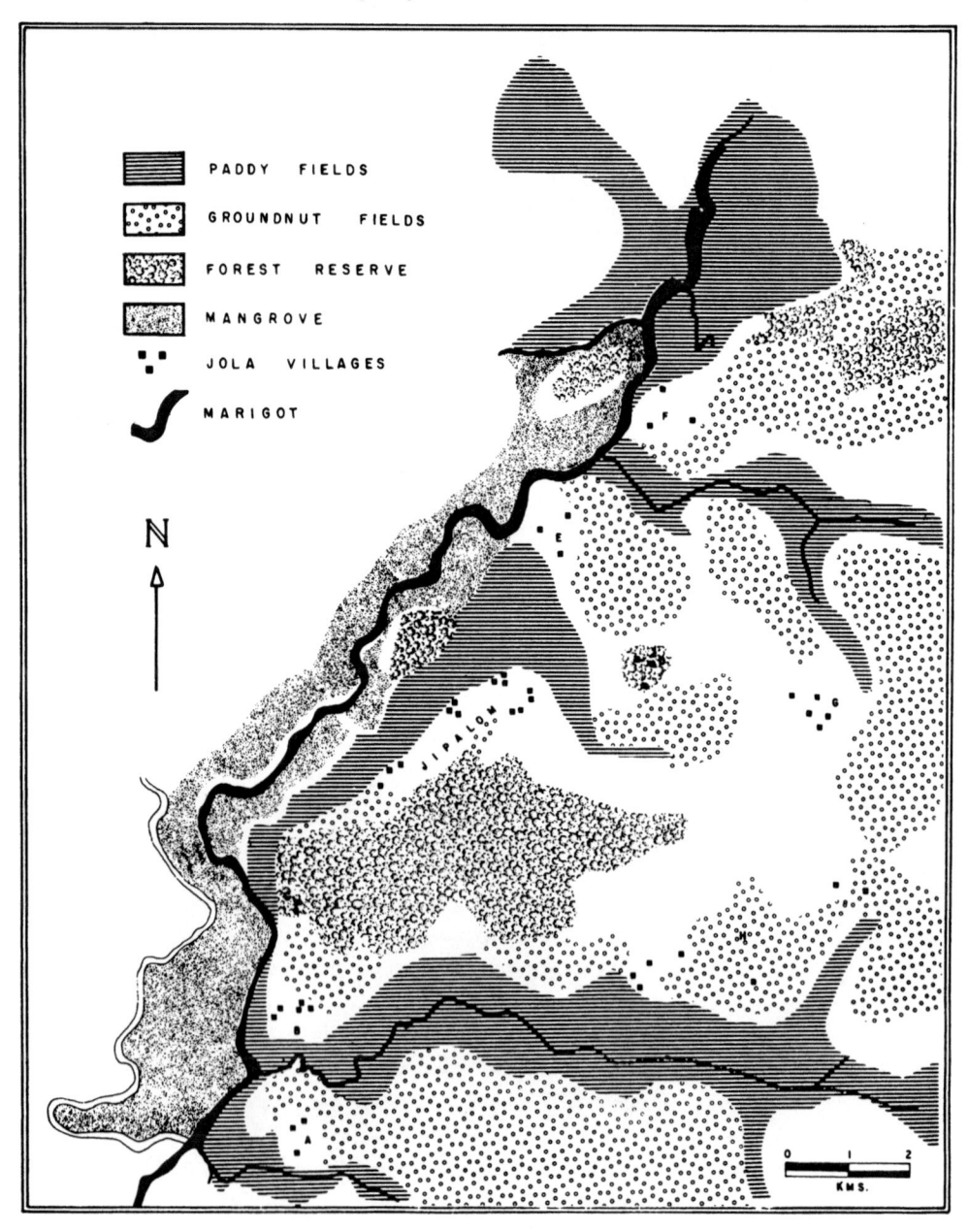

friendship and reciprocity with Muslims living in villages that have a surplus of land. Lenders and borrowers should consider themselves to be "brothers" under the tenets of Islam. They should, like all good members of the Qadiriyya brotherhood, lend each other land. The case for borrowing extra fields is not always made successfully, however. Although land is expected to be lent freely, or perhaps exchanged for small, voluntary gifts and the expectation of reciprocity at some future date, lending is often denied. The role of land-lender or *ajawáati* (host) is very important among the "Mandingized" Jola discussed presently (Part III). Among those groups, host-stranger relationships have emerged as an integral part of an established system of Islamic values stressing hospitality and generosity among a wide community of friends and believers. Among the Kujamaat Jola of Jipalom, however, the host-guest or *ajawáati* relationship is not particularly well developed. This contributes to the insecurity that surrounds the land-borrowing process. For lenders are not always certain that borrowers can be trusted to behave as "brothers" under the nascent banner of Islam. And good plateau land is rapidly becoming scarce.

In this process women are kept altogether out. They have no usufructuary rights to groundnut land. Although they invest nearly 17 percent of their time helping their husbands cultivate groundnuts, they cannot borrow land on the plateau and go into business for themselves. Nor can they control any part of the product. When their husbands sell the groundnut crop after the yearly harvest, they are expected to buy clothes for their wives and children, but it is up to each individual to do so. Beyond gossiping and complaining, the wife has no other indirect way to enforce her claims (Linares 1985).

To reiterate, groundnuts are a new, export cash crop based on the impermanent cultivation of bush-fallow fields. Men must borrow extra land by activating – not always successfully – long-distance ties with members of the wider Islamic community. In contrast, rice agriculture is an ancient, symbolically elaborated, and socially integrated subsistence system. It is based on the permanent cultivation of agnatically inherited, or matrilaterally secured, fields. Not surprisingly, labor relations are organized differently in the two systems. This is so regardless of whether we are referring to the labor of the conjugal family pair, of kin and other assorted relatives, or of associative groups. In neither case, however, is this work organized along ritual lines as in Sambujat. On the other hand, Islam is appealed to as an explanation, albeit a justification, for some of the imbalances in labor inputs that have emerged with the coming of a cash crop.

130 *At the crossroads: the Kujamaat Jola of Jipalom*

The conjugal family and the labor process
It is often assumed that when subsistence-based, relatively isolated peoples enter the world market, social relations of production become "profoundly disturbed" (Oboler 1985:1). The encounter between economies of very different scale is expected to generate marked changes in the social organization of agricultural tasks; across all segments of the peasant economy.

Not all tasks, however, or all aspects of the labor process, necessarily change in the same direction with the introduction of cash crops. It is still possible for some organizational features to carry over from "traditional" crops. In Jipalom, for example, few structural changes have occurred in the social division of labor by gender after groundnuts were introduced. Much of the labor that goes into the cultivation of both rice and groundnuts is still generated within the conjugal family unit. As in Sambujat, the sexual division of labor is still interdependent. Men ridge and furrow the paddies as well as the upland (millet and groundnut) fields. Women seed and transplant the rice, and also punch-hole seed the groundnuts. Women weed rice and millet.

Plate 13: Two Jipalom closely related conjugal families working together. (Courtesy, J. David Sapir).

What has changed with the introduction of groundnuts into Jipalom's economy, however, is the time and effort that men versus women invest in agricultural work. Let us assume that what goes on now in Sambujat was also in some ways characteristic of the pre-groundnut situation in Jipalom. In Sambujat, the burden of work in the rice fields is equitably shared by both spouses. Thus, in 1981 when I did a comparative time-expenditure survey, Sambujat women were investing an average of 105 eight-hour long work-days a year in agricultural work, and their husbands an average of 108 work-days, or virtually the same. In Jipalom, on the other hand, for the same year, women were investing 111 work-days a year in the combined crops of rice, millet and groundnuts, but men were investing an average of only 87 work-days in the same crops. Thus, women worked the same number of days, or slightly more, than their Sambujat counterparts, but the men worked much less than both their Sambujat counterparts (87 vs. 108 work-days yearly), and the women.

Besides the work they perform transplanting and harvesting rice, wives regularly help their husbands in the latter's groundnut fields. They plant the seed and help with the winnowing of the crop. Wives also helped to weed their husbands' millet fields. Thus women's work-load has not been significantly reduced with the advent of a cash crop that gives them few monetary rewards. They have simply had to redouble their efforts, from rice-field work to millet and groundnut work.

The same is not true, however, of the Jipalom men, whose work-load has diminished with the advent of animal traction. In 1964, before the ox-plough was adopted, Jipalom men averaged 153 work-days a year in agricultural work (58 for rice work, 16 for millet, and 79 for groundnuts). This is more than their Sambujat counterparts. After the introduction of the ox-plough, however, the men's work-load dropped to 58 work-days for rice work (which is the same as before), but 24 work-days for groundnuts and only 5 work-days for millet. This is because the ox-plough is employed in land preparation for both these crops, but not for rice.

If the Jipalom wives were more willing to work in each other's fields, their tasks could be made less onerous. But though Islam has encouraged polygyny, it has not guaranteed cooperation among co-wives. Co-wives may get along well, in which case they may cultivate their fields together. But the truth is that they often don't, in which case they are forced to cultivate apart. The husband can exert only a limited amount of pressure on his wives to encourage them to cooperate.

As I have indicated, the gender-based division of labor within the Jipalom conjugal family has not changed in structure – both genders work on both types of crops – though it has in numbers of hours worked by women in contrast with men. The division of labor by age, however, has changed in subtle ways with the coming of Islam. Again, taking Sambujat as the "original" pre-Islamic, pre-cash-crop model, it is to be noted that a married son helps his parents cultivate, as well as the reverse. In Jipalom, on the other hand, a father never works in the fields of a son. Elders do not help juniors with physical labor. The Jipalom obligation to parents has therefore become asymmetrical; from son to father, but not the reverse. This is explained as the filial duty of a pious Muslim, to help his parents.

Hence, the advent of a new religion has provided the Jipalom inhabitants with a timely rationale. Islam is used to explain imbalances in the workloads of men and women, elders and junior men.

Men's associative labor

As with other Jola groups, Jipalom's household labor requirements are not fully met unless extra sources of energy can be secured from outside the extended family unit. During the 1960s, additional labor was enlisted through associative work. Men participated in various kinds of overlapping work-groups called *sikáf* (pl.), *ekáf* (sing.). The *sikáf* were organized along residential and/or loose age-grade criteria. Three such groups operated regularly: (a) the first *ekáf* included the more active men; these were the unmarried 18 to 24 years old, and the married men in the early 30s and 40s; (b) the second *ekáf* included older men, roughly over 40 to 50 years of age; (c) the third *ekáf*, of a rather residual sort, included children 12 to 14 years old, who could already use the *kajandu*. Members of the same *ekáf* were likely to have been initiated (done the *futamp*) together in the sacred forest. That is, they formed a flexible kind of age-grade. This was true whether the men were married or not, as in the first *ekáf*; for even though a young man has been circumcised, it often takes a long time to find a wife.

A fourth *ekáf* ignored all differences in age. It was made up of all the adult men in the ward, including the young, middle-aged, and elders. What this group earned was automatically saved up for the time when the boys' initiation had to be staged. For it is the case that the elders are still in charge of the circumcision. The money the other three kinds of *sikáf* made could be used for other things besides the initiation ritual. It could be lent out to needy members, split evenly among the members of the work-group, invested in building a new school or repairing the little mosque.

Although associative work was, and still is, cast in terms of mutual help and reciprocities, the fact remains that there were marked differences among individuals who benefited from associative, *sikáf* labor. In 1965, most elders of the Bojas ward received considerably more free help from the men's association than did junior men, though not always in the same manner, nor for the same reasons.

Once a year, the fourth *ekáf*, comprising all the men of the Bojas ward (more than 30 in total) would ridge and furrow the deep *marigot* fields of Afaru, the ranking elder in the village. They were joined by two or more individuals representing the other wards in Jipalom. In return, Afaru gave them a good meal accompanied by rice beer, which is more appreciated than millet beer. The beer was made by the wife whose fields were being prepared, with the help of Afaru's oldest living son. A week later, the men worked in the fields of the second ranking elder of the Bojas ward, for beer also. He was considered to be a particularly pious Muslim.

In Table IIb, I have summarized the sources of labor that went into the preparation of the fields of 12 men belonging to the Bojas ward. The data were gathered during the 2 months of a non-drought year (August and September of 1965), at the height of the agricultural season, when the rice fields were being furrowed and ridged. This is an arduous, exclusively male task. The table lists the percentage of the total area of *biit* (rainwater-fed fields, the most abundant land category) prepared by 3 types of people: (a)

Plate 14: Before the introduction of animal traction, Jipalom men prepared each other's groundnut fields by associative labor (the *ekáf*). (Courtesy J. David Sapir).

134 *At the crossroads: the Kujamaat Jola of Jipalom*

Table IIb: *Flow of labor from different sources for Bojas agnates in Yentam (i.e. rain-fed rice fields) preparation during one agricultural season.*

Agnate	No. of parcels	Total area square m.	Prepared himself %	Prepared by B,S, kin %	Prepared by men's *sikáf* %
A*	72	4,991	0	19	82[a]
B*	43	2,954	24	4	72[b]
C*	18	4,647	36	0	64[c]
D*	42	4,088	45	3	52[b]
E*	32	3,709	50	4	46[b]
F*	40	5,529	67	12	21[d]
G	36	2,565	90	10	0
H	22	2,988	82	18	0
I	32	4,684	77	23	0
J	36	4,728	47	53	0
K	51	3,026	46	55	0
L	6	838	100	0	0[e]

Note:
* elders
[a] *Sikáf* from a Jipalom ward other than Bojas.
[b] Agnates from Bojas ward.
[c] Men from the village of Jatuke, where agnate Cs daughter is married.
[d] Agnate F is an elder and a classificatory brother of C; the Jatuke men did his fields also.
[e] Agnate L lives mostly from his fees as a native curer.

the conjugal unit alone, (b) the conjugal unit with the help of close kin, (c) members of *sikáf* or associative work-groups. A glance at the data reveals that elders (A, B, E, F), and middle-aged men (C, D), received on the average more *sikáf* labor than younger men.

It has been argued, mostly by Marxist scholars, that in precapitalist societies labor tends to flow "upwards," from younger men who are dependants, to elders who control the means of reproduction (Meillassoux 1964). The problem with this argument, however, is that it assumes the prior existence of a structure of differentiated statuses based on age criteria. The Kujamaat Jola of Jipalom have not developed a homogeneous class of elders. Thus, for example, in Table IIb elders D, E and F do about half of all the work themselves, whereas elder A does none. Moreover, elders may be allowed to pay for *sikáf* labor with beer and food for different reasons: because they enjoyed a great deal of prestige (elder A), or because they were infirm and could not do much heavy work (elder B), or because they were childless and had no-one to help them (elder F). Other elders (C, D, E) were expected to pay for *sikáf* labor with remittances sent by their sons working in town.

Thus, the Jipalom elders cannot simply command directly the labor of younger men or dependants by withholding wives or political patronage. The services elders provide as family counselors, arbitrators in disputes, representatives of the group and general upholders of the Islamic order, may be reciprocated through labor contributions that are, in a way, asymmetrical and sometimes free.

There is an obligation, of a specially asymmetrical type, that the Jipalom inhabitants consider to be their duty as good Muslims. Unlike the men of Fatiya discussed in the next chapter, the Jipalom men do not set apart a special field which they cultivate in groundnuts for some well-known marabout living elsewhere. Nevertheless, a number of total strangers, who had settled in Jipalom when I was first there in 1964, cultivated regularly for a resident Jola marabout with whom they lived:

Jerending accompanied his brother Jeju, who came to Bojas to be cured by Lamin, a marabout and an agnate of the Bojas ward. When Jeju became cured, he became Lamin's student. In return, Jeju and Jerending did all of Lamin's cultivation for him, both in the rice fields and on the plateau. More than was considered good by others in the ward. In addition, Jeju was always giving Lamin money.

Contributing free labor to a marabout can be thought of as a ritual obligation, for marabouts are holy men and as such demand services and respect. On the other hand, working for an elder who is acting as host to a distant matrilateral relative is not thought of as a ritual obligation. But this does not make it less compulsory.

Twenty-seven years have passed since my first lengthy stay in Jipalom. At that time, male associative *ekáf* labor was the principal way in which the men got their groundnut fields prepared. It was customary at the time for all the men of the Bojas ward to work together in one large *ekáf* numbering about thirty men. This was the only work-group in Jipalom who could command a bull for a day's work. Since that time, however, all male *sikáf* labor in the groundnut fields has totally disappeared. The pattern has been replaced by one in which people scramble to buy their own ploughs, oxen or carts – or borrow them in any way they can. If they cannot, they still have to do the work by hand. In recent years, a few lucky individuals have also hired a tractor and got their plateau fields prepared. Whatever arrangement they may make, it is obvious that the cultivation of a cash crop has promoted a more individualistic pattern of work and new attitudes towards technology.

A technology that is not used in the old rice-growing system, and certainly not by women.

The women's associations
In a discussion of gender differences in the control of economic resources, Friedl (1975: 62) has argued that the crucial variable is "which sex has the right to command the labor of others or the product of their labors." This point was carefully documented by Guyer (1984b: 381), who demonstrated that differences in seasonal rhythms in two West African societies were related to "women's relatively limited institutionalized means of mobilizing labor."

It cannot be categorically asserted that Jipalom women lack the rights, or the actual means, to secure the labor of others. However, their ability to hire outside labor is limited by their inability to get hold of cash while in their village setting. Women cannot sell the rice they produce, or partake of the profits from the groundnut harvest, despite having helped to produce it. But they can, and do, occasionally sell their labor-power. A woman can do individual work for another woman, who pays her in kind, or whose husband pays her in cash. A good harvester gathers about 20 bundles of rice a day, and gets up to 4 bundles of rice weighing 3–4 kg. apiece for pay. That a woman got paid as much shows how precious her labor is, and how difficult to get. For, after a week's work on their own rice fields, and on their husbands' groundnut fields, women have little spare time to sell.

In the last instance, women are forced to rely on associative work among themselves to get their fields done. And in the process of doing so, they may also earn some cash. Two types of female work-groups, or *sikáf*, existed in Jipalom in the 1960s. The first work-group was composed of the in-married women (the *kuseek*). They worked together in the rice fields of one another, on a voluntary, usually rotational basis. In working for each other, the *kuseek* were really working for the conjugal pair as a unit; that is, they worked on the fields that had been allocated to the wife as well as on the fields that her husband controlled. Not surprisingly, most often it was the husband who did the remunerating in cash or in kind.

When they planted or winnowed the groundnut fields, the *kuseek* worked exclusively for the men. For this work they were paid a certain sum which they saved up or kept as a fund against which to borrow in times of need.

The second type of female work-group involved in agricultural work in the 1960s comprised small clusters of female agnates married elsewhere (the *kuriimen*). They worked only intermittently. When they did so, they worked for each other and for their brothers, seldom for the latter's wives. Hence, as

The impact on social and productive relations 137

with other aspects of their social life, namely out-marriage and polygyny, the practices that are encouraged by Islam have helped to underscore differences in the degree of power enjoyed by two separate categories of women. For example, during the 1960s, the association of locally born female agnates was headed by one of its members. The association of in-married female affines, however, was headed by a man who had the title of "president." He was in charge of "storing" and "investing" their money, deciding for whom the *kuseek* would work, lending to those women who were in need.

By 1985, after a decade and a half of drought, some changes in the use of female associative labor could be observed. Women still helped their husbands by punch-hole seeding and winnowing the groundnut crop. In this context, they seemed to be using associative labor (the *ekáf*) more often than they did before, because the men were cultivating greater surfaces in groundnuts and millet. And they were being paid twice as much as in 1964. For the reverse reason, because much less rice was being done, the women obviously used much less *ekáf* labor in their rice fields than before. In fact, in 1985, the *ekáf* was used in rice-field work only five times during the entire season. And when the women used associative labor, it was mostly to weed the rice fields, rather than to transplant upon them, or to harvest. This was because, during the drought, direct-seeding was the only alternative, even though it increases the weed problem. Other changes in the forces and relations of production had also occurred during the last decades.

Plate 15: The in-married women's *ekáf* works for a resident male agnate. They are beating the dried plant to detach the nuts. (Courtesy J. David Sapir).

Changing forces and relations of production

The years that have elapsed since I was first in Jipalom have been years of hardship and long-lasting drought. Not surprisingly, there have been major changes in Jipalom's organization of agricultural labor. In the late 1970s, after nearly a decade of drought, the people of Jipalom were unable to cultivate rice as they had before. Associative work had not entirely disappeared, however. The largest of all the work-groups, composed of all the men in the ward, was busy furrowing the special fields set aside for the boys' initiation (the *futamp*), schedule to take place in a few years. Hence, in rice-field work, "traditional" ritual activity still continued to underscore productive activity. But only to a limited extent.

To this day, work in the rice fields is largely centered on the conjugal family unit. In contrast, groundnut farming was, until a decade ago, primarily a male collective endeavor. As Table IIc shows, in 1964 men were investing 71 adult days/ha in groundnut work. At the lowest level of segmentation, a man worked mostly in the company of his closest male kin, often his sons or married brothers. At the most inclusive level, the work was done by all the men in the ward organized into one large *sikáf*. They would do each other's groundnut fields, starting with the elders' fields, for a feast and abundant millet beer. However, they also received some help from the women. Alone, or in groups, the women usually planted the seed at the beginning of the rains, and helped their husbands beat and winnow the groundnut plants at the end.

By 1981, however, the plough had made its appearance in Jipalom. The men were only spending an average of 24 adult days/ha on their groundnuts. Animal traction is a great labor-saving device (Table IIc). It has been calculated that a team of oxen and a plough reduce labor inputs by 70 percent (P. Richards 1983: 59). In that year (1981), in Jipalom, a village of 115 married men, there were only 3 complete plough teams (called *equipes*), including oxen and carts to transport the harvest. The only person that owned the special two-bladed plough the Jola use to plough the rice fields was Landing, the *atalibao* (Koranic instructor) of one of the wards. In 1985, there were 11 complete *equipes* (with or without the rice plough), plus 5 more lacking the cart. Hence, in 4 years, the number of ox-plough teams had at least quadrupled. Although the number of households that owned an ox-plough was still very small, less than ten percent, an increasing number of individuals used some form of animal traction in their groundnut fields. A man might lend his oxen out to a Jipalom neighbor in the morning, provided the latter would lend him his plough in the afternoon.

It has been argued by Boserup (1970: 32–34) that high population density

Table IIc: *Labor input by gender in Jipalom[a] (adult days/ha)*

	Women	Men	
		(hoe)	plough[c]
	1981	1964	1981
Wet rice[b]	85	42	
Millet	10[e]	16	5
Groundnuts[d]	16[f]	71	24
Totals	111	129	87[g]

Note:
[a] From Berger, 1981: "Program for the Development of the Baila *marigot* in Casamance." Report, Ministry of Rural Development (Senegal) and US AID. Also from my own 1981 data.
[b] If the average amount of rice land cultivated is 0.85 ha, then the yearly labor investment in ricefield work would be 75 days for women and 49 days for men.
[c] Labor inputs drop by 70% if using the oxen-drawn plough (P. Richards 1983, footnote 8, p. 59). This makes it 24 adult/day ha for men for groundnuts and 5 days/ha for millet. The figures remain 16 days/ha for women.
[d] The average size of a groundnut field cultivated by a household head would be about one hectare.
[e] Includes long hours some women spend year-round pounding millet to feed the oxen (at least 8 hrs weekly).
[f] Does not include post-harvest processing.
[g] Total includes the 58 days/ha doing rice.

has prompted the adoption of plough agriculture in the developing world. According to her, "the advent of the plough usually entails a radical shift in sex roles in agriculture." Because everywhere men monopolize the new-plough technology, "men's burden of work usually increases while that of the women diminishes." In the Kajamutay, however, exactly the reverse has happened. For the wives of those lucky male individuals who own oxen, there is more, rather than less, work in sight. Oxen are fed special diets of sorghum which women must pound for hours every day; this is in addition to working in the fields. In 1985, women continued to help their husbands by punch-hole seeding the groundnuts and beating them to separate the nuts from the stem. Generally then, groundnut cultivation has contributed to making mature men wealthier, younger men who are in charge of driving the oxen-team somewhat more independent, and women more overworked (Linares 1985). And Islam has also enabled some elders and Muslim clerics to claim a privileged status, while imputing religious ignorance to women who are expected to work as hard, or harder, than before, with little time left over after work in the fields and household chores to rest or pray, as men do.

Conclusions to Part II

Islam and groundnut production have had a disruptive effect upon the social organization of production in Jipalom. A community located in the Upper Baila basin, Jipalom is "typical" of the region north of the Casamance River known as Kajamutay. In all this area, the effects of Islam have been mostly indirect. By being historically and conceptually linked to the cultivation of groundnuts, Islam has augmented peoples' dependence on external markets. By eroding old beliefs and ritual practices, Islam has gradually contributed to the dissolution of productive relations. Until recently, a plurality of spirit-shrines underscored a coherent system of social action that brought co-resident men and women into relations of reciprocity and respect. Nowadays, the spirit-shrines bring mostly disease and misfortune. In the many years between my first and last visit to the area, neither a viable syncretism between old and new religious practices, nor a more vigorous form of Islam, have emerged.

The kinds of practices performed at life-crisis rituals, such as the prestations to the matrilateral kin, are crucial. Important usufructuary rights to land are secured by activating matrilateral ties. This applies particularly to usage rights over rice fields. Also, conflicts over land are traditionally mediated by the uterine kin of the compound, that is by the *kusámpul*. Today, the system is in flux. Islam is eroding the rituals that buttressed uterine relations, with the concomitant adverse effects on land-use patterns.

When it comes to borrowing groundnut and millet fields, the practices that have emerged are opportunistic; persons borrow land where they can. Although good Muslims should be generous with each other, Islam does not regulate extra-domestic relations. Moreover, owing to several recent developments – the introduction of the ox-plough, the increasing shortage

Conclusions to Part II 141

of land, and the drought – plateau lands are becoming scarce, and the personal networks that made borrowing possible are fast disappearing.

Not only land-tenure, but also labor patterns, are being affected by new, emergent opportunities. Whereas associative work was once important among the men, even though some benefited from it more than others, the use of the plough is making male cooperative labor obsolete. This appears to run against Islam's emphasis on male joint activities. In reality, however, Islam in Jipalom is only a half-way house. Praying and politicking together, as do men in the third village we will be considering next, have not yet become the rule. The weak presence of Islam is the result of many factors, among them the distance from the centers of power, the absence of local Islamic clerics, the importance placed on French rather than Koranic studies, and the attitude of distrust towards people like the Wolof or Manding who, though Muslims, are not Jola.

Whereas associative work continues to be practiced by the women, there is an increasing tendency for their work-groups to be headed by men. Among the men, a patronage system is emerging, revolving around the use and loan of ox-ploughs on plateau lands. The increasing emphasis being placed on growing groundnuts for cash is eroding rice production.

Rice for the Kujamaat Jola has more than simple economic importance. I have argued elsewhere (Linares 1985), that rice is a social glue. It serves to cement social relations through rituals in which paddy or cooked rice is distributed to kin and acquaintances. But the role of rice is not only public and political; it is also domestic. Practices governing storing, cooking, and eating rice reinforce and clarify relations among household members. They distinguish between persons on the basis of gender, generation, age, and status position.

I have also argued that, in clear contrast to rice, groundnuts are not a ritually important crop; for they do not enter either the ritual or the domestic sphere. This statement must be somewhat modified, however. It is true that the men of Jipalom do not set apart a special field which they cultivate with groundnuts for some well-known marabout living elsewhere. (They do so regularly in the villages of the Kalunay, including the community of Fatiya that I will be describing in the next section). Nevertheless, as I have indicated (p. 135), some strangers who were living in Jipalom when I was first there in 1964, cultivated regularly for a resident Jola marabout from the Bojas ward with whom they lived.

The combination of practices the Jola attribute to Islam (though not always accurately) has also eroded the status of women and taken away the power they used to exercise in the pre-Islamic context. Instead of controlling the shrines, which gave them the power to cure disease and bring good things to worthy villagers, the in-married women's participation in ritual activities is increasingly being relegated to such practices as female excision. It is true that agnatic women still have a say in agnatic affairs; but they use this option mostly on their brothers' behalf. And even though in-married women have usufructuary rights to paddy land, these rights disappear once their husbands die. Unlike the women of Sambujat, the women of Jipalom cannot buy or sell the product of their labor, namely rice. On the other hand, they benefit very little from the sale of the groundnut crop which their husbands monopolize. Even though they can earn some money doing *sikáf* labor for the men, and even though they can occasionally sell their labor-power individually, they have very little of it left over from their own arduous work for this to constitute a serious option as a money-making device.

Undeniably, then, Islam in its local version has depressed women's status without increasing their access to new political positions and new technologies. Jipalom's women work harder than ever, without enjoying the autonomy, both moral and economic, enjoyed by the Esudadu women of Sambujat discussed in the previous chapter. Instead, Jipalom's wives are urged in the name of piety to respect their husbands, to help them with agricultural tasks and to perform domestic work without complaining.

With regard to the new technology such as ploughs and oxen, these can be rented or bought from state-owned agencies, but few men, and no women, have the money, or live near enough to a town, to do so regularly. And even if they were able to buy or rent equipment, either the price would fall or the rains would fail. More than being under-capitalized, the Jipalom economy appears to be partly in, partly outside, the monetary system.

Scarce labor is ultimately available, or equipment can only be borrowed, by activating ties of kinship and friendship. And these ties need to be reinforced constantly through coherent ritual activity. Yet many of the old ritual practices that once helped to structure relations of reciprocity are falling into disuse. They are not being substituted, in their specificity and in the particular social work they performed, by equivalent Islamic rituals. Thus, by accepting Islam, the Kujamaat Jola have begun to turn away from the complexities of their religiously sanctioned forms of reciprocity. And by adopting groundnuts, an Ajamaat is operating in a wider political sphere that places him, if not at an outright disadvantage, at least in a dependent state.

The underlying question remains, why do the Kujamaat Jola seem so much at a loss at the present time? The argument I have tried to put forward is both a structural and an ideological argument. Neither Islam, nor cash cropping, have been accompanied by a new, coherent model of society. "Seldom in the first phases of its penetration in tropical Africa can Islam have been taught as a comprehensive theology" (I. M. Lewis 1980: 58). In the Kajamutay, a new ideology has created contradictions in the social fabric at large. And it has specifically contributed to the unstructuring of social relations of production by eroding those very rituals that, in the "traditional" context, would promote the lending and borrowing of things like ox-ploughs. In the next chapter we will see how a totally new model of structural relations has emerged in the Manding-influenced community of Fatiya. Here, a completely separate social and sexual division of labor has been adopted, with interesting consequences for the system and the individuals within it.

PART III

MANDING MODELS AND FATIYA MORES

5

Ideology and legitimation

This chapter analyzes a process that, for want of a better name, has been called the "Mandingization" of Jola society (Thomas 1958/1959, Pélissier 1966, Linares 1981). In the literature on the Jola, emphasis has been placed on how "traditional" Jola culture has become transformed by the introduction of new norms and values borrowed from the Manding. Pélissier (1966: 799–800) has expressed this point of view in an impressionistic yet insightful way:

> The Jola, hard working and after profit, essentially anxious to accumulate rice and to augment their cattle, have borrowed from the Manding, not only their religious conceptions, but also their life-style and their hierarchy of values. These peasants, rustic and concrete, have become, in the image of their models, contemplative and attached to long words. Real wealth is no longer based on material things; their love of work and sense of land have singularly diminished. At the same time, women have assumed in this new society a role comparable to the one occupied by women among the Manding.

The implication of this statement is that the "Mandingized" Jola have wholeheartedly adopted Manding ethnic identity. In crossing ethnic boundaries, the Jola have undergone a systematic shift in the system of meanings through which they construct their identity. And, further, that this shift has brought with it fundamental changes in gender relations.

As Epstein (1978: 100) has ably argued, however, no one ever carries a single identity. Members of all societies simultaneously hold a whole range of identities in the same way as they occupy a number of statuses and play a variety of roles. The Jola of Fatiya, a community in the Tangori district of Lower Casamance at the edge of the Kalunay Forest bordering on Manding country, do indeed accept that many of their attitudes and practical behaviors reflect *buŋarabu bati kumandingaku* ("the path, the way of the Manding"). They will even signal out those religious practices, social institutions and productive arrangements which they believe, rightly or wrongly, to have been "borrowed" from their Manding neighbors. Their attitude to this is neither pride nor shame but a straightforward recognition of the diversity underlying custom and practice.

Nevertheless, while acknowledging that they have been greatly influenced by the Manding, the inhabitants of Fatiya think of themselves as being first and foremost Jola. They will point to their language, and much of what they consider to be "traditional" Jola ways, to prove their point. Thus, ethnicity must be seen as a self-labeling phenomenon. Ethnic groups are no more, no less, than the diverse categories of identification and ascription that members make for themselves (see Barth 1969). And individuals can identify in one way, while behaving in another way and questioning those with whom they share close affinity. As P. Richards (1984) usefully suggests, ethnicity can be viewed in network terms. He quotes from the work of Van Binsbergen (1981: 62) to the effect that new beliefs and rituals "impose new networks for the flow of people and goods (tribute, pilgrims offerings, healers' fees etc.) over wider areas." In doing so, they actually re-shape supralocal relations of production.

The purpose of this chapter is not to sort out the degree of choice vs. imposition in Manding–Jola cultural interchanges. For it is impossible to ascertain to what extent a particularly Jola group was ever in a position to embrace, or to reject, Manding cultural hegemony. Furthermore, "Mandingization" is obviously not a fact, but a subtle, two-way process that is still going on at the present time. Rather, the aim will be to analyze the central role that Manding-type Islam has played among the Jola. Differential access to land and other productive forces, limited eligibility to political offices, social asymmetries and segregated tasks have been institutionalized through various channels: Islamic rituals, secular Manding routines, state-promoted economic practices and national political policies.

The process of "Mandingization" can be analyzed from the point of view of a flexible political strategy that facilitates many things: the incorporation of migrants into local social networks, the economic linkage of local communities with larger towns, the institutionalization of privileges, the extension of kinship loyalties, and the formation of unisexual work teams. Access to kinship networks, as P. Richards (1984) also suggests, may be achieved in the context of patron–client relationships, by mastering the necessary cultural skills. Translated into Fatiya's community practices, this means the adoption of mutually advantageous relations of clientship and patronage through aspects of land ownership, political control, and religious comportment. With its authoritative sanctioning of knowledge, political power, economic profit, and domestic relations, Manding-type Islam has legitimated new cultural practices and social forms. At the same time, Manding-type Islam has been molded in the Kalunay Jola context by the very same practices it has tried to subvert.

The first part of chapter 5 takes up two related issues: the role of Islam in Manding history and society and the way Islam is practiced in the Jola community of Fatiya. The latter part of chapter 5 touches upon the effects of the adoption of Islam and aspects of Manding "culture" on social and economic behavior. Emphasis will be placed on the role of Islam in legitimating new status relationships, such as those between village founders and immigrants, elders and younger men, patrons and clients. The implications of these new relationships for access to political positions and material forces – that is to authoritative and allocative resources – shall be explored in the last part of the chapter.

The Manding: a brief history
When Portuguese traders first arrived in the middle to upper reaches of the Gambia, Casamance and Geba rivers in the 1450s, they described peoples living along the shores in terms that suggest they were part of a Manding-controlled commercial and political network.[1] The explorer Cadamosto (Crone 1937: 70), for example, remarks of the people he met in the area between the middle Gambia and the middle Casamance River as "men who frequent other countries, not remaining tied to their homes" . . . "but all recognize one God and some hold the tenets of Muhammed." These persons, who were probably Manding traders and or itinerant marabouts, had apparently displaced, exterminated or incorporated the previous Bañuñ inhabitants. "It seems likely that the first Mandinka [Manding] migrants into the lower Gambia–Casamance area found Bainounk [Bañuñ] living there, with the heaviest Bainounk [again Bañuñ] concentration in the south near the Casamance" (Wright 1977:9). Subsequent accounts again refer in passing to Manding presence in the headwaters of important rivers.[2] "In times and sequences yet to be determined, Mandinka traders extended their commercial networks to link the upper Casamance, Cacheu and Geba rivers; and Mandinka leaders founded the states of Casa along the upper Casamance River, Birassu/Braco along the upper Cacheu River, and Badour along the upper Geba River" (Brooks, 1980b: 16).

Historians (Lauer 1969, Rodney 1970, Curtin 1975, Wright 1977, Barry 1981) have traced the origins of these Senegambian Manding populations to the actual movements of peoples occupying the savanna lands of the interior, towards the coast. The westward movement of the Manding, ultimately from somewhere in the Upper Niger River, is thought to have taken place in two different stages: the first stage, which may have started as early as the ninth or tenth centuries, before the consolidation of the Mali empire, was more of a trickle than a wave; the second stage dated from the thirteenth and fourteenth centuries and involved larger movements of people and more aggressive conquering techniques. "The Mandinka [i.e. Manding] who came west to settle in the Gambia and Casamance regions were part of the important Manding civilization that shaped life in the Western Sudan throughout most of the second millennium" (Wright 1977: 12). In his study of Niumi, a Manding state existing before and after Cadamosto's and Diogo Gomes' visits to the Gambia River, Wright (1977: 15) defines the political situation as follows: "along the south bank, [of the Gambia River] and down across the upper Casamance and Geba Rivers, Mali's rulers (*mansa*) exercised authority through local rulers who were most likely ethnic mixtures of Mandinka and peoples indigenous to the area."

More recently, Wright (1985) has raised an alternative explanation for the Manding presence in the Senegambia. He suggests that the so-called western movements of Manding peoples may have actually represented a slow process of "cultural transferal" rather than massive migration.[3] Wright does not rule out the possibility that some ancestors of the present-day Senegambian Manding may have been actual traders who came directly from Mali to set up stations in far away lands. But he puts the emphasis where it should be, namely on the problem of distinguishing between subtle shifts in ethnic identities and the actual movements of people. For it is a fact of Senegambian history that ethnic labels and identities have continually shifted. This is what has happened to the "Mandingized" Jola groups living in the Kalunay.

According to Dalby (1971), the term Manding should be restricted to the ethnic groups otherwise known as Mandinka or Malinké, Bambara, and Dyula. Except for the Bambara, the other two groups trace their area of origin and expansion to the Upper Niger region, once the heartland of the Malian empire. In Senegal, the term Manding (*amandiŋao* in Jola) refers to the Mandinka or Malinké groups of the Senegambia and Guiné Bissau; it has been used in that sense throughout this book. From the Gambian to the Geba River one finds three Manding groups. First, there are the Manding living along the south bank of the Gambia River, from its mouth to the interior; they constitute about 40 percent of the total population. Secondly, there are the Manding who dominate the Middle Casamance, from the

Soungrougrou River east to the town of Kolda, where Fulani or Toucouler country begins. Thirdly, there are the Manding groups located in what is now Guiné Bissau, beyond the reaches of the important rivers, away from the coast. Whereas the Manding of the Gambia and Guiné Bissau had strongly centralized political organizations, those of Middle Casamance had weak governments. Their unity depended upon common membership in the community of Islam.

If we see their distribution in spatial terms, it is clear that the Manding form an arch around the Kaluñay or eastern border of Jola territory. They encircle the Jola on all sides except westward, along the sea. However, up to the fifteenth century, contact between the Jola and the Manding or "Mandingized" populations who had settled in the Middle Casamance and Gambian rivers was probably sporadic, indirect, and even hostile. Not until after they had completed their take-over of the Bañuñ-occupied lands north of the Casamance River between the eighteenth and nineteenth centuries, a process described in part II, did the Jola confront the Manding directly. In the 1840s, the Manding had two important kingdoms within the Foñi region itself, Kombo and Kiang (Quinn 1972: 34–35).

As mentioned in chapter 3, during the nineteenth century the Jola turned to gathering forest products for profit in the form of trade in palm kernels and palm oil, followed by trade in red rubber from the vine *Landolphia*. This trade ushered in a pattern of migration to the Gambia that brought the north-shore Jola into direct contact with their Muslim neighbors and hosts. Yet good relations between the Jola and the Manding continued to be hindered by the Manding-led *jihads*, or holy wars of religious conversion.

The maraboutic wars, together with French intervention, created the kinds of social dislocations and disruptions that eventually laid Jola territory open to outside influences. The *jihads* also re-kindled religious awareness among the Manding themselves. For them, the nineteenth century was a period of Islamic resurgence. It reminded them that they had duties as Muslims, to take the role of peaceful proselytizers among the Jola north of the river when conditions permitted.

Salient features of Manding society
The pre-colonial, nineteenth-century social organization of the Gambian Manding (or Malinké) states such as Wuli and Niumi, was hierarchical and stratified (Quinn 1971, Wright 1977, Weil 1984). At the top of the Manding sociopolitical ladder were members of the royal–commoner caste. In the past, these persons did not farm. Instead, they had slaves to do their work for them. Craftsmen, namely blacksmiths, leather-workers, and praise-

singers, or *griots*, were also constituted into castes; they did not farm either. During the early twentieth century when slavery disappeared, "nobles" turned to farming, slaves also became independent farmers, and many specialists became traders and middlemen (Weil, 1980, 1984). Yet many aspects of Manding caste and class persisted to this day.

It should go without saying that the Manding (Malinké) are not a homogeneous people, unvarying in their cultural practices or social institutions.[4] However, there are certain synthesizing "currents" in Manding society that the Jola of the Kalunay have perceived and incorporated, albeit in a modified fashion. The Manding, or Malinké, have been described by Schaffer and Cooper (1980: 9) as an "intensely religious and intellectual" people. Their study focuses on three villages belonging to the former kingdom of Pakao, located in the Middle Casamance, within the Department of Sedhiou (Seju). Living within an old Islamic center, the seat of considerable religious power in the past, the inhabitants of Pakao show certain features of Manding social organization in their more exaggerated form. Thus, their system of castes is as developed as it is among Malinké society in Mali (Camara 1976). The roles of chief and *imam*, of elder and junior, of women and men, are also carefully distinguished.

Answers to the question of why, and how, the Manding seem to be surrounded with an aura of piousness, which they seem to cultivate assiduously, must be sought in their historical role as spearheads in the Islamic revolution that swept across West Africa from the late eighteenth century throughout the nineteenth century. As a consequence of their heritage of political greatness from the Sudanese empires – the Mali Empire in particular – the Manding have now a "reputation for piety and long-term contact with the Muslim world" (Leary 1970: 5). However, this reputation is not due to their having created an effective political machinery. In the Middle Casamance, the Manding have always lived in autonomous villages within amorphous territories. These regions lack supravillage political or administrative bureaucracies. Probably for this very reason, Islam has acquired special importance as the principal organizing force in Manding society. It has created its own sub-culture through what Leary (1970: 41) has called "a commonality of life styles and systems," or what Pélissier (1966: 561) refers to "as an element of cohesion, of organization and social discipline."

The role played by Islam in Manding social organization has been documented by Weil (1971). He has discussed how Islam actually enters into the process of political socialization among the Manding of the

Gambia by being appealed to when various parties wish to reach consensus at village meetings. These gatherings are held any time an issue of interest to all the villagers needs to be brought up for solution. One of the ten principal speakers or elders is always the *almamo* or head of the mosque. Although in most such occasions the elders carefully orchestrate the reaching of consensus among the litigants, sometimes it comes to pass that an acrimonious disagreement among them flares up. At this point, the chairman calls those present to prayer. At the next daily prayer, the *almamo* gives the sermon of unity under Allah. "It is primarily conflicts which immediately threaten the unity of the whole village that are adjudicated directly by Islam in the form of mosque prayers by the *almamo*. Moreover, Islam often provides the ideology and logic of debate and mediation" (Weil 1971: 259).

The Manding also draw a clearcut social division between "owners of the land" and more recent immigrants. It is a pervasive underlying feature of their social organization, and it is sanctioned by Islam. Having defeated the infidels, village founders are considered to be guardians of the lands owned by Allah. Thus, a Manding village is divided horizontally into two clear and distinct groups: the founders (*angsarlu*) and the strangers (*falifalu*). Members of the class of founders share the same patronym. They are in charge of initiating all political processes. They are basically regarded as patrons, whereas the strangers are regarded as clients: "The strangers thus have a form of second-class citizenship in the village; it is the founders who hold the highest local position of steward over the village land" (Weil 1971: 254). Within a particular Manding area, the oldest lineage, the one that first established rights to land, controls access to the means of production; they lend fields to subsequent immigrants. The legitimating fiction for this situation is provided by Islam. Founding lineages act as senior stewards over land belonging "ultimately" to Allah. "Land is distributed to other patrilineages as they join the village on the condition that they will act as junior stewards over it and that they will respect the senior authority of the founding lineage and its elder head, the village chief" (Weil 1981). Although the founding lineages have claims to rice lands, this does not apply to newly cleared land which is owned individually; or to a new category of land such as irrigated rice land (Dey 1981). The immigrants or strangers (the *falifalu*) work in public projects, join the military, and also give political as well as material support.

In short, Islam plays a central role in forging Manding social realities, starting with the juridical system and, as I will try to show, ending up with domestic relationships.

The role of Islam in Fatiya society

Islam also plays a central role in shaping social relations within the Jola community of Fatiya. The community is right at the border of the Jola region known as the Kalunay, within the administrative circumscription (*arrondissement*) called Tangori. The Kalunay is a vast upland area, partly covered by a forest reserve and divided from the Middle Casamance, where the Manding are located, only by the Soungrougrou River. Fatiya itself is only several valleys over, to the east of Bignona, on the highway to Dakar. With its hospital, post office and public buildings, the Bignona *préfecture* includes the largest town north of the Casamance River. In 1981, Bignona had some 17,400 residents (about 18,000 in 1988), in their majority Jola (Cheneau-Loquay 1988, table 4: 145).

Fatiya is still a pioneer village; its population grows year by year. In 1958, the official village census for Senegal listed the village population as being 142; in 1964 it had grown to 182. By 1972, the population was 233, which means a yearly increase in 8 years of about 3.5 percent, as compared with the general figure of 2.8 percent for Senegal as a whole (Decraene 1985: 15).[5] By 1980–81, the Fatiya population was close to 320 persons. Fatiya's demographic growth contrasts markedly with the stagnation of Jipalom, whose population is either stable or actually declining. The reason for this growth is not very far to seek: Fatiya's founding families are constantly encouraging new immigrants to come and settle – something the immigrants do willingly, for the village is very well-placed.

The original inhabitants of Fatiya came from the town of Sindian at the time of the Manding wars of the nineteenth century. With its present (1981) population of over 2,500 persons, Sindian, is located about 20 km north of Bignona, halfway to the Gambian border. By 1905–1906, Sindian had become an important trading town where more than 300 Manding traders had settled permanently (Leary 1970: 214). Here, Manding influence has gone beyond religion to affect Jola social behavior, economic practices and organizational forms.

The first Jola inhabitants of Fatiya, the Sane, are said to have come from Sindian at the time of the maraboutic wars. Elders of Fatiya still remember when Sindian was constantly under siege and the town had to be palisaded. Oral histories clearly indicate that Fatiya was founded by conquest. By the Sane crowd taking over by force from unknown peoples – some of whom may have been Bañuñ – the land they now cultivate. It is this act of appropriation that now legitimizes the rights of Sane descendants to be considered owners of the land.

Ideology and legitimation 155

Plate 16: Aerial view of Fatiya: (1) the highway to Dakar, (2) ward A: houses with enclosed orchards, (3) ward B: houses with enclosed orchards, (4), (5) groundnut/millet fields, (6) palm groves, (7), (8) rice fields. (Courtesy, Service Topographique, Dakar)

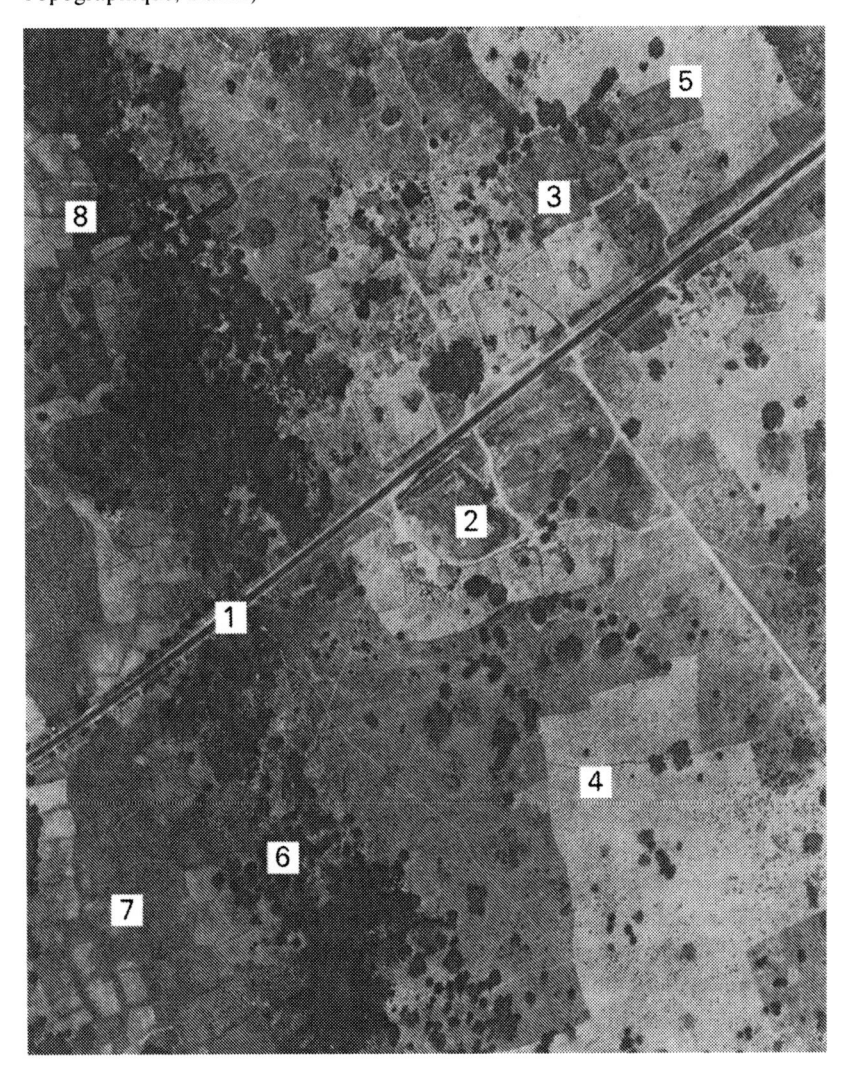

The elders of Fatiya converted to Islam in the first decades of this century, at about the same time as the Jipalom elders. In fact, the Fatiya elder who leads the daily prayer converted when he was about fourteen years old. In Fatiya, as in Jipalom, praying can take place individually, at a person's home, or collectively, at designated places. In Fatiya, there are two small prayer houses (*miserey*), one in each ward. But there are also larger mosques (*ejamon*, from Manding *jamango*, where Friday prayers can be said), located in the neighboring towns and communities. Devotion, like socializing, is more intense during the slack agricultural season. At this time, the men say their five daily prayers inside the *miserey*, led by a Sane *imam*, a member of the founders' lineage. Women cannot go inside the *miserey*. If and when they join the men in prayer they do so from a distance, outside on the grass, under the direct sun or the pouring rain. Incidentally, the women of Jipalom must also pray outside the *miserey*, but they do so from within a covered porch.

In Fatiya, as in Jipalom, there are two kinds of schools: the Koranic or "Arab school" and the French school. Because their holidays do not overlap, a few Fatiya children can attend both schools. The "Arab school" costs money and this is the reason given for why it has fewer students. Out of the 25 or so students attending the Arab school, only 5 or 6 are girls. In the 1960s, there were more girls learning the Koran than now; during the drought of the 1970s, they were taken out because their fathers could not pay. In 1981, the Arab school costed 200 francs CFA a month (less than one US dollar), which went to pay the Koranic instructor or *atalibao* so that the students would not have to work in his fields. When I mentioned the Murids (Mourides) of Senegal, the well-known Muslim sect in which the disciples or *talibés* cultivate for their marabouts, my Fatiya friends were emphatic: their *talibé* relationship was not like that.

Even though the inhabitants of both communities converted at about the same time, and even though the new generation of boys has received some Koranic instruction, Islamization (*bungarab bati Islam* or "the road to Islam") has gone further in eliminating old beliefs and ritual practices in Fatiya than in Jipalom. Doubtless, this is partly because Fatiya is only a few miles from Bignona and on a major highway to Dakar, compared to Jipalom, which until recently was isolated by bad roads and crumbling bridges for much of the year. However, it is not simply a matter of access to towns with their mosques and centers of Islamic learning. It is because, being strategically located at the edge of the Kalunay, the Fatiya inhabitants enjoy constant contact with Manding traders and clerics living nearby.

Plate 17: The Arabic school: 17A: a *talibé* teacher writes arabic on his tablet. 17B: his students display their skills.

When I was in Fatiya in 1985 there were no Manding living inside the community. But the next village over called Ngoram had 5 Manding resident families living among 25 Jola families. The present chief of Ngoram recounts that when his Jola ancestors first settled, there were only Bañuñ living there, who they promptly displaced. Then a great marabout (*amorao*), from the Manding holy center of Pakao mentioned previously, moved to Ngoram with a host of his disciples. When the Jola residents finally converted to Islam it was largely owing to his efforts. He also attracted a few Manding families to come and settle. When they first came, the Manding families lived in a separate compound. Later on, when more Manding families moved in, they joined the Jola families in the same ward, though in separate courtyards.

It bears emphasizing that the first Manding families were welcomed because they were in a position to lead the local inhabitants in the learning and practicing of their new religion. Subsequently, when more immigrants came, the Jola inhabitants of Ngoram used the very same Manding notion, that founders are "owners of the land," in order to welcome other Jola and Manding families, and thus build up the population of their community. To the newly arrived they extended usufructuary rights to land. I will have more to say later on about how everyday relations between Jola and Manding are structured in such mixed villages as Ngoram. The point to emphasize here is that each benefits from joining the other's social networks: the Jola gain access to the prestigious world of Islamic learning and to people who are expert traders; the Manding gain access to land on the plateau where they can grow groundnuts for cash.

Islamic law tends to structure the entire social field of its practitioners. "The Koran regulates not only all the juridical aspects of life: marriage, repudiation, emancipation, but also all domestic acts: nourishment, clothing, housing, etc. For all strictly personal behaviors, such as bodily cleanliness, adornment, women's fashions, a Muslim is subject to the traditions of the Prophet and his wives, the Sunna" (Gaudio and Pelletier 1980: 15). However, it is also important to keep in mind that African Islam is not an undifferentiated whole, a uniform set of practices adopted everywhere and in the same manner. Quite the contrary; Islam means different things to different peoples. And this is clear from the way Jola Muslims practice their religion in different contexts and areas.

Although they see Islam as a total way of life, the Fatiya residents usually described their faith in terms of the practices that it prescribes, permits or forbids. A person will readily talk about the attitudes all good Muslims should share, such as a love for one God, a sense of brotherhood, generosity and respect for others. More often than not, however, he describes his faith primarily in terms of what he should do as a good Muslim, and not in terms of what he needs to know. Without in any sense implying that their faith is superficial, it is important to emphasize that the Jola are concerned with correct behavior; with the "doing" aspect of their new religion. The bundle of practices they perform is, for them, Islam. This allows me to argue that religious practices help structure other, seemingly unrelated behaviors, like the social division of agricultural labor.

What Islam prescribes as correct behavior is set out in several places: in the Koran, the Sunna, which are the traditions drawn from the Prophet's actions, in the Ijamâ, or consensus of the learned and faithful, and in the Qiyâs, or reasoning by analogy (Guèye 1977: 13 and nn 31–34). This corpus, often referred to as the "devotionals," regulates every aspect of behavior, from the way one should perform bodily functions, to the way one should behave during the pilgrimage to Mecca. The detailed manner in which daily routines are codified makes African Islam, at least as it is practiced by various Senegalese groups, amenable to inspection by outsiders (like myself).[6]

First, one may note that the Jola (in Fatiya as well as Jipalom) not only know how to pray correctly, but are also deeply concerned with the mechanics of how one does the ablutions (washing parts of the body in proper sequence, and for the prescribed number of times). Literally everyone, men, women and grown-up children, know when and how to prepare for the five daily prayers. They are also conscious of the need to observe a host of other Islamic practices. Among these are: the fast of Ramadan; the taboo against eating certain animals (not only pigs, but also monkeys, dogs, horses and mules, things that have died naturally, hyenas and scavenging birds, etc.); the proper procedure to follow when a Muslim person is dying, or when he or she needs to be buried; the killing of an animal by cutting its throat, rather than by any other method; and the interdiction on drinking alcoholic beverages (which applies to palm-wine but not to millet-beer).

When it comes to abstract questions, however, such as what are the five pillars of Islam, or what the differences are between the Qadiriyya, Tijaniyya and Muridiyya brotherhoods, only those Fatiya inhabitants who have received formal instruction, or who are otherwise conversant with Islam, will voice an opinion. Few women, but most men, know that the Qadiriyya is the oldest of the brotherhoods, whereas Tijanism and Muridism are relatively recent departures.

Even though they are sanctioned by the "official" version of Senegalese

Islam given by Guèye (1977), the Islamized Jola often take exception to some Muslim practices. The laws of inheritance are an example. Whereas, according to Guèye (1977: 125–127), the Koran allows a widow to inherit from her husband (a quarter of the property if the deceased left no descendants, one eighth if he did), and a daughter to inherit from her father (the quantity depends upon the presence or absence of other sisters or brothers), Jola Muslim inheritance laws are patrilineal; wives or daughters do not inherit from husbands and fathers. The retention of Jola customary practices also applies to marriage. For example, whereas the Koran forbids a man marrying two or more women who are sisters, this is a regular Jola procedure, greatly preferred because it lowers bridewealth payments.

The Jola of both communities, Fatiya and Ngoram, have also added a few ritual precepts of their own that are not prescribed in the Koran. Among these are the interdictions against eating ducks, which Jola Muslims consider dirty; against burying more than one person in a grave, which orthodox Islam permits while traditional Jola practices forbid; or against having sexual relations during Ramadan, which Jola Muslims permit after the daily fast is over while the Koran forbids it. In short, the Jola version of Islam departs, in minor or major ways, from the "orthodox" version of Islam as codified by a prestigious authority.

Concomitant with the adoption of Manding-type Islam has been the rapid demise of the spirit-shrines or *sinàati*. If we recall, in Jipalom traces of the non-Islamic religion still remain and the shrines still sanction life processes to some extent. Not only Jipalom's men, but also Jipalom's out-married females (the *kuriimen*), control important shrines, with their accompanying rituals. In Fatiya, however, because of the constant pressure from Manding religious clerics and sundry marabouts living in Bignona, only traces of the "old" religion persist. The Fatiya inhabitants describe the *sinàati* by using terms such as *sibanban* ("they are finished"), or *sijupuorit* ("they are few"). Even the old men who had converted during their lifetime had difficulty remembering the names of the shrines. Most "traditionalist" (non-Islamized) elders have died. In 1971, there was still a married couple alive who were described as *pankuraan* (from the derived verb *raan*, to drink); in 1985, only two old animist ladies remained in the village and by 1990 both had died. The old shrines are spoken about entirely in negative terms: as the product of Satan, that is, as the forces of evil.

True there are a few *sinàati* still around. The ones that have persisted – originally, the most important – are all in the hands of members of the Sane lineage, who, as we will shortly see, are descended from the village founders and hence "own" the village. The principal Sane shrine is *Kaneewak*, the

Ideology and legitimation 161

male agnatic shrine that keeps the patrilineage together. In addition to *Kaneewak*, the Sane "own" a few other shrines. Thus, the chief Abdulay has an *enáati* (a spirit) named *Fuseek*, which he inherited from his father. Abdulay did not particularly want to continue "doing" the shrine, but people with an unmistakable skin disease kept coming to him to be cured. Because he was the chief, there was no way for him to refuse to entreat the *Fuseek* spirit. The chief's brother also owns an *enáati*. It "traps" by making the throat swell so that a person cannot drink. Another Sane brother has one called *Fulef*, who makes a child not want to eat. In addition, a few old agnatic women are still around to do the shrines. The chief's father's sister has an *enáati* which is simply called *Bakiin* (spirit); it makes the body swell.

In reality, however, few really important Fatiya shrines are still active. Thus, when someone gets sick the first thing he/she does is to go to a Muslim curer (an *alaak*) and it is up to him to decide whether an *enáati* is responsible for the illness, and whether it should be propitiated. Often he advises the sick person to go to the Bignona hospital instead. Thus, most of Fatiya's *sináati* have been reduced to their lowest common denominator. They function purely in the context of giving and curing diseases. They no longer stand for social categories, as spirits always do in Sambujat and to some extent in Jipalom. Under the impact of a persuasive and universalistic religion, the Fatiya *sináati* are rapidly falling into disuse. Today, their presence is only justified by the persistence of disease and the ever present fear of death.

Legitimating ideologies: social hierarchies and status asymmetries
The sorts of dynamic transformations that Kalunay Jola society has undergone, as a result of exposure to Manding cultural influences, point to an increase in power differentials taking the form of subtle shifts towards more hierarchical organization and asymmetrical interaction. A growing distinction begins to emerge between founders and immigrants, seniors and junior men, patrons and clients. Among the communities of the region, including Fatiya, patrilineal descent from the lineage of village founders or first arrivals becomes an important juridical, political and behavioral principle. It is not the notion of descent *qua* ideology that has become greatly elaborated, for there is no coherent set of ideas, such as we find in other West African societies, linking the transmission of life-giving substances like blood and semen with the presence of lineages. It is that residence patterns, political offices, ritual roles, all have become focused around the Manding-derived cultural construct dividing persons who are patrilineally descended from the original founders from more recent

immigrants who lack these ties.[7] In 1981, the Fatiya class of founding families comprised 16 married agnates in the elder and junior generations. Twice as many married agnates belonged to the immigrant category. The majority of immigrants, like the founders, had also come from the land-hungry town of Sindian. The oldest members of the immigrants class came to Fatiya about 30 to 40 years ago, when it was a small Sane village with lots of untouched forest nearby. This fact, as we will see, is important. It is expected of an immigrant that he will at first have to borrow all the fields he cultivates.

Fatiya is divided into two wards (*kalol*) of roughly equal size. They are thought of as "upper" and "lower" divisions of the village, in much the same way as Manding villages are conceptualized. Each ward is in turn divided into courtyard groups called *fank* (sing.) or *unk* (pl.), as in Jipalom. However, in Fatiya only the 3 courtyard groups belonging to the Sane descendants of the original founders are named. These named units comprise a clearly defined set of 3 interrelated patrilineages whose members can actually trace descent to a common ancestor and also live in close proximity. Founders are referred to as *kucilom esúk*, "those who own the village." The remaining population of Fatiya is composed of immigrants who are grouped into separate, genealogically shallow patrigroups, living in dispersed courtyards. Many immigrants are absolute strangers to each

Plate 18: Transporting the rice harvest to the chief's compound.

Table IIIa: *Fatiya household types[a] according to two criteria: co-residence and co-production[b,c,d]*

Household "types"	Solitary	Elementary	Multiple	Fraternal	Grand
Co-residence	0 (2)	17 (17)	5 (10)	3 (6)	4 (14)
Co-production	0 (2)	19 (19)	2 (4)	2 (5)	5 (19)

Note:
[a] For a definition of household types see Table Ic, note 1.
[b] Number of CFUs in parenthesis; total is 49; 61% co-reside in complex (multiple, fraternal and grand) units; 57% co-produce in complex units.
[c] Compare with Sambujat's households (Table Ic).
[d] In the one Jipalom ward I studied intensively, out of 15 CFUs, 13% co-resided in complex units and 40% co-produced in complex units.

other, having come to Fatiya from entirely separate villages. Again, it should be emphasized that Fatiya's residence and descent principles are radically different from those of Sambujat and Jipalom, where there are no founding families, no strong descent ideologies, no recent immigrants, and very few resident "strangers" (only in Jipalom).

The social distinction that is made between founders and immigrants also emerges at the level of household composition (Linares 1983). In Fatiya, a conjugal household unit comprises a man, his wife or wives, and their children. The husband usually has his own bedroom, and so does each of his wives. This, as we have seen, is also a customary practice among Jipalom's married couples. But, contrary to Jipalom's residential practices, and in startling contrast to those of Sambujat, a married son in Fatiya rarely moves out of his parental home. Instead, the house is enlarged to accommodate the new conjugal unit, which now occupies a separate room, usually facing the exterior. Additional rooms in this "porch" area are occupied by unmarried sons, widowed sisters, the elder's widowed or retired wives, and "strangers" or guests. The entire extended family shares a living room, a vestibule and a porch. Hence, as in Manding villages, co-resident units in Fatiya are quite large, larger than in the other two other Jola villages I have been discussing (Table IIIa).[8] Fatiya's households are not only larger and more complex, but within Fatiya itself founders' households are on the average larger than immigrants' households (Linares 1984). Again, this is a feature of Manding society.

Members of Fatiya's founding lineage also monopolize political and religious offices. The Fatiya chief is always drawn from the *fank* called Kalaab, recognized as being the oldest in the village. He always bears the patronym Sane, which is of Manding origin and the exclusive prerogative of founders. The Fatiya chief must always be drawn from among the members of the founding lineage, even though the person who actually occupies the post must be ratified by all village members, including the immigrants. Power to make binding decisions is also monopolized by members of the chiefly line. It was always a member of the founding lineage who headed the groundnut cooperative first established under the (now-abolished) official Senegalese department ONCAD (Office National de Coopération et d'Assistance au Développement). The authority of founders is not complete, however. Immigrants, especially those with longtime residence in Fatiya, have an active voice in the general village congress, where most local land-tenure decisions are made. But even though they can voice their opinions, they cannot introduce new policies nor implement decisions.

Not only do they monopolize political, economic, and as we will see ritual offices, but founders are the only persons with inalienable rights to live forever in the village. A member of the founding lineage can be absent from the village for any period of time, and he can behave in a "difficult" or even dishonest manner, with complete assurance that he will never be expelled from the community. Members of the immigrant class, however, are not secure even with respect to residence. Although an immigrant in good standing would probably never be asked to leave, instances are known of difficult or troublesome immigrants who have been ejected out of village lands.

In addition to immigrants, there are a number of "strangers" living in Fatiya. They are Lobé, a Fulani or Tukulor-related group who have been Muslims for a long time. They are married to Lobé women and live in their own courtyard. Although their wives cultivate right alongside other Fatiya women, the men do not work the land. Instead, they are craftsmen, making mortars, pestles, canoes, and other modern implements. In theory, if a Lobé proves himself worthy, he will be allowed to marry a local Jola woman; however, no such marriages are in evidence at the present time.

If one were to draw an overall village hierarchy, one would place the Lobé strangers partly outside the system. One would begin with Fatiya's recent immigrants, especially with those lacking close kin within the village, and place them at the bottom. Next, one would place the older immigrants, especially those who enjoy a measure of security by virtue of having taken as a wife a member of the founding lineage. The two highest positions in this hypothetical ranking system would, of course, be reserved for the founders themselves, followed by their matrilateral relatives. It should be clear by now that an equivalent social schema would be impossible to draw for an Esudadu community, not even for one in the Kajamutay.

Underlying the notion of founders vs. immigrant is another legitimating concept, that of seniority or elderhood. As we have seen, in Sambujat the notion of elderhood is built around the activities elders perform to control supernatural powers. An elder who is in charge of an important spirit-shrine is respected, and in a way even held in some awe. "He is strong, he controls a very mean Spirit," they will say of the ritual elder or *ai*. But the elder's actions are still hedged by prohibitions and restraints. He must exercise his power to appease a shrine on behalf of, and never in opposition to, the will of community members. And whatever authority he has over a shrine, it is not extended to the rest of society. An elder in Sambujat does not own more land, nor have access to extra labor, by virtue of his age or genealogic position. He does not mediate in disputes directly, nor seek consensus. That is the duty of the chief. He is not the head of an extended household since his sons have usually moved out to establish their own separate conjugal families. And he certainly does not control junior members by withholding bridewealth payments. An elder who is in charge of a shrine is not necessarily regarded as a wise or socially persuasive person. His activities are confined to the sacred domain. An elder must above all be forceful: he must "sit upon" a spirit, "bribe" it through offerings of wine and sacrifice, keep it from "attacking" when feeling neglected.

As can be expected, the construction of elderhood in the Mandingized community of Fatiya, whose inhabitants are all Muslims, is very different. It is more secular and paternalistic, closer to our own notion of seniority as a privileged status attributed to persons who are wise in the art of achieving consensus and seeking compromises. A respected elder is talked about as having "a shadow." An old man's shadow refers to his ability to protect younger men who take refuge under him. If an old man or elder is "not good" (i.e. generous, wise, comforting) he is talked about as "having the shadow of a ronier palm." A respected Fatiya elder is often a member of the immigrants' group. One of the wisest elders I knew, the father of my principal assistant, was a man of considerable stature, admired for his character and intelligence. Many foreigners, including myself, as well as younger members of the founders' group, benefited greatly from "being in his shadow."

The importance of seniority, and the political or economic processes that are built upon it, have been the focus of considerable anthropological debate. Some authors (see L. Mair 1962: 69–81, for example) have focused on the functions of age classes and/or age grades in the organization of important tasks of public interest among East African societies lacking well-defined classes or centralized political institutions. Other authors, mostly French Marxists like Meillassoux, Terray and Rey, have developed the theme that in West Africa "age is a vector of social stratification" (Abélès and Collard 1985: 10). Doubtless the best known of these theories is the one proposed by Meillassoux concerning the domination of juniors (*cadets*) by elders (*aînés*) through the latter's control over the circulation of women at marriage.

Despite its undeniable ingenuity, Meillassoux's argument has met with considerable criticism. Not only has he tended to gloss over the obvious fact that elderhood can only be a temporary status because juniors will eventually become seniors, but this sort of argument ignores the more fundamental question of how, through what mechanisms, are notions like that of seniority actually constructed (Abélès and Collard 1985). Put differently, treating seniors as if they constituted a unitary category ignores the various phases of this status. It impedes looking into the reasons why some aspects of this status, and not others, are incorporated into the intellectual and practical constructs of a particular peoples. In the words of Augé (1977: 78–79), it is important to investigate how a society establishes the sum of what is thinkable and possible. Or, in the words of Donham (1985), it is necessary to gain some idea of how these ideas are expressed in social practice.

Land tenure: those who own and those who borrow
The social hierarchies and status asymmetries that emerge in the founder vs. immigrant, elder vs. junior, distinctions are mediated through practical aspects of land tenure and land transmission. Like the Manding, the Jola of Fatiya associate conquest as a mode of settlement, with Islam as a sanctioning dogma, and lineal descent as a mode of defining exclusive rights to resources. Thus they make a clear-cut division between a land-owning privileged class of founders and a land-borrowing and dependent class of more recent immigrants. This gives to the Fatiya land-tenure system a totally different cast from Sambujat's or Jipalom's land-tenure system. Even though differences in wealth and seniority may be marked in Sambujat, and status and gender differences may be recognized in Jipalom, in neither of these two villages do we find anything like the incipient class system of Fatiya, with its founding families who control material and political resources, and a class of immigrants and strangers who are entirely dependent upon them for their livelihood.

To emphasize once more, the rights of Fatiya founders to own and distribute community lands is based on a Manding model, whereby "owners of the land" is a pervasive and legitimizing idiom in all land-tenure transactions. Not only Manding (or Malinke) described by Schaffer and Cooper (1980), but also other Mande people like the Bambara make this equation. Talking about a Bamana (i.e. Bambara) community near Segu in Mali, V. D. Lewis (1979: 45) has this to say: "The first clearer of virgin bush and his descendants become the owners (*tigiw*) of that land (*dugukolo*), just as the first settlers and his descendants become the chiefly clan (*dugutigiw*) when his settlement reaches village (*dugu*) size."

In Fatiya, a specific historical rationale underlies the division of the community into two groups, founders and immigrants. The original founders of the Fatiya community, the Sane, are said to have left the ward called Bujaken in the town of Sindian, to escape from the Manding *jihads*. Armed with European guns, the Manding were raiding for slaves to sell to other wealthy Manding for their use as labor in the groundnut fields. The Fatiya elders recount that when the Sane first came to the area, they joined the local Jola inhabitants and together they drove the Bañuñ away. The Bañuñ were thin on the ground; one of their villages may have had only three houses in it. Once settled in Fatiya, the Sane staked out large tracts of land, much more than they could cultivate themselves. Gradually, they attracted other Sindian families to come with their wives and settle. To this end, they lent them parcels of cleared land. Thus, the Sane became the "hosts", while the immigrants became their "guests", or "dependents." If he has a particularly strong personality and is intelligent, an immigrant man may wield considerable influence. However, in the last analysis, he lacks inalienable rights to the means of production. For all intents and purposes he belongs to a de-franchised class.

By virtue of the legitimizing construct that founders, and only founders, have rights of disposition over land, the kinds of conflicts and litigations that were a pervasive feature of the Jipalom land-tenure situation have been eliminated from Fatiya. As members of the same lineage, the Sane do not dispute land ownership among themselves. As land-borrowers, rather than land-owners, the rest of Fatiya's inhabitants who are immigrants have no voice in this matter. They may grumble among themselves that the Sane are not being generous enough, that they have not lent them enough rice parcels for all their wives to work. But their only recourse is to public opinion in the hope that "shame" will pressure the Sane into lending them a few additional fields that they or their wives can cultivate.

The actual mechanisms of land inheritance or acquisition are fairly straightforward. Within the founding families, ownership of paddy fields, as well as plateau fields, devolves in the usual Jola manner, that is patrilineally, from father to son at the time of marriage. The son keeps the upland fields to work himself, but he extends complete usufructuary rights over his rice fields to his wife. Every time he adds a new wife, his father adds one or more rice parcels.

In contrast, a new settler who comes to Fatiya must ask one of the Sane founders for usage rights to land. Groundnut and millet fields are made on upland areas, on the plateau surrounding the concessions. They are under a "typical" bush-fallow, savanna-type, short-cycle, shifting cultivation regime (Boserup 1965: 29–34), as in Jipalom. When new immigrants arrive (they usually come in groups) the founders get together and decide how many upland fields they can spare; the immigrants, in turn, must decide how many fields each one needs. The household head of each immigrant family makes its own arrangements with a particular member of the founders' lineage so that he gets enough upland fields to cultivate. As can be readily appreciated, the situation is complex: a multitude of simultaneous contracts are usually going on between founders and immigrants, each requiring separate negotiations. Land distribution is not done every year, but only when, and if, several immigrant families are in need of more upland fields.

Because women are not at all involved in groundnut or millet cultivation, the number of wives an immigrant has is irrelevant for borrowing land on the plateau. It is nonetheless crucial for the business of borrowing paddy fields down in the valley. Every wife works at least two large paddy fields, one of which she hoes herself, the other which the female work association or *comité* helps her prepare (more on this point below).

To summarize, in Fatiya two distinct land-tenure processes operate simultaneously; the first involves permanent alienation of paddy land through agnatic inheritance within the founding families; the second involves temporary contracts over usage rights between founders and more recent immigrants. Founders are under an obligation to lend out fields, for this is considered a moral obligation and bad form to refuse. But some men do refuse: "there is one or more in every village" I was told. Immigrants, in turn, owe political allegiance to the founding members and are also under a moral obligation to help them with agricultural tasks. They must always return borrowed land at the owners' request.

It is to the founders' advantage, however, to be just and generous. Much of a chief's political success, for example, depends on maintaining correct relations with immigrants, for he ultimately depends on them for political support in the village congress. For different but equally compelling reasons, it is also important for immigrants to align themselves with particular founders, men who can exert a significant amount of influence with local authorities.

It is also possible, however, for an immigrant to clear his own upland plot from the forest. This land he will own outright. However, by 1970 no more forest land was available for clearing, and rural government agents (*les Gens de l'Eau et Fôrets*) were unwilling to "de-classify" reserved forest areas. Hence, Fatiya's immigrants were more dependent than before on borrowing upland fields from the founders.

Clearly, in Fatiya, immigrants are engaged in the kinds of relations that have been described in the literature as clientship, not only with village founders, but also with sundry land-lending hosts. For, in order to increase the number of fields he is rotating, a Fatiya man, like a Jipalom man, often must borrow groundnut fields in other villages. To do so, a Fatiya man usually displaces himself for the entire season, not just for a short period. In addition, he must pay his *ajawáati* or host, who is often a Manding, a charge of 10 percent of the profits from the groundnut harvest. In exchange, the host feeds his male guest during the entire stay. Again, this practice is differently construed in Jipalom, where an individual stays for part of the season only, bringing with him his own rice and often a wife to cook it. Thus, Jipalom men keep a certain social distance from their hosts, unlike Fatiya men who have become quasi-dependent clients of their patrons or hosts.

Clientship, or more accurately patron–client relations, have in turn been defined as "inegalitarian patterns of exchange that are marked by a certain reciprocity and affection rather than domination and exploitation, and by personal and diffuse linkages rather than class power and control" (Fatton 1987: 93). It has been argued by Fatton that within the wider Senegalese scene, patron–client relationships "have perpetuated traditional patterns of domination and subordination." The salient example of a patronage or clientship system cited for Senegal is that of the marabout and his *talibés*. "The marabouts were enmeshed in a patron–client relationship whereby, as patrons, they extended to their peasant clients the material and spiritual support of belonging to a prestigious Islamic brotherhood. In return, the marabouts expected the devotion, allegiance, and free labor of their clients" (Fatton 1987: 97).

Clearly, however, patron–client relationships are not the same everywhere. A large body of literature has focused on the spatial, as well as the temporal, variations in patronage systems (e.g. Michie 1981, Bradburd

1983, Eisenstadt and Roniger 1984). In the Fatiya community under consideration, the relationship of host to stranger, immigrant to founder, is much less exploitative than the *marabout–talibé* relationship described later for the Murid brotherhood of the Groundnut Basin of Senegal. It is more like a situation whereby a patron provides economic aid and protection against outsiders, including government officials, and the client pays him back with "intangibles" such as admiration and esteem, the promise of political support, and relevant information. Moreover, not only is the Fatiya situation much looser, less structured, and potentially exploitative than in the Murid case, but it is also more individuated. Founders and immigrants do not constitute themselves into opposed, monolithic blocks. Particular Fatiya individuals are involved in patronage networks in different ways, with different peoples and to different purposes (e.g. Michaelson 1976). Elderly, wealthy immigrants, for example, or young men who have been in the Army or have received formal instruction in Koranic studies, tend to be more independent from founders than more recent, less worldly, less educated, or poorer newcomers.

A reason why immigrants enjoy a measure of independence, and in some occasions even exercise ascendancy over some of the founders, is because they are not under the formal obligation to contribute their labor, or part of their produce, to the founders in exchange for usage rights to land. The Fatiya system has the in-built potential for autonomy and flexibility which other systems lack. Nonetheless, it is still founded on the tacit recognition that relations between non-overlapping dyadic categories of persons, namely patron and client, founder and immigrant, host and guest, are based on social asymmetries and inequalities of power. These relationships are totally alien to the Esudadu Jola, and only structure part of the social field of the Kujamaat Jola. But they are a pervasive way of thinking about social relations among the nearby Manding, who have provided the cultural logic and practical model for their existence among the so-called "Mandingized" Jola of the Kalunay.

This is not to assert that patron–client relations are an exclusive Manding phenomenon. Quite the contrary; clientship is an ubiquitous feature of numerous societies around the world. Among the Mandari chiefs of the Nile Valley, for example, heads of lineages not only own the land, but they also provide ritual specialists for their clients, to whom they extended protection. In the Interlacustrine Bantu states of East Africa, where the aristocracy was made up of a pastoral class, clientship was based on the transfer of rights in cattle (Mair 1962). And so on. But what is specific about the host–guest, founder–immigrant model, which the Kalunay Jola have adopted, is that it follows closely Manding practices. It encourages the constant renewal of useful networks of nonetheless asymmetrical patron–client relations by basing them on the legitimating fiction that all men are equals and brothers under the eyes of the Prophet. The idea that men who are brothers under Islam owe each other favors and are bound by rules of reciprocity operates both ways. In Jola villages located further inside the Kalunay, it is the Jola who are founders of the village and owners of the land; it is the Manding who are the later-day settlers and immigrants; it is they who must secure rights to use the land from the Jola founders.

Not only productive resources, but also reproductive resources in the form of marriagable women, form an integral part of the networks of strategic connections linking individuals in various communities of the Kalunay. For, like land and other goods, women form part of the cycle of economic prestations and ritual reciprocities that men command. And like these other "resources," women enter into the kinds of dependent relations that underlie other aspects of Kalunay social life. The chapter that follows (ch. 6) gives a general sketch of gender relations in the community of Fatiya and shows how these are reflected in domestic arrangements. It then broadens out to include making linkages with other communities through marriage negotiations. The last part of the chapter is concerned with how the principles of social opposition and differentiation, that are embedded in distinctions made between founders and immigrants, elders and juniors, men and women, domestic and public acts, are played out in social practice. Here, I will be considering the labor process and forms of cooperative or associative labor.

6

Social relations of production re-structured

Marked distinctions in social status and political power underlie much of Fatiya's public life. The same is true to some extent of more private household and domestic contexts. These also are permeated by subtle power differentials pointing in the direction of increased inequality and social separation between the genders and the generations. There is nothing surprising in this. Public roles are a continuation of private roles, and there is a dialectical interplay between sacred acts and secular routines. In Fatiya, gender relations permeate domestic organization, and this in turn is the result of marriage strategies that facilitate access to the labor power of women. The social organization of production extends beyond the household domain to embrace cooperative forms of work and labor contributions. The present chapter traces these complex relationships. It is an effort to explicate how changing ideologies of power, brought about by exposure to Manding ways, has led to a re-structuring of social relations of production. In the community of Fatiya, and indeed in the whole of the Kalunay, the social separation of cropping systems is the result of a pervasive ideology that makes clearcut distinctions between different categories of people and the roles they play.

Constructing gender relations
Basic processes of social separation lie at the center of gender relations. In Fatiya, institutionalized relations between men and women, and between the elder and younger generations within each gender, are generally modelled after Manding social organization. This is explicitly recognized by the actors themselves. But the knotty question still remains as to what precisely is a Manding model of gender relations, and how one is to grasp its essentially qualitative dimensions.

Most experts on Manding social organization nevertheless make a special point of emphasizing the strict separation that exists, at the level of thought and action, between the sexes. Camara (1976: 48–57), himself a Manding, refers to gender relations among the Malinké of Upper Guinée as comprising a "sexual hierarchy." Men monopolize authority in all spheres of life: political, religious and domestic. Women are considered (by men) to lack social maturity. Camara (1976: 54–55) summarizes Malinké gender relations as follows: "Malinke society is a male society, directed by men, within which a woman is condemned to assume an eternal condition of minor, serving as a pawn in the game of matrimonial exchanges among groups of men . . ." According to him, Islam has aggravated this situation by denying a woman the right to gain access to paradise except through her husband's recommendations.

There is no denying that Islam makes a clear statement concerning the areas where men and women are, or are not, the same. Guèye's guidelines (1977: 177–178), specifying the obligations and interdictions that all good Muslims should observe, are revealing in this context. As a respected Islamic cleric and scholar, Guèye seems to represent the orthodox version of Senegalese Islam. According to him, the Koran affirms that both sexes are identical in the following respects: in their faith; their religious practices; their legal rights to work and own property; their equality before the law; their access to knowledge and culture; and their dispensations from prayer when ill or travelling. However, as he clearly states: "I do not think that there can be total equality between men and women since their proper nature excludes it" (Guèye 1977: 177). The areas where women are not equal includes such things as serving as witnesses before a judge, where a man is worth two women; being unable to repudiate a husband; having to wait at least forty days after a divorce to remarry, and so forth. A woman is also excused from observing a number of rites, such as the Friday prayer, fasting during her monthly period and serving in holy wars.

At first glance, the sexual differences mentioned above do not seem to be that fundamental, or even serious. After all, in legal and economic matters, men and women enjoy the same rights. In practice, however, they do not. In a number of crucial areas, women's status in Fatiya is subordinated by Islam. Here I will touch upon three areas: worship, politico-religious roles, and schooling.

A woman is forbidden from entering a mosque to pray; she must always pray in the back. In the *miserey* (small mosque) this means praying outside, on the ground. The big mosques in towns have a section, quite apart from the main hall, where women pray separately. In daily occurrence, women do not go near the *miserey* to pray, whereas men regularly pray together, inside. It was explained to me (by men) that women disrupt the prayer; men will be unable to concentrate. As an elder put it, Islam dictates to women: "do not place yourself in front, or the men will look at your behind, and that God does not want." In the eyes of men, women are not only sexually inciting, but also potentially polluting. For example, if a woman is menstruating and goes near a mosque where a marabout is doing the *virdei* (praying using beads), she risks ruining his prayer. In the eyes of women, however, the same prohibition receives a slightly different interpretation. They explain it as being dangerous to their bodies; as causing bleeding and difficulty in breathing. Whatever justification is provided, the reality is that women must always remain outside holy places.

Women are also forbidden from participating fully in life-crisis rituals. Thus, at funerals, women remain spectators; if the deceased is a man, women do not participate at all in the arrangements. If the deceased is a woman, they are only in charge of bathing the body and covering its private parts with a small cloth. Afterwards, men take over; they carry the body into the room where it is wrapped in white cloth by a marabout, who also recites verses from the Koran; they bury the woman and pray for her. Once the burial is over, at the *esadai* (communion) only men are given rice flour with sugar and kola nuts to eat. However, visiting women may stay over after the ceremony to be fed, a matter that, at least on one occasion I recorded, caused strong protest from male members of the deceased.

Additionally, in Fatiya all politico-religious posts are outside the reach of women. Thus, women can never become marabouts, *awadanis* (persons who call to prayer), nor, of course, *alimams* (those who lead the prayer) or *talibés* (student-cultivators). Men must always fill these posts. The post of *awadani* may be filled by a man who has a strong and clear voice. The *alimam* must be a male member of the founders' lineage, however.

Insofar as schooling is concerned, women are also at a disadvantage.[1] Koranic instruction serves solely to enlighten girls; to help them bring their future children up as good Muslims. Boys have many more options open to them. If they have studied the Koran, they can become marabouts and earn money by curing through prayer and herbal medicines, by becoming instructors, and by having disciples work for them; they can receive alms and free labor from the community. In fact, those who display particular talents for learning Arabic may go on for further studies to the Franco-Arab schools in the big cities, which are subsidized by the Senegalese State. It should be noted, however, that Jola marabouts cure by prescribing roots and leaves, which the patient pounds and mixes with water before bathing in it. Manding marabouts, on the other hand, cure by writing on a wooden tablet, washing off the ink and giving it to the patient to drink. It is usually the Manding marabouts who make amulets and bless objects.

Like many other religions (Judaism, for example) Islam emphasizes sexual separation; the fact that women are different from men, for they have separate obligations, privileges and dispensations. But in the Mandingized region of Kalunay, and in the particular communities of the Tangori district such as Fatiya, Islam serves to rationalize subtle aspects of female subordination and inequality. These emerge not only in ritual situations, but also in minute details of everyday actions which demand of women that they show deference and demeanor in front of men. A woman greets a male traveler by curtsying, or kneeling in front of him. To show respect for a husband, a woman will not butcher an animal, a chicken or a small goat. She gives it to her husband to cut its throat (the Muslim way). Not being able to dispose of barnyard animals amounts to not being able to eat meat without her husband's consent. Women claim that even if they are beaten when pregnant, to the point of aborting, they will not flee. For their suffering and their humbleness women will be recompensed by God after death.

The fact is that women are trapped in a bind. Because women must work from sun-up to sun-down, they have very little time to pray. When they rise, they may say the morning prayer, and when they prepare to sleep, they may make-up the lost prayers. But women generally know fewer verses of the Koran; their prayers are thus shorter and more perfunctory. Despite their claims to rewards in the other world, their lack of time and formal instruction obviously places them in a ritually inferior position. In short, all Muslims are supposed to display patience and respect for others, but Fatiya's women are called upon to exercise these qualities more often than are men.[2] Their degree of self-denial becomes obvious when one sees men, chatting and lolling about on the *bantaba* (Manding for the talking platform), while their wives are still out, working in the rice-fields, or caught in the drudgery of endless domestic chores. Whereas the Koran says that men must feed the family, the reality is otherwise; women's rice is used solely for this purpose. Men can sell their millet and their maize; women cannot sell their rice.

There is, then, a distinctive style of male religious comportment in which Fatiya women do not share. I. M. Lewis (1986: 106) puts the matter well when he discusses the marginal rituals that Tunisian women perform when compared with the men's saints' cults: "The burden of religious orthodoxy is depicted as falling primarily to men as the pilgrims and pillars of Islam, whose religious devotions count also for their womenfolk, who are thereby exempted from an equivalent degree of direct religiosity." In the discussion that follows, I will describe the girls' circumcision ritual in Fatiya and compare it with the boys' initiation. The purpose of this comparison is to show how differently both ceremonies mold the adult statuses and behaviors of men versus women.

Few institutions have received as much controversial attention from the anthropological literature – the feminist literature in particular – as female circumcision. Some of the issues involved have been touched upon in my description of the girls' excision ritual in Jipalom (pp. 109–111). To repeat, this is a thoroughly Manding (and also Fulani) custom. In Senegal, neither the Wolof, nor for that matter the Sereer, excise their girls.

The Manding circumcise their girls in rites that, according to Schaffer and Cooper (1980: 99), "parallel that of boys and evokes similar images of maturation." Although they state that structural similarities between male and female rituals "suggest a conceptual equivalence of the sexes," the reality they describe seems to point in the opposite direction. By all counts, the girls' circumcision seems to be a much less elaborate affair than the boys' circumcision. Among the Manding (Malinké) themselves, the boys' initiation is a fundamental aspect of the age-class system. Those who have been circumcised together are bound for the rest of their lives by obligations of mutual aid and reciprocity (Charest 1971). Within his own age class, a young Manding boy learns to assume political responsibility, to display religious competence and to work in groups. In the girls' ceremony, a single relationship is emphasized throughout, namely the relationship between novice and "older sister" or "guardian." During seclusion, the girls live with their guardians who drive home the values of hard work and the need to cooperate with one another. The whole proceeding is directed by the "queen" and her elder assistants: "The girls' circumcision ritual establishes a source of power for the queen, validating her leadership and on-going authority over the village women" (Schaffer and Cooper, 1980: 101). In short, the ritual seems to stress compliance and submission rather than maturity and independence.

The same seems to be true of the equivalent ceremony taking place in Fatiya. Here, the *eñakey* or girls' circumcision is often preceded by a small ceremony called *sunay*, when the girl is actually excised. The *sunay*, which the Manding also perform, is often carried out when a girl is about ten years of age. It allows her to marry when she becomes of age. A girl who had the *sunay* must eventually undergo the full *eñakey* ordeal. Otherwise, she is thought of as being *setut* (unclean), and her prayers will not be heard.

Fortunately, the Koran simply says, "do not cut too much" (Gaudio and Pellitier 1980: 54). The following description gives a feeling for what goes on at the girl's circumcision:

Aramatulai has just come out of the forest (in November 1981), where she was circumcised. She was one of more than 100 girls; their stay in the forest was for two months and ten days. The excision ("they will cut only a little") was performed by a trained "nurse" *en masse*; another "nurse" cured the wound. It hurt a great deal "so I could not walk" she said to me.

In charge of the proceedings were elder and mature women who constantly give advice to and reprimand the initiates. Often, they beat the girls with a long whip for past wrongdoings or present misbehaviors. During the entire stay in the forest, the girls could not bathe. They washed their faces with dust (a Muslim procedure when preparing for prayer away from a water source). The mature women would bring diverse dishes that they threw together in a mixed mush. "It made me nauseous and I could not eat; for that reason I was whipped". It was awful, Aramatulai concluded. "I wouldn't excise my daughter; the Wolof don't do it. The Koran says it is obligatory only for men".

As with the Manding, the Fatiya girls' *eñakey* ceremony socializes women to age-grade solidarity. It also creates special relations among categories of women who are present at the ceremony: dependence in the case of initiate and officiant; support and solidarity among initiates, and between them and older sisters; deference and respect from younger to older women. The girls' ceremony takes place routinely, every two or three years, involves relatively few persons, is seen as an obligation, sets up age distinctions within the female community, and may, in fact, lessen a woman's chance to enjoy sexual relations. These are clear indications of the place women are destined to occupy in the male-oriented world of the "Mandingized" Jola.

La Fontaine (1985: 162–180) and others have documented the important point that in societies where girls as well as boys are initiated, it is important to understand how one event relates to the other since "both are a part of a single ritual complex that must be analyzed as a whole for either to be understood" (La Fontaine 1985: 164). As might be expected of a "Mandingized" Jola community, the boys' circumcision has a definite set of cultural connotations attached to it that are different from those attached to the girls' excision ritual. For a girl, excision means a ritual cleansing previous to marriage. It allows a woman to pray, and it is held at the place where her mother actually lives. If the mother has re-married, this may not be the girl's natal place. For a boy, initiation marks an important transition to adulthood and full participation in political and economic affairs; it is held at the place where a boy is born, amidst his own agnates.

Manding models and Fatiya mores

The Fatiya boys' initiation called *futamp* departs from both, the Sambujat and the Jipalom models in that the Fatiya boys are circumcised twice, first in the Manding *futamp*, then in the Jola *futamp*. The Manding-style *futamp* takes place every three years and is usually held in Fatiya itself, in the regular forest, for there is no sacred forest here, as there is in Sambujat and Jipalom.[3] A place is chosen within the forest, a big hut (*egúut*) is built, and the boys are secluded in it for up to 30 days. Nowadays, the actual operation is performed by a Jola marabout (*amorao*) from the neighboring town who lived for a long time among the Manding. In order to marry, a Fatiya boy must be circumcised in the Manding fashion.

The second type of boys' circumcision is closer to the "traditional" Jola *futamp*. It is usually held in the sacred forest (*kareŋ*), in the town of Sindian, where the majority of Fatiya's inhabitants originated. However, if a recent Fatiya immigrant comes from another village where the *futamp* is still being celebrated, he will send his children there to be *futamped*. The Jola-style *futamp*, which is held every 15 years or so, takes place after the Manding style *futamp*; in principle, it is a precondition for marriage, but in actual fact it is held so infrequently that men marry without it. Although, in general, the "traditional" *futamp* is very similar to the Jipalom *futamp*, there are predictable alterations: there is a reduced emphasis on matrilateral prestations; there is a very short stay in the forest; and more attention is paid to contributions by agnatic than uterine kin.

To summarize, the Manding version of Islam the Fatiya population has adopted has reinforced gender distinctions. As an ideology, it attributes to women a host of arbitrary qualities, positions and tasks. In a way, it subordinates women by emphasizing quite subtly their dependent status and lack of parity with men. In addition, a number of everyday practices reinforce social and generational distinctions. This becomes obvious when a younger wife cooks for an older co-wife, or when she genuflects in the presence of a stranger, or when she asks to be pardoned even if her husband was at fault. Doubtless, Manding-style Islam has contributed to making women feel ritually inferior and politically unimportant.

In contrast, the "old" pre-Islamic religion served to uphold gender equality by investing women with substantial ritual power. In the previous chapter on Jipalom I mentioned the shrines that women "owned." Thus, the in-married women had *Furamben*, whereas the out-married female agnates had *Ebune*. Although some villages surrounding Fatiya celebrate *Ebune* with some alacrity, for it is an agnatic shrine, they do not regularly do *Furamben*. Only a few villages still do the affinal female shrine. In Fatiya, however, neither shrine is done anymore.

Manding-type Islam has also molded "appropriate" male behavior. This includes acquiring such talents as the ability to speak well, to play host to strangers, to extend protection to young men, to be even-handed with wives and, of course, to be pious and patient. Together with these qualities goes a certain arrogance and assertiveness, characteristics that are difficult to explain in any other than subjective terms. Fatiya was the only village where men would remark to me, albeit in jest: "I'll give you in marriage to X" or "there goes the new wife of Y" (my very respectable assistant). My Sambujat and Jipalom friends would have considered this sort of aggressive bantering in very bad taste.

The kinds of cultural constructs surrounding gender relations in the Kalunay community of Fatiya find expression, first and foremost, in the domestic arena. For it is within the household where power differentials are forged, and where control over resources is first instituted. But this institutionalizing of power relations goes further in the Kalunay than elsewhere, in that the very nature of the household has changed in structure, meaning, and actual composition (Linares 1984).

Domestic relations and resources

In Fatiya, when a son marries he does not usually move out of his parents' home, as he does in Sambujat. Instead he enlarges it to accommodate his new family. Multiple, fraternal, and "grand" households, with several brothers, married to several wives, all living together in the same structure, under the supervision of their elderly father, or of the older brother, are not uncommon, especially among the class of founders (Linares 1984). As can be expected, interpersonal relations in these types of households are complex. Within the conjugal family, there is a strict rotation, at least in principle, of who cooks when, which wife contributes rice to what meal, and what wife's turn it is to share her husband's bed. In reality, however, a senior wife often stops cooking altogether. Like the male elder who has stopped cultivating, she is said "to be resting." When this happens, a younger co-wife, or a daughter-in-law, must cook for her. Cooking takes hours and is considered to be an onerous job, especially after a full day's work in the rice fields. A man eats apart from his wives, in the company of a married son or an older brother, and younger boys eat with them. Although an elder is fed by his own wives, his daughters-in-law regularly send him a bowl of rice. Women eat with other women, together with their babies and female children. Solitary persons cook and eat apart. In all cases, conjugal units living under the same roof share only some, by no means all, tasks of cooking and eating.

In addition, senior wives stay home while younger wives travel with their husbands to attend to their needs. Elderly wives are "retired" and younger wives cultivate for them. A household head, if he is old and has many helpers, may stop cultivating his millet fields altogether. The elder son takes over the organization of his younger brothers' work. Small children are pampered by their parents, older children go to school but help their parents on days off and during school vacations, and young unmarried men are often in charge of the oxen used to plough the groundnut fields. These domestic relations are important, for they pave the way for the very different options that are open to each gender, and each generation, to control and distribute resources.

The totality of rice that feeds the family is produced by women. Storage practices vary from household to household, but the same general principles hold. Co-wives who get along – and not all do so by any means – store their rice crop in the same granary (*buntúŋ*). If they do not get along, each will store her rice with another woman, the wife of a husband's brother, for example. Older wives store their rice apart. In all cases, the *buntúŋ* is located above the kitchen where the wife cooks. As a man said to me: "I built my wives' *buntúŋ*, so they must feed the family and I will tell them to cook rice for strangers when they visit." In addition to the family rice, younger wives must give their husbands one of every ten bundles of rice that they harvest. This rice is described as being for *charité*. This is the term used for the rites that take place after a Muslim burial, on the same day, a week later, and on the 40th day. This rice is for a man's exclusive use. He can use it to feed strangers or to distribute at important occasions like baptisms or weddings. In the last analysis, he can even sell it if he so wishes. Hence, men do not only own the means of production, they own the means of profit as well.

In a good year, male heads of households can sell a certain amount of surplus millet, plus other garden crops and, of course, groundnuts which they grow solely for the export market.[4] Men have a significant source of independent income, some of which they are supposed to invest in buying things for the family. But women often complain, with some justification, that their husbands do not clothe them adequately, or pay for the necessary expenses for their children. Perhaps they would do less complaining if they could sell rice, when, and if, they produced a surplus.

So far, we have been talking about domestic relations as if a household were a self-contained, self-serving, independent unit. But marriage is never divorced from wider social processes. Households come about and persist through what are essentially political strategies. The following section will give some idea of how the movement of women at marriage reinforces aspects of male social control.

Marriage and the circulation of women

In Fatiya, marriage presents endless opportunities for male members of various communities to extend their political networks by exchanging sisters and daughters for wives and mothers. These alliances work both ways: they reinforce, as well as cut across, ties based on succession and descent. In the male-centered game of making a strategic marriage, women have become the instruments of male political activities, and part of their constituency of dependants.

Fatiya's marriages take place over considerable distances. In most cases, the wives' natal villages are more than 25 km away, not within easy distance by foot. The 82 wives married into the Fatiya community in 1981 came from 24 different villages.[5] Only 7 percent of the wives came from Fatiya itself. The wife-giving communities are, like Sindian or Kañaru, (Kagnarou) often large, overcrowded, and suffering from a land deficit. These larger villages tend to provide the bulk of the wives for the inhabitants of more recently established, less crowded, smaller villages like Fatiya.

Clearly, the spatial dimensions of Fatiya marriage practices differ from the spatial dimensions of Sambujat and Jipalom marriage practices. As I have indicated, village in-marriage is common in Sambujat, and marriage within a circle of 6 villages is the rule in Jipalom. In Fatiya and the rest of the Tangori district, on the other hand, women have lost much of the influence they exerted within their own agnatic environment by having to move far away from their own natal villages to marry (Linares 1988).

Another factor that may depress the status of women, at least in the case of younger wives, is polygyny. In Fatiya, plural marriages are the ideal, if not the rule. Duogyny is as common as monogamy, with an additional 10 percent of all marriages involving 3 wives. Moreover, heads of households in Fatiya's founders' category have 2.3 wives each; heads of household in the immigrant category have only 1.24 wives each. The chief has 5 wives; 3 out of 5 individuals having 3 wives apiece are members of the founders' lineage. A few enterprising immigrants have taken as their second wife a daughter of one of the founding families. Hypergamous marriages in Fatiya are not simply a matter of changing social status; they determine access to resources in a very fundamental way (e.g. Goody 1976: 119–120). A male offspring of this union will eventually inherit land, thus shifting in social category from land-borrower to land-owner. Again, the Fatiya situation is in strong contrast to the situation in Sambujat, where monogamy and in-marriage are the reality, and even contrasts with Jipalom, where polygyny is limited, and women can still go back and forth to their natal communities with considerable ease.

There is also a definite preference in Fatiya for what has been called in the anthropological literature restricted exchange. A man can take a wife from the House where his father has given a sister.[6] These marriages are common. In this type of marriage, men from different villages consistently exchange women. That is, they give sisters where they secure wives, with the result that women move back and forth between villages. Actually, in Fatiya restricted exchange involves the exchange of women between individual patrifilial groups.[7] It is even common in Fatiya for a man's sister to take her daughter and give her back to her brother's son. This is the most clear example of direct exchange. In a sample of 62 Fatiya marriages, 25, or 42 percent, could be classified as restricted exchange. To be more precise, they could be put into the categories of direct exchange, or delayed direct exchange of women as discussed by Keesing (1975: 78–90). In this system, marriage serves to create, and continually reinforce, alliances between particular, localized lineages.

In talking about women as exchangeable items, I have been deliberately using a sex-biased terminology. I have done so because Fatiya's men refer to women in such terms; as facilitating the reproduction of vital political relations by their movement in space. Not only Fatiya's men, but also the women use the idiom of exchange when referring to marriage. A woman will say, "I will get my husband's daughter and give her in marriage to my own brother's son"; a man might say, "my father's sister will get me a wife"; another may complain "the Manding do not give us their daughters in marriage." In fact, a girl is commonly fostered by a woman with the sole purpose of eventually marrying her off to one of her own agnates. In this respect, the surrogate-mother role is not unlike the role of female, high-status elder in Kpelle secret society (Bledsoe 1980: 75–79).

Clearly, then, an element of transacting with women's reproductive capacities is present in the marriage system of Fatiya. Daughters and sisters, nieces and wards, are steered into making certain kinds of marriages that are advantageous, not only to male agnates, but also to senior women. In fact, women are still highly valued as reproducers of lineage relations, in both a social and a biological sense. Hence, marriage payments are steep. They take the classical form of bridewealth payments; that is as contributions from the groom's parents to the bride's parents.

There are a series of "ideal" steps that need be followed in order to comply with Manding-style marriage negotiations, including with the bridewealth prestations they imply. These steps were summarized for me briefly by various Fatiya male friends: (A) A young man meets a girl and wants to be married to her. He then asks his father to search for a

Social relations of production re-structured 183

"delegation." This should be composed of the groom's "real" brother, plus a friend and/or a brother of the *fank*. This group visits the girl's father several times, carrying different amounts of kola nuts: on the first trip, 5 kola nuts for the father; if the girl agrees to the marriage, she will also chew on a nut; on the second trip, 10 kola nuts for the girl's father's brother; he has the right to "speak," especially if he is opposed to the marriage; on the third trip, enough kola nuts for the entire *fank* of the girl (her real, or classificatory, fathers and brothers); the last trip is with kola nuts for the entire ward; this may be quite costly. At each of these visits, the groom's "delegates" may have to do some "fast talking" to overcome various objections to the marriage. At the end of these negotiations, the male ward members of the girl reach consensus: she can marry. Note that all initial approaches were done carrying kola nuts; this is an Islamic custom (non-Muslim Jola do not usually chew kola nuts). (B) If ward members agree to the marriage, the groom must send them a whole lot of additional gifts (see below), to be distributed to the male household heads in the girl's natal ward. (C) After this, the groom's other expenses are to go to the girl's immediate extended family. The girl herself, and her father, ask for money. In addition, the groom must buy a grand *boubou* (the embroidered full-length robe Muslims wear) for the father, with plenty of cash in the pocket; often, the girl's father gives the *boubou* to one of his brothers as a gift. The groom should also give a prayer mat to the father, a great deal more kola nuts for him and his cohorts, a goat to the bride (this is seen as the Muslim equivalent of the Catholic's ring), one very nice *pagne* (cloth), worth a goodly sum, for the girl's mother, or her sister if the former is dead. This cloth is called the *bamburaŋei*, from the word for the cloth that women use to carry babies on their backs. If not considered nice enough, the *pagne* will be returned. The girl herself gets a token 20CFA francs (less than US $0.10), to signify she is married and must not run around; if she does, the groom may ask for the bridewealth back. The longer the interval between the negotiations and the ceremony, the more the groom will have to pay to keep the relationship going. (D) The marriage ceremony itself also costs the groom and his family lots of money: the marabout who "talks" must be paid, the bride's sisters who accompany her must be also paid, a bull must be killed to feed the girl's matrilateral relatives, all visitors must be given goat meat seasoned with purchased products like onions, tomato paste and olive oil, and rice to eat. The rice often has to be bought because the groom does not yet have a wife to grow it. The conclusion of marriage festivities is marked by the husband buying large amounts of soap and having the unmarried girls in his ward wash the guests' clothing (called the *kaposak* from the verb *kapos*, to wash). (E) For several weeks after, the bride sits outside her new home and receives gifts from visitors; a chicken here, a clay pot there.

As I said, these are the "ideal" steps that have to be followed in a proper, Fatiya-style Muslim wedding. If we take a look at the actual bridewealth payments that one particular individual made for each of his three wives, however, we will see that there is a great deal of room for maneuver. K., as I will refer to him, is the son of a long-standing and respected elder, who is an immigrant into the Fatiya community from the large town of Sindian (thus, K. is not a descendant of one of the village founders). As we will see, his wives "cost" K. different amounts, depending on who were their respective fathers, what the particular "status" of the bride was, and what was the order in which they were married. When figuring out what these expenses "mean" in relative terms, it should be kept in mind that at the present time (1981) the income of a Fatiya man from the sale of groundnuts, and sometimes millet, averages 25,000 to 26,000 CFA (about US $100) according to the Berger Report of 1981, pp. 10–39. My own calculations of men's income at the time yielded a higher figure, about 50,000 CFA francs ($200) for an able man like K.:

1. K.'s first wife, Satu, was born in Bujoke, a ward of Sindian. He married her in 1952. I learned via the grapevine that this was an arranged marriage. K.'s father had set aside 10,000 CFA francs (about $40.00 US dollars) to "pay" for the expenses listed below. He also killed a bull on the marriage day (15,000 CFA), and K.'s mother emptied her granary of all the rice she had. The day of the *kaposak*, the father killed a goat (2,000 CFA). Satu's father was not a Muslim, so K. gave him three large calabashes filled with purchased palmwine (500 CFA francs?). K.'s father paid for the following expenses with the 10,000 CFA francs he had saved up: a *boubou* (worth at least 4,000 CFA francs), with pocket money in it (about 500 CFA), for the father's brother (who was Muslim), 3,000 CFA francs for Satu's clothes, 1,000 CFA to the *kuseek* who accompanied the bride, 500 CFA francs for the bride's cohorts, and 500 CFA for the *griot* (praise-singer, usually a Manding) who sang and played at the *bugur* dance. Total costs: *about 28,000 CFA francs*.

2. K.'s second wife, Bintu, is the daughter of one of Fatiya's village founders. She had once been married in a nearby community of Tangori, where Bintu had been brought up by her father's sister (her *asopapor*). It is common for an *asopapor* to bring up a brother's daughter and "give" her to a husband's son to marry; this is considered to be a Manding "custom." Since Bintu had left behind a son when she divorced and gone back to Fatiya to live with her father, she was considered to have "reimbursed" her husband and his kin; they could not complain. K.'s negotiations for Bintu started in secret. He began by talking with her brother, man called Unfali, who had lent K. a large groundnut field and some paddy land for his first wife, Satu, to work. Unfali

agreed to the marriage; K. gave him, 4,000 CFA. Unfali said that K. must also see Bintu's older brother; K. gave him 2,500 CFA. Next, K.'s father sent an emissary, K.'s mother's sister's husband, a very respected man, to "close" the deal; K. gave 1,000 CFA for him to take to Bintu's father. Other costs were as follows: 4,000 CFA more to Bintu's father in cash, plus 1,000 CFA in kola nuts, 5,000 CFA for Bintu's ward-"brothers," 1 goat for Bintu herself, plus 500 CFA cash, and 2,000 CFA more to buy two sheets and earrings. *Total costs*: about *22,500 CFA* francs. Because Bintu was divorced, K. did not have to give the *boubou* to her father, or the *pagne* to her mother which Muslim custom demands. Neither did he have to pay for a large wedding party. He figured he had saved at least 15,000 CFA francs.

3 K.'s third wife is called Sajo; she was born in Jacoi Banga, more than 20 km. north of Fatiya. She had also been divorced and living with her father when K. married her. For Sajo, K. paid 6,000 CFA to her father, 4,000 CFA to her to buy clothes. He gave the women of her ward one sheep (2,500 CFA) and to Sajo herself 300 CFA. In addition, he paid 500 CFA for the taxi to bring her to Fatiya. Total: *13,300 CFA* francs. Sajo was definitely "not expensive."

The Fatiya elders bemoan the time when bridewealth payments were smaller. When asked why they are so steep now, they invariably answer "*buŋarab bati Kumandingak*": "it is the road, (the way), of the Manding." Incidentally, bridewealth payments among the higher strata ("noble" castes) in Manding society are extremely high. They sometimes go up to 60,000 CFA francs, though there is room for *kakaanoor* (haggling; discussing). It is of interest to compare the bridewealth payments that K. made for his three wives (28,000 CFA francs, 22,500 CFA francs and 13,300 CFA francs respectively) with the bridewealth payments that his father, an elder, made for his wives. This was at the time when few people in the village had converted to Islam. His father had "paid": 1,500 CFA francs and a goat for his first wife; the second wife came to him via the *bulaañ* (widow remarriage). Her deceased husband, who was a classificatory "brother" of the old men, had not finished paying off his bridewealth obligations. Hence her new husband, K.'s father, needed to give her only a goat.

In Fatiya, as in Jipalom, marrying a widow via the *bulaañ* is one way open to a man to scale down bridewealth payments. Another way, namely "wife stealing," with the full consent of the bride of course, is an option open only to a Jipalom man. It is a common practice in Kujamaat villages, where Manding influence is slight, where bridewealth payments are substantial, where the economy is under monetized, and where women are more independent, to practice "wife stealing." If a Fatiya man attempted such a thing, it is said that the police would catch him and beat him up.

Not only are Fatiya women more directly under their husband's control than in either of the two other communities I studied, but also in-married women are more under the control of agnatically born, senior women. A man's female agnates (his *kuriimen*, that is his sisters and father's sisters) play an active role in surveying and disciplining his wives. In case of conflict between spouses, or between co-wives, it is the *kuriimen* who are brought in to mediate. They make great efforts to redress the situation, but if settling a dispute seems impossible, they may send a wife home to her kin, permanently or just for a cooling-down period.

Thus, a marked element of sexual and social asymmetry characterizes the Fatiya marriage system. Wife-givers have higher status than wives-takers; practices leading to direct exchange of women are encouraged; hypergamous marriage (with a daughter from a founding family) is aspired to; founders have more wives than immigrants; and women are under the direct control of their husbands and the latter's sisters. All this makes sense in the context of the Mandingized version of religiously sanctioned social relations which the Fatiya residents have adopted.

The labor process: kinship and seniority

In previous sections I have tried to place historical priority, seniority or relative age, and gender, in the context of conversion to a new religion and adoption of Manding ways. A marked social and sexual division of labor is both a cause, and a consequence, of a pervasive cultural ideology that sets up distinctions between men and women, founders and immigrants, older and younger people, marabouts and commoners. As we have seen, these distinctions are played out in social action through minute religious rituals and routines. Ritual practices structure all social relations by specifying the manner in which individuals and role categories should behave towards each other. But it isn't ritual *per se*, nor household routines, that dictate who works with whom, and who appropriates the product. In the analysis of productive relations it is the entire social setting that has to be kept in mind.

In this discussion, I am concerned with the cross-cutting ways in which seniority and gender relate to each other in the contexts of the organization of household-centered agricultural work and associative (i.e. cooperative) labor in Fatiya. What are the constraints on labor that people perceive, and through what structures is it organized? How do ritual and belief enter into the organization of practical tasks. What are labor's cooperative and individualistic dimensions? Who works for whom and under what conditions? How does the Fatiya labor process differ from that of Sambujat and Jipalom?

The Fatiya labor process is based on the almost complete gender separation of cropping tasks. Men grow plateau crops – millet, sorghum and groundnuts – by a bush-fallow system, often with the aid of animal traction. Women grow rice in permanent fields which they alone hoe manually and also weed, plant, transplant, and harvest. In their separate tasks, women and men employ altogether different tools and techniques.

Again, this sexual separation of cropping tasks is a well-established pattern among the Manding. For at least 300 years, rice cultivation among the Gambian Manding has been in the hands of women. As warriors, merchants and proselytizers, men were kept away from home for long periods of time, leaving women to do the subsistence farming. Millet and sorghum cultivation have been in the hands of men, at one point mostly slaves, for as long if not longer. Thus, the separation of cropping tasks among the Manding probably preceded Islamization and the adoption of groundnut cultivation. This is an important point. Doubtless, groundnuts pushed women even further into subsistence production, marginalizing them from the cash sector of the economy. This situation was aggravated further by the spread of Islam, with its emphasis on male control over social and political transactions. But neither groundnuts nor Islam can explain the Manding sexual division of labor. Its roots lie deep in the history of this warring, trading, state-forming peoples. It is this particular "brand" of gender-related Islam that the Fatiya Jola have adopted.

In what follows, the first section is concerned with men's work in their millet and groundnut fields. The second section is concerned with female-centered work on the rice-fields.

In the so called Mandingized Jola villages of the Kalunay, the men of the extended household cultivate together, under the direction of the oldest male working member. As head of household, he is supposed to organize the yearly use of land and labor by each member of his extended family.

Osuman Baji (an immigrant) and his unmarried brother (Sankum) by the same father, plus Osuman's two married sons (Lansana and Ibreima) cultivate millet and groundnuts together. When the crop is sold, the money is turned over to Osuman who will redistribute a certain amount to Sankum, Lansana and Ibreima but still keep about half of the proceedings to pay for the family needs throughout the year.

More often than not, if an elder is fortunate enough to have several married sons, he stops cultivating. In the chief's family, for instance, a total of five married sons cultivate together while their father "rests." Even though an elderly father has stopped cultivating, he continues to make important political and economic decisions. Only in the unlikely event that an elder does not have sons – for this category includes the sons of a deceased brother – will he be forced to cultivate himself. If an elder is "resting," his eldest son, who is an active cultivator, organizes the male labor of the household. Although he might be under his father's control in other matters, the oldest son is in charge of planning out agricultural tasks on the plateau. He also makes sure that the "resting" father is fed from their common produce. If an elder is obliged by circumstances to cultivate, he still exercises the privileges of seniority by never cultivating in the fields of a son. The latter, on the other hand, regularly works in his father's fields. (If we recall, in Sambujat fathers work in their sons' fields as well as the reverse. In Jipalom they do not.) Labor contributions are therefore asymmetrical, from son to father, but not the reverse. Thus, in Fatiya, the construction of seniority begins with the most basic relationship, that between fathers and sons.

Beyond this relationship, the concept of "brotherhood" takes over. Two married, mature men of approximately the same age, usually "real" brothers, but sometimes co-resident men who share the same matrilateral kin, often prepare their groundnut and millet fields together. Below, I have listed the working arrangements that were made in 1981 between adult married men in the Fatiya immigrant category:

Malam used to cultivate with all of his married sons. After he died, his son, who lived in the same house as himself, began to cultivate alone. His three other married sons, however, continued to cultivate as a group even though all did not live in the same house. (b) Malam's full brother, Unfali, has all along cultivated with his own married son plus his deceased brother's married son. (c) Bakati, an old man, does not cultivate. Two of his "real" married sons used to cultivate together while his brother's son cultivated apart. When one of the "real" sons died, the two remaining "brothers" joined forces. The case of Osuman is given above. He cultivates together with an unmarried brother, and two married sons. (d) Ibreima Sane and Matar Jeju are from different villages but they live in the same *fank* and cultivate together. (e) Nine men cultivate apart even though some are related and/or live in the same *fank* (see below). (f) Lansana used to cultivate with his classificatory brother Ciemo. After Lansana died, Ciemo continued to cultivate with his unmarried sons. (g) Sembu used to cultivate with his two married sons. After he died, each of his sons began to cultivate apart. (h) Seku Baji lives with his youngest married son, and they cultivate together. His two other married sons who have built separate houses also cultivate with him. (i) Seven households heads cultivate apart. Three of them are full brothers; they are mature men but not yet seniors; they do not have sons of working age. The other four men who also work apart are unrelated to each other. Similarly, they are youngish men with immature children.

The example given above confirms the fact that the extended family (with more than one married generation) usually works together as a group. The main stages in the developmental cycle of the group are as follows. When a father is alive, he regularly works with his sons. This is always true for his unmarried sons, and often true for his married sons as well. When a father dies, however, some (though by no means all) of his "sons" may opt for cultivating independently; it is usually the deceased's brother's son who leaves the group. When the family is not "extended," the household head, whose sons are usually young, commonly works alone, whether or not he has a brother in the same circumstances as himself.

There are definite advantages to cultivating together. First, it adds flexibility; men can rotate their upland fields together so that some are in use while others are under fallow. Secondly, men can share technology so that one household may own the plough, while the other the oxen or the cart. Thirdly, there is greater security; if a man falls ill his brothers will continue to share his work-load until he can resume cultivating. But there are also disadvantages, namely the problem of who has authority. And here is where seniority plays a part. Sons always work for their fathers. When brothers cooperate, the age differential is greater than when brothers do not.

The seniority principle is also important with reference to the chief and other "notables." The chief, if he is not too old and is still active, must cultivate like everyone else. But every year he can ask a few men from each of the Fatiya houses to help him. It was made clear to me that a chief asks for help and does not order it. Furthermore, he gets help because he is an old man, and elders have the right to ask for help from village men. The fact remains that only elders and no one else get extra help for free. And so do the Islamic marabouts and *alimams*, whether they live in Fatiya or in a neighboring village, because they do not cultivate. One well-known marabout from Sindian has a very large field which the Fatiya Sane have lent him. Every year it is planted in groundnuts and then harvested by all Fatiya men working together. They do so for free, "in order to thank him." Even the women contribute their labor by helping stack up the groundnuts on the drying rack, something they never do for their husbands.

In 1970, when I was in Fatiya for several months, unrelated men still regularly worked together in cooperative groups (called *sikáf* as in Jipalom) that were constituted along general age-grade lines. The young, middle-aged or elderly men (if still active), who came from a particular ward or *kalol*, worked in separate groups ridging and furrowing each other's groundnut fields in exchange for a good feast. They used the short-handled Manding hoe (the *eronkatoŋ*), rather than the *kajandu*, the Jola tool *par excellence*, to the sound of Manding drums.

The introduction of the plough into Fatiya's agricultural economy

190 *Manding models and Fatiya mores*

Plate 19: All the village men do a day's work for a renowned marabout. They dig up his ripe groundnuts (19A, top), and stack them up to dry (19b, bottom).

during the last decades is fast rendering male associative work obsolete. Ownership of ploughs is distributed as follows:

In 1985, out of 7 founders' households, 3 had the complete "team" (the oxen, the two-bladed plough used on the plateau and the cart), whereas 1 had only part of the equipment; the rest had nothing. Out of the 6 Baji immigrant families, 2 had the complete team, 3 had part of the equipment and 1 had nothing. Out of the 5 Jeju immigrants, 4 had the complete team, and the other had part of it.

From the example given above it is obvious that the Sane founders do not own more farming equipment – in fact they may own less – than the immigrants. This makes sense in view of the fact that founders can exert considerably more pressure on immigrants to borrow their equipment than the reverse. But not without having to reciprocate in some fashion, as the example given below may show:

The chief and his sons own the oxen and the plough. But their cart (the *charette*) is not in working condition. The cart is essential. It is used to carry wood, building materials and, at harvest-time, to haul the groundnuts to a nearby village for sale at the cooperative. The chief's sons, who cultivate together, have made an arrangement with Malamini (an immigrant) to borrow the latter's cart when they need it. In exchange, they have (in 1985) used their ox-plough team three times to prepare Malamini's sorghum, millet and maize fields. Malamini's only surviving brother is married to one of their sisters (a daughter of the chief).

The rest of the men who are neither founders, elders, nor Islamic clerics, lend each other equipment on a reciprocating basis. A man may lend his oxen in exchange for the use of a plough; another a seeder in exchange for a donkey to pull the small cart. However, the owner of the oxen is entitled to four days of plough-use; the owner of the plough is entitled to only one day of oxen-use. Despite the occasional disagreement, the feeling that men should be generous and trusting towards each other is very strong. It is sanctioned by Islam. That all Muslims are expected to "behave like brothers" is a commonly made remark.

Women's work in the rice fields
When we come to analyzing women's work a totally different pattern emerges. As I have indicated, in Fatiya as well as all "Mandingized" Jola areas, the separation of cropping systems by gender is almost complete. Women grow rice exclusively; aside from their house-gardens (see below) they do not grow other crops. In turn, men hardly ever go down into the rice fields, and when they do, it is only to help their wives carry the harvest to the conjugal granary. It goes without saying that women do not have access to animal traction. As Boserup (1970: 53–56) and others have indicated, the

192 *Manding models and Fatiya mores*

Plate 20: Past and present technologies: 20a: men still use the short-handled Manding hoe (*eronkatoŋ*) in light tasks such as weeding. 20b: They prepare their plateau fields with the ox-plough.

tendency everywhere is for introduced technology to be monopolized by men.

Without access to their husbands' labor, or to the plough, women must rely on each other for help hoeing and harvesting; the weeding is usually done individually. Ideally, co-wives are supposed to work together. The same is true of a daughter-in-law and her mother-in-law, provided they live in the same house. In reality, however, the ideal of cooperation is achieved in only half the cases. In a small but randomly chosen sample of conjugal units, there were 10 units in which co-wives cultivated together and 9 in which they did not. That the ideal of female solidarity is achieved in only half the cases should not surprise us. The word for a co-wife is *abetom*, loosely glossed as "my wrestling partner," from the verb *abet*, to trip someone. A young wife often prefers to cultivate with her husband's son's wife rather than with her own co-wife. In polygynous societies such as Fatiya, the age differential among co-wives may be considerable. Obviously, a younger woman will be at a disadvantage when working with an older co-wife who cannot do as much.

Under these circumstances, a woman must rely on her same-age mates, from outside her household, for extra help with work in the rice fields. To this end, women are formally organized into work-groups. Commonly referred to in daily conversations as *comités* (the Jola word is *fupal*, as in *apalom*, "my friend") recruitment to these work-groups is by age class, especially in larger wards (in smaller ones women of all ages may work together in the same *comité*):

> One *comité* is formed by the younger married women; in the ward where I lived it numbered 24 women; the other *comité* is made up with the older ladies (the *kumerak*, from *mère*, mother), who number 14. These two *comités* always work apart. They work for each of its members in rotation, but only once, and for pay. A third, somewhat different work-group is made up of the *kujaŋa* or unmarried girls. They do not constitute a *comité*, but are instead described as a *société*. They work for anyone that pays them. However, when they work for one of Fatiya's adult women, they must adjust payment downwards.

Fatiya's female *comités* are very large, larger than any equivalent group in Sambujat or Jipalom, and they are also formally organized, with a woman at the head. She is charged with collecting a penalty fee from any woman who is late or absent from a work-party. Women share few real or putative kinship ties with each other. Without formal rules to enforce cooperation, women could not be counted with to work together at times when large work-groups are most needed. In a "typical" week, women work an average of three days for themselves and two days for their *comités*;

194 *Manding models and Fatiya mores*

for two days they rest, except at the height of the planting season. The money a *comité* makes is distributed evenly among the women. It may be as much as 8,000 CFA francs a day, but when divided among 20 women, it doesn't amount to much (to one dollar fifty cents a day).

Still, Fatiya's women often feel the need for help over and beyond the labor they get from the *comités*. This is especially true at harvest time, when

Plate 21: The married women's *comité* works for one of its members. They turn the soil in the rice fields using the long-handled Manding hoe (*ebara*).

the crop must be in before it is eaten by birds, or before it lodges. Because their opportunities to earn cash are not extensive (pp. 197–198) women cannot often pay for hired labor. Instead, they must wait until a woman from a place like Sindian, where rice fields are scarce, comes along and offers to harvest in exchange for three to five bundles of unmilled paddy (called *fukok* (sing.)/*sikok* (pl.), these weigh an average of 4.5 kg. a piece) for a day's work. In addition, a few women may join together to form a *fusaleŋaf* (sing.)/*kusaleŋaf* (pl.) (from the verb meaning to measure, to prove oneself). The members of these small groups work for each other in rotation, for free.

Now, it is easy for an outsider to assume, while watching large groups of women harvesting in *comités* and singing, that they are cooperating easily and spontaneously; that they are content, or at least resigned to their arduous work. The subject of their songs reveals a different picture, however. Often, women sing about their own troubles. For example, one song asks, "what do you trust?" and a woman answers "my *ebara*" (the woman's hoe); the same song then asks "what do you fear?" and another woman answers, "my *ebara*." The point, succinctly made, is that some women work hard while others fear work. The most popular class of songs concern marital problems: "I went to a marabout, and he told me to do a *charité*, so my marriage would improve"; "how am I going to marry that man, he smells"; "Amadu Ba says he will repudiate his wife Kadi. Kadi says, that is nice, a man who insults me insults my mother"; "he says he will not marry me because I am ugly – does he insult me because I have no granary?"; "when I work I have no problems with my husband, but if I go dancing, he beats me"; "one side of my husband's family is Muslim, the other pagan; I do not want to live among them, but I must stay"; "the *kuriimen* (the husband's sisters) are here, looking around; they will find me sitting quietly." And so forth.

Clearly, women's songs do not celebrate happiness and harmony. The whole tenor is very different from the songs women sing in Jipalom; or from the songs men sing in Sambujat (where men do the singing). In fact, Fatiya women make up songs to "get back" at their husbands. A woman who has had a bad experience makes up a song about it and sings it out in the fields. She does so while away from the men, in the company of her women friends, who are her main support. Her friends show that they stand behind her by chorusing back in response. If a woman is not a good singer, she goes to one that is, tells her what has happened, and asks her to compose a song about it. As a male friend of mine once confessed: "my wives said they would make-up a song about me, and I said to them, if you do, *c'est finis*" (the marriage).

Table IIIb: *A comparison between female labor inputs in agriculture*

	Hrs/Are[a]	8-hour days per 1,000 square m.	Days/year[c]
Fatiya	15.78	19.73[b]	90
Jipalom	10.88	13.60	126
Sambujat	8.35	10.44	150

Note:
[a] An are is 100 square meters
[b] Fatiya women work a 6-hr day; for purposes of comparison, however, the data have been converted to an 8-hr day.
[c] Calculated as 20 work-days a month during the agricultural season. At least half the time is spent doing *sikáf* labor for others.

The reason why women do not always seem to be content cannot be explained by simply assuming that they work too hard. In table IIIb I have summarized Fatiya's female labor inputs into rice cultivation, then compared them with female labor inputs from the two other villages under discussion. Obviously, Fatiya women do not get much help from the men, so they must invest more labor per unit area of paddy land (per 100 square meters) than do women elsewhere. But, on a yearly basis, their work load is less than the work load of Sambujat or Jipalom women because they cultivate a smaller total amount of land. This is also true on a day to day basis. Compared with Sambujat women, who leave for the fields at dawn, Fatiya women do not leave their compounds much before 8:30 to 9:15 in the morning.

A concern with female systems of farming has been part of a wider concern with the impact of capitalism, and various forms of colonial government, on the productive relationships of African farmers. Boserup (1970: 5) was unequivocal on this point: "Economic and social development unavoidably entails the disintegration of the division of labour among the two sexes traditionally established in the village." Recently, Swindell (1985: 71) has re-stated the problem thusly: "The sexual division of labour within farming groups can be materially altered by the introduction of new crops as the demand for labour rises in general, or at particular points in the cultivation cycle." In many parts of tropical Africa, he goes on to state, changes in the social division of labor, and in the roles women play, have been extensive and profound. They have been brought about by male monopoly of cash-crop production and wage-labor migration, leaving women to do the subsistence farming.

In fact, Oboler (1985) has focused an entire study on changes in gender roles, and women's declining position within the new economic order, among the Nandi of Kenya. "Is Nandi society marked by a greater or lesser degree of sexual stratification now than what it was in the precolonial period?", she asks (Oboler 1985: 2). Not surprisingly, the author concludes that the economic position of women has worsened in many ways as a result of colonial policy and incorporation into an export economy. The richness of Oboler's data, and the solid contribution she has made to the problem of defining male and female spheres of action are undeniable. Yet I remain unconvinced that formulations in terms of degrees of sexual stratification advance our understanding of women's complex position very far; among the Nandi or elsewhere. At best, Oboler gets trapped in the usual quagmire over what is meant by male dominance and how it is to be measured. At worst, she imposes her own value judgments on those of the Nandi, female or male. As she herself points out, Nandi women do not view their situation in quite the same negative terms as she does. It seems to me that Guyer (1984b: 5-6) is more insightful on this issue when she insists on the need to take into account peoples' perceptions about their own situation. Despite the heavy work load and the limited work opportunities that modern Beti women living in Cameroon experience, they clearly perceive their new situation as an improvement. Beti women do not consider themselves to be unambiguously worse off than before: "it is difficult to sustain an unmitigated 'decline' theory in the face of disagreement from the very people it concerns."

Thus, the assumption that commercial agriculture often leads to a decline in women's status since it is men who monopolize cash-crop production has not gone by unchallenged. Again, Guyer (1984b) has argued that among the Beti of Southern Cameroon conditions have changed, in some ways for the better. During the first half of the twentieth century women continued to grow food crops for family use while men became engaged in the cocoa export economy. But this was a temporary condition. By the 1970s "women farmers had developed a market orientation to meet the rapidly expanding urban demand for food in Yaounde, the national capital."

It would be difficult to assert that Fatiya's women have developed a "market-orientation." Nonetheless, as Guyer has demonstrated, female farming systems are not a frozen, unidimensional mode of production, but an ongoing, dynamic process, the outcome of complex, and often contradictory, forces. In fact, the women's situation in Fatiya has improved in the last decade. During the sixties and seventies, Fatiya women paid a daily rent of 10 to 20 CFA francs for the right to sit under the hot sun in the Bignona market and sell the small amount of vegetables they grew in their individual gardens. They walked to market every morning during the dry season, carrying the same kind of perishables, and often returned home at night with some of it unsold. By 1981, however, male "promoters" from a (now defunct) government agency (PIDAC) had convinced the women to make a large common garden, on which they could grow vegetables during the dry season using well irrigation (see p. 216). The "net" profits the women make from the sale of their vegetables (6,000 to 7,000 CFA francs) is little when compared to the 40,000 CFA francs or more the men make from the sale of groundnuts and millet. But still it is something.

If we are to argue convincingly that a monopoly of cash crops or wage-labor migration "causes" a demise in women's status, we must somehow be able to demonstrate how this is done; through what prior economic constructs, and in terms of what pre-existing rationalities is the monopoly of remunerative activities by one gender or the other to be justified in the first place? Let me give an example which, though seemingly banal, does probably help to explain why Muslim Jola women do not participate in petty trade, or move about as much as the men. There is a widespread notion (spread by men?) that the Koran forbids women to ride bicycles. Bicycles, of course, are the main source of mobility in rural, backwater areas. Women who ride bicycles risk the danger of becoming sterile. Since sterility is actually common, and so is child mortality, women are reluctant to put themselves at risk, just in case this might be true. Thus, they walk everywhere. This means that they cannot be itinerant traders, for they cannot compete against bicycle users, nor visit relatives often, nor make contacts and cultivate useful persons. Obviously, bicycles are not *the* reason why they cannot do these things. But it is through constructs such as the interdiction on riding bicycles that women's subordinate position is maintained. (See also Martin 1988: 95.)

Clearly, then, a satisfactory analysis of differences in the ways in which Jola women living in the three communities under consideration have access to land and labor resources must take account of the total way in which social relations are constructed and legitimized in each of these settings. For, as indicated, in Fatiya gender distinctions are part and parcel of a cultural system in which all sorts of other social distinctions are drawn along generational, religious, and kinship lines. And these are based in turn on an ideology which accommodates itself easily to inequalities in status and asymmetries of power.

To recapitulate, principles of sexual separation and seniority underlie the dynamics of labor-organization in Fatiya. Elders of either sex work shorter hours than do younger persons. Marabouts (*alimams*) do not farm at all.

Instead, other men work for them. Men work fewer hours than do women. In 1981, for example, women were hard at work planting rice at the beginning of August while men were already through with all heavy work and were only doing some intermittent weeding. Generally speaking, in Manding or "Mandingized" villages women work longer hours in agriculture than do men. In the Manding village of Genieri, in the Gambia, male farmers work under 600 hours a year on crops, while female farmers work under 1,100 hours. Aside from total working hours, "the seasonal patterns of male and female work are completely different" (Cleave 1974: 39).

Once they are through ploughing and planting their fields, Fatiya's men settle down to endless conversations on the "talking platform" (*bantaba*) next to the highway, where other men circulate. This is considered important, for it is through greetings and conversations that particular social networks are forged; especially with persons who can exercise political influence, or have special access to things or services. It is considered of utmost importance for men to maintain useful "connections" while keeping themselves informed and spreading information selectively. It is considered to be "gossip" when women do the same.

Associative work in the three Jola communities: a comparative note
It may be helpful here to summarize the various forms that group labor take in the three Jola communities under consideration, to give an idea of how differently social relations of production are constructed in each, despite their close proximity.

A: Sambujat
In this community, the monogamously married conjugal family is a co-resident unit that performs much of the agricultural work. Both sexes work the same number of hours. In addition, two closely related conjugal families, say parents and a married son(s), or two married brothers, (the *buaju* or extended patrilineal family), can also cultivate together even though they never reside together. (The closest analogy to Sambujat houses are our own one-floor, "apartment" or duplexes). When parents work with a married son and his wife, both couples work on one another's fields even though they never store the harvest in a common granary. The Sambujat men's associations are as important today as they were in the past, for *nobody* uses animal traction. Each named male association is built around a central shrine. Membership has different levels of inclusion (all the men of the *hank*, the men of two or more *hank* only, all the men in one of the two wards). Men often work for money, but when they work for a "local"

agnate they charge less than they charge outsiders. The male associations regularly work for the elders. When they do so, they get paid with a pig. All generations (elders, middle-aged men and often young boys) usually participate in the work done by the associations, but the mature unmarried young men (the *kukambani*) often go out as a group to work in other villages and earn money for their local "club" activities. The earnings from the mature men's associations are spent in ceremonies staged around the propitiation of important shrines. An individual who refuses to cooperate is expelled from the association. If he wants to be allowed back in, he must pay dearly by sacrificing a pig and contributing large amounts of wine to the shrine.

The female associations operate mostly at harvest-time; they are less involved with tasks like transplanting, which can be done a little at a time. Inclusion in the women's association is defined on the basis of *hank*; that is, they comprise all the in-married women who are married to a group of real brothers or "semi-agnates." The local, agnatically related women do not form a separate group by virtue of the fact that half of all women are locally married female agnates. The women also, spend the money they earn on propitiating their shrines (the *Sihuñ* or female shrines). Women do not work for elders, though they may work for an elder's wife. Women work for other women, who either pay them directly (women can sell rice and have money to pay laborers), or depend on their husbands to do so since they, also, often have their fields done at the same time.

B: Jipalom

In the Kajamutay, the introduction of groundnuts as a cash crop has created two parallel systems (Linares 1985). Women still grow rice in the alluvial lands. Men additionally grow groundnuts and some millet in the upland lands of the plateau. The division of labor by gender, however, is still cooperative: men prepare the ground in the rice fields; women help their husbands plant the groundnuts and process them; women also help their husbands weed the millet fields. What has changed in all this is not the structure of family labor *per se*, but the amounts of time each sex spends working in the fields. In 1985, women were spending an average of 111 work-days (a work-day is 8 hours) in agricultural labor; in contrast, men were spending only 87 work-days. This was quite a change from the 1960s, when animal traction was not employed. At that point, Jipalom men worked as hard, if not harder, than women, because they had all the land preparation to do, in the rice fields as well as in the groundnut fields.

Although the genders may cooperate between them, they do not necessarily cooperate within them. In Jipalom, co-wives do not always help each other with agricultural work. There is a great deal of rivalry between them. Brothers do not always cultivate together in the rice fields. The same is true for Sambujat. But in Jipalom two brothers often grow groundnuts on a cooperative basis. This lends some flexibility to the system; brothers can take turns working in their groundnut fields or their rice fields; they can also rotate their fields in and out of fallow together.

In Jipalom, the division of labor by age has also become more segregated. Young men work for their fathers; but not the reverse. Young women do not work with, or for, their mothers in law. Male group labor was (until recently) organized in terms of associations or *sikáf* (pl.), *ekáf* (sing.). These are non-named groups defined in terms of residential and/or loose age criteria. There were at least three *sikáf* in operation in every ward: the mature men's *ekáf*, including the fully adult but yet unmarried young men, the elder's *ekáf*, which always worked apart, and the young children's *ekáf*; they often worked in the nurseries where lighter soils prevail. By way of contrast, in Sambujat, if we recall, all generations tend to work together when doing group labor. Jipalom elders receive more help than mature "junior" men. This is the same as in Sambujat. But whereas in the latter community elders are helped because they provide important ritual services, in Jipalom they are helped for very different reasons: because they can pay, because their in-laws help them, for *charité*. A few strangers and matrilaterally-related "outsiders" cultivate regularly for their hosts in exchange for usage rights to land. It should be emphasized, however, that the introduction of animal traction has changed all this. By 1985, associative work by men in the groundnut fields, had all but disappeared. When I was last in Jipalom (1990), the men's *ekáf* had not been used at all in the groundnut fields, and only occasionally, in preparation for the boys' initiation, in the rice fields.

The women's associations are also referred to simply as *sikáf*. In contrast to Sambujat, where all women work together, in Jipalom there are two totally separate female *sikáf*, one composed of the in-married women, or *kuseek*, one composed of the out-married women, or *kuriimen*. The former work for themselves, doing work in the rice fields as well as the groundnut fields; the latter work for their brothers, and only in their rice fields. The women's association occasionally work in large groups: the *kuseek* to do the *Ebune* ceremony on their behalf; the *kuriimen* to raise funds with which to help their brothers meet the expenses of the *futamp* (the boys' initiation).

Whereas the association of the *kuseek* or in-married women is headed by a man, the association of out-married female agnates is headed by one of its members.

C: *Fatiya*

When we come to Fatiya, however, and the whole of the "Mandingized" Jola area known as the Kalunay, a totally different pattern of labor relations emerges. The descendants of the village founders own the means of production (i.e. the land). They also monopolize control over village affairs, both secular and religious. In a way, immigrants represent a de-enfranchised class, even though some immigrants of long-standing status have earned substantial respect.

The sexual segregation of cropping systems is complete. Women work only in the rice fields; men work only in the plateau fields. Husbands do not help their wives prepare the land; wives do not help their husbands with the planting of groundnuts or the weeding of millet, as in Jipalom. Co-wives work separately, rather than with each other, about half the time. The women's rice nourishes the family, feeds visitors and is given out sweetened with sugar at funerals. Unlike women in Sambujat, but like women in Jipalom, women in Fatiya cannot sell rice or give it away. Their husbands command the joint granary of the household.

The gender separation outlined above is accompanied by a generational separation as well. Elderly men stop working altogether; their sons do the cultivating for them. Elderly women stop cooking for themselves; younger co-wives or daughters-in-law cook for them. On the other hand, the conjugal family loses importance as a separate economic unit. The joint male labor of the household, which is now a large, extended, co-residential unit, is organized by the male elder (the father or an older brother). Often, the earnings from the groundnut harvest are shared jointly by the men.

Nowadays, Fatiya's men participate little, if at all, in associative labor that goes beyond the extended household. Their fields are prepared by animal traction; their weeding can be done individually. On the other hand, women continue to work in associative groups known by the French term *comité*. These are organized strictly by age classes: the married women's *comité* works separately from the elderly women's *comité*. The young, unmarried girls also work separately, for money. The mature women's *comité* is very large; it includes all the women in the ward, not just the women in a particular *fank*. The *comités* are formally organized, with a woman at its head and a treasurer, who fines any member that is late or absent from work. The women's *comité* works for each other in a strictly rotational basis; once around for field hoeing, once around for harvesting. If a woman loses a turn, say because someone dies and the women have to go off to the funeral, she is out of luck.

Renowned Muslim clerics, that is marabouts, have fields set aside for groundnut production, which are worked by all the men and women of the village together, in one enormous group. This is the only time that women work in upland fields; to help stack up the marabout's groundnut harvest and winnow it. Male elders who are in the category of "owners" of the village lands, receive substantial labor contributions from younger men and recent immigrants. Thus, in Fatiya, a "Manding" model of gender and age relations has been adopted, with obvious implications in the direction of increased sexual and generational separation, and increased political and economic subordination.

Conclusions to Part III

The Jola of Kalunay are adapting a multitude of foreign practices to their own needs. No less than the native Jola religion, Islam developed in dialectical relationship with novel economic and social pursuits. To attempt to identify foreign, as opposed to indigenous, traits, is a sterile exercise; they evolved together, as a coherent cultural whole. With Islam as the legitimating idiom, the Kalunay Jola have adopted a particular Manding pattern of social relations that emphasizes descent, gender, and relative age. Yet these transformations did not occur in isolation. They are part of an emergent social system characterized by patron–client relations of production and control over vital resources.

There is more to the so-called process of "Mandingization" than a mere label. On the surface, it describes the substitution of old practices by equally old, but different, practices. In a more fundamental way, however, what I have been describing as Fatiya's new "way" is only a particular juncture in the time–space dimensions of the Kalunay Jola. Marzouk-Schmitz (1981: 4) implies that the "Mandingization" of Jola society has somehow come to an end: "One does not know why this phenomenon has stopped suddenly in time (end of the 19th century) and within precise geographical boundaries." But social change is not a simple process, nor a one-time thing. The process of Manding–Jola adjustment is still going on, in interesting ways.

As in all situations of cultural contact and change, the Jola are adopting Manding practices selectively. They are incorporating what they perceive as Manding ways, while in reality projecting many of their own cultural constructs on their Manding neighbors. What they have incorporated has been done partly from choice, because that way of life privileges certain individuals, such as founders and males; and while alienating women from power positions, a clear-cut division of labor grants them a certain autonomy to make productive decisions. And even though the legitimating fiction, that founders are sole owners of the lands has introduced a large measure of inequality, it has also brought in a certain measure of internal peace.

The structure of productive relations that now dominates the lives of Fatiya community members has been the result of more general social changes. These changes are not only quantitative, they are also qualitative and behavioral as well. Placing social processes squarely within a cultural context helps us to understand changing economic relationships (Geertz 1984: 520). In Fatiya, senior men outrank junior men, senior wives outrank junior wives, men outrank women and so forth, and this is shown on the practices surrounding who works with whom, who lives where, who cooks for whom, and who eats together. In Fatiya, patterns of land transmission, of marriage and the reproduction of children, practices pertaining to agricultural labor and the consumption of food crops, have been restructured to conform to new social circumstances. As Gourou (1984: 154) points out, these new circumstances include establishing relations of cultural dependency with their Manding neighbors.

Although it should not be interpreted as wholesale adoption of Manding ways, nonetheless many of the fundamental differences between Fatiya and the two other villages discussed previously can be traced to a long and complex history of contact with the Manding. There is nothing particularly "natural" about Fatiya's women, or for that matter Jola women living in the Kalunay, cultivating rice while their husbands cultivate upland crops. For it should be obvious to anyone that the sandy, light soils of upland parcels are, if anything, easier to work than the heavier paddy soils. Nor can the sexual division of labor be attributed solely to the appropriation of cash crops by men; or to gender ideologies imposed by Islam. As we have seen, the population of Jipalom, our second village, is also Muslim, and its external economy is also centered on the production of groundnuts for cash. Yet the sexual division of labor in Jipalom resembles that of Sambujat in being structured in more egalitarian ways. In Jipalom, both men and women work on both kinds of crops, though not to the same extent.

The sex polarity underlying Fatiya's system of production is only one aspect of the total manner in which social relations are organized in a "Mandingized" Jola village. Where all kinds of distinctions based on descent, ritual status and gender are emphasized, it comes as no surprise that there is a complete sexual separation of agricultural tasks. The tendency to increase social distance, and to hierarchize social relations, is largely the outcome of ideological forces, beginning with resistance to

Islam, then penetration by, and finally cultural domination by, their devout Manding neighbors.

However, only some, but by no means all the more salient aspects of Manding culture and organization have penetrated Jola society of the Kalunay. For among the "Mandingized" Jola there are no castes, no developed age grade systems and no fearful cult of masks. What has occurred is illustrated in Fatiya by a shift in the direction of increased gender and generational polarization. And by the emergence of more differentiated social statuses and politico-religious roles.

It should go without saying that "Mandingization" is a process and not an event. It involves a continuum, a gradation in the degree to which Manding cultural conventions and organizations have penetrated different village settings in the Kalunay. As we have seen, Fatiya is on the edge of the Kalunay, not very deep within the Manding sphere of influence. A cursory glance at social arrangements in another Jola village, squarely within the Kalunay region, will illustrate a different stage in the process of accommodation to Manding cultural practices:

Jijipun is next-door to Beme, a Manding center of some importance located near Marsassoum, where Manding territory begins. Six of the twenty families residing within Jijipun are Manding families; they came to Jijipun searching for land. The founders of the village were Jola; they came to Jijipun at the time of the Manding wars from the village of Jimand further east. The Manding families now live intermixed, in the same wards, with Jijipun's Jola families. Although each family has its own house, members of either group often eat together in unisexual clusters. Each group speaks its own language at home, but when they speak together, they use mainly Jola.

Manding men and Jola men cultivate together in *comités*; and so do the women. Members of either ethnic group may pair up together to do groundnuts, sharing the profits. Whereas the village chief is a Jola, the *alimam* is a Manding. It is said that even though in days past the Manding knew the Koran better than the Jola, they don't now. The son of Jijipun's chief is the *awadani* (he calls to prayer); he was trained for 15 years in Koranic studies in Beme. There, he studied with a learned Manding marabout from Kaabu, an important Manding Islamic center. Today, the only school in existence in Jijipun is the Arabic school. In order to go to the State school and learn French, the children must walk to the next village. The relationship between both ethnic groups was described succinctly by a village resident: "Jola children are trained in the Koran by the Manding; the Manding, in turn, work the Jola's land. This is why we live together."

A "Mandingized" Jola can be identified by other Jola by the fact that he employs the long greeting ceremony that the Manding use, by his constant use of prayer beads, and by the way he dresses. Because, like the Manding, he stops work at mid-day, a "Mandingized" Jola is always well-dressed, for he has had time to go home, wash, and put on his *boubou*, a white frock. The Jola also say that a Manding, or a "Mandingized" Jola, can be distinguished by his suspiciousness; he needs to have a great deal of information about you before he welcomes you. Moreover, a Manding woman needs her husband's authorization to do everything. "Even if her father died, a Manding (or a 'Mandingized' Jola) wife would need her husband's permission to attend the funeral, whereas a Jola woman would not even ask; she would simply go." Such cultural stereotypes are revealing, for they point in the direction of asymmetry in the codes that sanction social and sexual behavior.

In all this, the Jola never were, nor are they now, mere passive pawns in the game of power and prestige. There are some south-shore groups like the Esudadu who have simply refused to become Muslims, to grow groundnuts, or to accept foreigners. Other groups like the Kujamaat Jola of Jipalom are caught between relations of autonomy and dependence. A third, if perhaps less attractive option for those who admire "traditional" ways, has been chosen by the people of the Kalunay. In re-structuring aspects of their social relations to conform to a Manding model of what a proper Islamic community should be, they have been successful in organizing agricultural production in an efficient, if inegalitarian, way. In attracting strangers from other villages to come and settle, the inhabitants of Fatiya have been able to build up their community. And in drawing their wives from among a wide range of communities, they have built up political networks. These are useful for gaining usufructuary rights to land, and for the multitude of small economic transactions that go on in everyday life. Nevertheless, at the same time as they have enlarged their sphere of useful contacts, the people of Fatiya have been increasingly drawn into an unstable world-market for export crops. And they have also become more dependent upon the political patronage of regional marabouts. In the chapter that follows, I have attempted to place the micro changes that have taken place in the transformation from a Sambujat-like, to a Fatiya-like, situation, in the macro context of the Senegalese political economy and national religious ideology.

EPILOGUE

THE JOLA IN THE PRESENT NATIONAL SCENE

Epilogue

How has the Jola society changed in the last decade? Do the patterns and practices described in the previous sections still characterize Jola society at the present time? Have the Jola remained outside the larger currents that have transformed the political economy of Senegal. According to Pélissier:

Outside influences, whether from other African societies or from Europe, have only recently penetrated Basse Casamance, and a monetary economy, with its usual retinue of upheavals, did not infiltrate this coastal zone until a few decades ago, despite it being frequented by western navigators for the last five centuries.
(1966: 673–674).

This is something of an overstatement. As we have seen, the Jola were in contact with European and Manding traders at least since the beginning of the sixteenth century. They also participated, as victims and profiteers, in the trade for slaves during the seventeenth and eighteenth centuries. After the 1860s, they even migrated seasonally to the Gambia in search of palm produce and red-rubber. And Jola women were involved in wage-labor, unloading ships in Ziguinchor, as early as the 1910s.

Nevertheless, Pélissier is quite correct in that certain important developments taking place further north during the past century took a long time to reach Lower Casamance. Thus, for example, by the 1850s, Islam and groundnuts had been adopted by many rural Wolof farmers surrounding Cap-Vert; by the 1920s they were just beginning to be adopted by the Jola of Lower Casamance. Dakar and St. Louis were connected by rail in 1885; Dakar and Ziguinchor were connected by the Transgambian highway in 1952. Since at least 1871 the inhabitants of four communes (Dakar, St. Louis, Rufisque and Gorée) were sending, like other French citizens, at least one deputy to the French Chamber of Deputies; the Jola were still fighting the French militia and being "pacified" in the 1910s. A cash economy was fully implanted in the Groundnut Basin (ancient provinces of Cayor, Baol and Sine-Saloum) by the 1870s; the Jola were still paying their taxes in kind rather than cash in the 1910s. Hence, for better or for worse, until relatively recently, the Jola of Lower Casamance were only loosely integrated into the political economy of Senegal. In fact, to this day the Jola will say, when going to Dakar, "inje bei Senegal" (I'm going to Senegal).

But this situation is changing fast. In the last three decades the young Jola population has become fully involved in seasonal, urban migration.[1] A burgeoning tourist trade is bringing in hundreds of Europeans a year to the beaches and resorts of Cap Skirring. Foreign technicians, aid donors, and Senegalese extension agents are everywhere, helping to build dams, dig wells, facilitate credit, disseminate new seed – in short, trying to raise agricultural production. Draft animals and the plough, dry-season vegetable gardens, milling machines, techniques which in the 1960s were rarely to be seen, are now in many Jola villages. The cities of Bignona and Ziguinchor doubled their populations in the years of drought between 1966 and 1976. Several Jola now occupy important government posts, including the Ministry of Public Works. These developments are dramatically reflected in the changes taking place within our three communities between 1964, when I was first in Jola land, and 1990, when I was last there.

Jola communities in 1990
Sambujat
When I was first in Sambujat in 1964, all residents were active practitioners of the "traditional" *awasena* religion. Yet neighboring communities in the Esudadu region had small populations of Jola Catholics (Baum, 1987, 1990).[2] By 1985, Sambujat was beginning to change in significant ways. Some of the young were failing to come back from school or city jobs to help their parents cultivate the rice fields. Renewed efforts were being made by a Catholic *abbé*, himself a Jola and a resident of a neighboring Esudadu community, to convince people to join the church. A prominent elder, a person who controlled one of the most important shrines, had died, and within weeks so had his wife and son. There was unease in the air and witchcraft was suspected.

When I returned in 1989, during the rainy season, things had, indeed, changed; for better or for worse. The Catholic chapel has been rebuilt under the insistence of the resident *abbé*. The elders had approved the project because the youth had requested it. While several of the Sambujat young went to Catholic mass regularly, many did not. "They go to mass and come back to the shrines" an elder explained. Few of the mature men and elders went to Sunday church, however, despite the efforts of the *abbé* to recruit them. One Sunday, while the *abbé* was giving mass, the chief was holding a meeting with the mature men to decide when the government extension agents (*agents des eaux et fôrets*) were to come and inoculate the cattle.

The unmarried youth (ages 15 to 25) now had a "functioning" *maison des jeunes*, where they held dances, accompanied by their *amplis* (amplificateurs, or loudspeakers). Boys and girls from the neighboring communities came frequently to hold their *concerts* as well as their *theatre* – skits and short dramas that they compose themselves. These activities have greatly helped to keep the *jeunesse dorée* of Sambujat coming back during the rainy season (their school vacation) to help their parents with work in the fields. More girls than boys came back, however, and several had small babies with them. Whereas giving birth out of wedlock was once strongly censured, it had now become very common. The local primary State school, where teaching was in French, was faltering. A gale had torn its roof some months before, and it was not being repaired very promptly.

Disaster had struck the village: a pig epidemic! Pigs were dying by the droves (I saw one die before my eyes). If we recall, pigs are the principal sacrificial animal, to be killed at the spirit-shrines. "All my pigs have died," Panding said (I did not see a single one in his courtyard). "Now I will have to buy a pig every time I need to do a *kawasen*." And you can't buy just any pig; it must be a good one, costing 10,000 CFA francs ($40.00) or more. Hence, the pig epidemic was having a big impact on the ritual system of Sambujat, and certainly on the political economy.

Next to the chief's place – and to the room where I slept – was a brand new building, too small to be a house. It was a shed to accommodate the new milling machine. The men had paid for it, to relieve the women from the onerous task of pounding the daily rice. The rice system was flourishing despite the obvious lack of manpower. Associative work was everywhere; and the youth's work groups were out. All in all, life seemed to go on, despite the pig epidemic and the doubts expressed over the chapel by the elders, and probably because of the *maison des jeunes*, the milling machine and, of course, the abundant rains. So much for the "timeless" traditions of an "animist" Jola village.

Jipalom

In 1985, when I was in Jipalom, the inhabitants found themselves awkwardly placed. They were half in, half out of a capitalistic market economy. Although they were cultivating groundnuts on an increasing scale – now with the help of animal traction and the plough – bad roads and faulty bridges meant they were still isolated from large towns such as Bignona. It took two hours to make the trip from the village to the city. Hence, men had difficulty getting their cash crop to the cooperatives. Women had stopped making pottery and baskets to take into town and sell in the market. A decade and a half of drought had left its mark; large sections of the rice fields laid abandoned. People were growing mostly plateau crops, and drought-resistant cultivars like manioc or maize were entering the subsistence system. Failing to bring rain and protect the people from sickness, the shrines were falling into disuse. Islam did not seem to be filling the spiritual and material gap in peoples' lives. In short, things seemed to be in disarray, and everyone was discouraged.

By 1989, major changes had transformed village life. After decades of relative neglect the Senegalese state was pouring money into Lower Casamance. The reason why was not hard to find: the Jola were now engaged in power politics at the national level (see pp. 220–221). In 1987, a splendid new road had been completed, linking Jipalom and neighboring communities with the town of Bignona.[3] The road cut down travel time from 2 hours to less than 30 minutes. Furthermore, public transportation had now become available; a *car rapide* went by daily, bringing people, products, and also the young back from Bignona and beyond to help their parents during the rainy season. The road allowed the inhabitants to sell their groundnuts directly to SONACOS, the groundnut oil refinery in Ziguinchor, thus bypassing the government-controlled cooperatives.

The community had now a *garderie* or nursery for the children.[4] It also had a *maternité*, where women were checked over while pregnant and also gave birth under the expert eye of a local, young, and well-trained midwife.[5] In addition, there was now a dispensary in the next-door community, a short walk by the new road from Jipalom. During the rainy season, a knowledgeable, State-trained male nurse took care of patients from all over the area.[6] He dispensed large quantities of anti-malaria medicine, and kept the inhabitants healthier than I had ever seen them before. Moreover, the "French" school was doing very well under a new (Sereer) instructor, who was effective and widely liked.

More startling yet was the fact that the wet-rice system was slowly coming back. Whereas in 1981, and also in 1985, the people were not making nurseries, transplanting, or preparing the heavier soils, in 1989 they had started doing all these things. Roughly three-fifths of the rice-growing area was again under cultivation. Only the salt-ridden fields (the *kafintak* and *weng*) near the tidal creek (*marigot*), lay completely abandoned. In 1990, however, the *kafintak* was transformed. Working together with the men from the adjacent village, the Jipalom men had constructed an impressive earthen dike, several kilometers long, to hold rainwater in the fields rather than let it drain into the *marigot*. In this endeavor they had been helped by the earth-moving machinery and technical help of a member of the Baptist church in Bignona. The rice field system was not as productive as it had been twenty-five years before, and household heads now had to purchase imported rice from Southeast Asia and the US to tide them over the loan season. None the less, once again, home-grown rice was contributing the bulk of the monthly diet, a vital development, since men would otherwise have had to spend all their earnings from the groundnut trade buying rice for their families. The price of imported rice had risen considerably after the Senegalese government had stopped subsidising it in an effort to increase local production.

The Jipalom women were again involved in dry-season remunerative activities. A few of them were making pottery. More important, they were making salt in large quantities. The years of drought during the 1970s had left a crust of salt on the sandy flats adjacent to the brackish waters of the *marigot*. Small groups of women from the same courtyard would collect the salt-laden sand, transport it to their work-station outside the courtyard in baskets, and there process it by extracting the salt through drainers and boiling it down in large cauldrons. The salt collected in huge baskets was fetching, in 1990, 1,500 CFA francs for 50 kilograms, and women were coming in from neighboring areas to buy it. Not in enough numbers to satisfy the sellers, but still enough to provide the only significant source of cash for the local women.

Fatiya

Major changes have also occurred in Fatiya during the last decade. When I was there in 1985 the ox-plough was regularly being used to prepare the men's groundnut fields, but it had never been used to prepare the women's rice fields. As usual, women prepared the land by hand, with the aid of the long-handled hoe. The following year, however, the men hired a tractor to prepare some of their wives' rice fields.[7] Note that it was still the men who commanded the new technology, for it was in their interest to help fill the family granaries. Unfortunately, the tractor could not be used in the men's groundnut fields which are full of tree-stumps. Once the rice fields were ploughed, small groups of women helped each other for free to do the broadcast-seeding and the weeding. Such a group was called a *fusalaŋaf*, meaning "to measure oneself." It was a fairly new form of labor arrangement. There was a new milling machine in the next community, but very few of the Fatiya women availed themselves of it. Most did their pounding by hand, to save money.

By 1989, however, the women were into making vegetable gardens during the dry season to sell the product to Bignona. The technique had been introduced by government extension agents from PIDAC (replaced in 1988 by DERBAC). Out of sixty women in the community two-thirds made vegetable gardens. The women were organized under a *président*, a man who served as the contact person between them and government agents. Each woman worked a plot measuring 1 by 10 meters for each of the three crops they grew, tomatoes, onions, and potatoes. Each woman earned 7,000–8,000 CFA francs (US $28–$32) a season, which they kept for themselves, except for the 1,200 CFA francs which they had to leave in the cash box for next year's expenses – buying seed, repairing the fence and purchasing insecticide. By way of an example, 6,500 CFA francs can buy 6 yards of printed ("Lagos") cloth; 7,500 CFA francs could buy a 50 kilogram bag of imported rice. The following year (1990) the women received a special subsidy through a Japanese technical mission (Japanese agricultural experts were there in force) to buy watering cans, new hoes, and more seed; they kept these materials in a shed built specially for that purpose.

Moreover, in 1989, some Fatiya men had decided to stop asking their wives for the year-end contribution or *charité*. This is a Muslim obligation consisting of part of the rice harvest which the men used for their religious rituals. Instead, a few individuals were each cultivating a large rice field, which they prepared themselves and even transplanted upon; their wives, however, still did the harvesting. The crop from this field, which was called the *champ religieux*, was used by the men in the community-wide *gamo* (*gamou*) ceremony, held on the Prophet's birthday.

Insofar as the rice system was concerned, women were again building small nursery mounds in the middle of the fields and transplanting from there. This is time-consuming work. In the 1970s, during the drought, they had broadcast the seed directly, which required less work preparing the land, but as a consequence they had many arduous hours of weeding to do. Transplanting is done, not only to get higher yields, but also because, when fields are full of water, the seed cannot be broadcast upon them. And full of water the fields were, for the rains had by and large come back; 1985 was an especially rainy year (1362 mm. in Ziguinchor). All in all, the Fatiya rice-system was doing well. And so was the community, which was now deeply involved in opposition politics.

What conclusions can we draw from these startling turns in the life of the inhabitants of the three communities? First, and most obvious, the inhabitants of all three Jola communities are now participating in State politics and national economic programs – but on their own terms, as independent farmers who own the means of production. Secondly, many of the changes that are going on, sometimes at an amazing speed, often have contradictory effects. For example, the flight to the city has lessened pressure on the land, eased the transition to a monetary economy, and brought in fresh ideas, new opportunities, better infrastructures, novel technologies. But at the same time it has led to severe labor shortages in the countryside, aggravated relations between generations, contributed to urban congestion and unemployment. This is true of many other developments. Thirdly, in some communities, such as Jipalom, the incomplete penetration of Islam has facilitated a new direction, one that is more open to "western"-style innovations (dispensaries, maternities, child-care nurseries) than one would otherwise have expected. This is not to say that Muslim villages do not have these amenities; or that the Jipalom people have stopped going to the marabouts to be cured. But it seems to me that the lack of resistance to these innovations was partly a product of the disuse into which the traditional shrines had fallen; and the absence of resistance from elders, Muslim clerics and other "conservative" members of society. Finally, there is the sense that, since this ideological course seems to be working, it is worth pursuing more vigorously. Thus, the Fatiya inhabitants are becoming more Muslim, and more Jola-style Manding than before – even to the extent of embracing the political philosophy loosely based on Murid ideology expounded by the Opposition PDS party.

On the political economy of the Senegalese State

The presence of the Senegalese Nation–State is indeed making itself felt more in the Jola countryside. For this reason, it is necessary to specify the kind of State we are talking about. Senegal is a very special country. It is one of the few multiparty democracies of Africa; a secular State with close ties to both the Western nations and the Islamic World League; a population that is 85 percent Muslim and 75 percent farmers; an economy once almost exclusively dependent on the export of groundnuts, but recently diversifying (by phosphates and fisheries); a net importer of foodstuffs, amidst which rice and sugar are the most important; a galloping birth rate; 30 percent of its seven million population in the cities; a net immigration rate; and large internal migratory movements. All these phenomena are interrelated and all form part of the Senegalese scene. However, the following discussion will mostly touch upon those aspects that have to do with the nature of the connection, at the level of the State, between ideologies of power, including religion, and the practices and policies surrounding agrarian production. For the changes that the north-shore Jola have experienced in accepting Islam and groundnuts as a cash crop are not isolated, unique phenomena; they are integral to more encompassing ideological processes. Even though Senegal is officially a secular State, religion has played a significant role in shaping agricultural practices and policies. As Coulon has pointed out: "Le Sénégal est bien connu pour être le paradis des marabouts et des confréries" (1983: 120). From the time they became firmly established during the last century, the Muslim brotherhoods of Senegal have profited from the new socio-economic order brought about by the French colonial regime. This was so despite their passive resistance to cultural and political assimilation.[8] With the cooperation of the French authorities, the brotherhoods developed a prosperous groundnut trade which became the mainstay of the new colony. Schumacher (1975: 4–5) has described this process among the predominantly Wolof farmers of the Groundnut Basin (Thies, Diourbel, Louga and the Sine-Saloum).[9] The marabouts could produce groundnuts at competitive prices because they had at their disposal a free labor force composed in large measure of Koranic disciples.[10] Since they also gave a boost to colonial commerce, "the Administration encouraged maraboutic colonies, with their disciples organized into work teams, to found settlements on virgin lands" (Coulon 1983: 105, my translation).

To this day, Muslim clerics, or marabouts, exert considerable pressure on the government to formulate economic policies that are favorable to them and their followers. These policies touch mainly on groundnut production and marketing. It is estimated (Cassell, quoted in Fatton 1987: 56) that "At the time of independence [1960], peanut production represented, alone, more than 80 percent of the country's exports. Peanut cultivation employed 87 percent of the active population and covered half of the cultivated land." Nowadays, groundnuts generate from two-thirds to three-fourths of the income flowing to the rural Senegalese population. Senegal's entire export economy is in fact greatly dependent upon this monocrop. Revenues from the groundnut trade help finance the large Senegalese bureaucracy, whose civil servants earn salaries many times higher than what an average peasant makes in a year (Hesseling 1985: 62). Although by the 1970s groundnuts accounted for only 40 to 50 percent of all exports, this is still a significant figure.

The most powerful of the groundnut-producing, exclusively Senegalese, Muslim orders is the Murid (Muridiyya, Mouride), incorporated formally by Ahmadu Bamba (c. 1850–1927) as an offshoot of the Qadiriyya. In recent years, perhaps as much as two thirds of Senegal's groundnut crop is grown by Wolof farmers, some 30 percent of whom belong to the brotherhood. In fact, according to some estimates, over half of all rural Wolof and Sereer are Murids; the brotherhood commands over a million members. Murid ideology is based on the idea that working the land is a form of prayer. The organization rests on the institution of the *dara*, or collective farm, made up of some twelve landless adult males who give their harvest to their saintly sponsor and at the end of some ten years of service receive their own plots of land (Cruise O'Brien 1975: 68). Under the saintly leadership of a supreme officer (the present Khalifa is Abdou Lahat, the son of Ahmadu Bamba), Murid disciples work for marabouts, who in turn convey they aspirations to government officials (Copans 1980: 192–199, 203–210).

The development of maraboutic colonies modelled after the Murid brotherhood did not directly involve the Jola of Lower Casamance. In fact, very few if any Jola belong to the brotherhood. For such acts of submission as are required of the Murid *talibés* are inacceptable to them. Moreover, there are few landless refugees in Jola society. All the same, those Jola living north of the river, who have for some time now been involved in the groundnut trade, are quite willing to recognize the considerable political power Murid leaders exert at the national level. During the drought of the 1970s, for example, the Khalifa general and his high-ranking marabout followers threatened that unless the government controlled price for groundnuts was not revised upwards they would advise their followers to withdraw from groundnut cultivation altogether and grow only millet (Cruise O'Brien 1979: 209–227). Faced with this threat, the government had no choice but to nearly double the price it paid the peasant for his crop.[11] The Jola were quite aware that, thanks to the Khalifa's intervention, matters did not become more desperate. For they could now sell their groundnuts at a reasonable price and buy much-needed rice for their families.

Marabout-follower relationships form an integral part of the ideology underlying interpersonal relations in all Muslim rural farming communities of Senegal, including "Mandingized" Jola communities (part III).[12] In the penetration of what Coulon calls a "Muslim political culture" into the Jola countryside, patronage and clientship have played an important part. It is in this light that we can understand why the residents of Fatiya once set aside a large groundnut field which they cultivated together – women and men – for the sole benefit of a famous marabout. He is Ousmane Badji, the controversial Jola *cheikh* from Sindian, whose miraculous deeds and earthly talents (visit to the Pope, financial aid from Arab countries) drew the spiritual and economic support of large numbers of Jola Qadiriyya and Tijaniyya adepts, both of whom he claimed to represent. "Indeed, since the patron–client relationship dominating the peripheral agricultural sector is profoundly imbued with Islamic fervor, it possesses a spiritual and religious dimension that imports to it [this sector] a relative stability and resistance to change" (Fatton 1987: 104–105).[13] This religious dimension to Senegalese agriculture can be clearly seen in the success with which Cheikh Ahmed Niasse, the young Tijani preacher dubbed the "ayatollah of Kaolak," has established an Islamic Institute for Agriculture, financed with the help of a number of Muslim nations (*Le Monde*, 10 April 1989: 6).

Despite the increasingly important role played by an Islamic ideology in the Wolof-dominated urban culture (see Ewane 1985), it is still important to keep in mind that Senegal is officially a secular State. And the Jola are not Murids. Thus, there is another level of relationship that we must consider. It has to do with the more "secular" aspects of Senegalese leadership, and how these have affected Jola perceptions of the State. For the Jola have had a long tradition of being in the opposition to centralized governments irrespective of its kind. First they opposed the Portuguese, then they opposed the French colonial administrators. Even after Senegal embarked on the road to independence (1945–1960), they continued to oppose whatever political leaders were residing in the metropolitan capital of Dakar. In the 1958 referendum, for example, Senegalese were given the option of either remaining as a self-governing republic within the framework of a French community, or of opting for immediate and complete independence. The majority of the Senegalese, including the marabouts, voted for remaining in the French community. The Jola voted for immediate termination of the French presence.[14]

In the 1963 national elections, the most important unified opposition to Senghor and his UPS party (Union Progressiste Sénégalais), came from the PRA (Parti du Rassemblement Africain-Sénégal). This was the same party that had led the campaign for full independence in 1958. When, in 1961, I first visited the Jola for a couple of months, a large proportion of the younger men and educated youth belonged to the PRA. Although the UPS won the elections, PRA continued in the opposition. At the end of my second, and longer, stint in the field (1964–1966), PRA had joined forces with the UPS; it stopped being the party of the opposition. For eight years

Senegal was essentially under a one-party system and the Jola lost interest.

An opposition movement, the PDS (Parti Démocratique Sénégalais), finally emerged in 1974, and some Jola began to give it their support. Given official recognition in 1976,[15] the party is headed by M. Abdoulaye Wade, a lawyer and professor of political economy (also ex dean of the *faculté de droit*) at the University in Dakar. M. Wade "advocates a form of *socialisme–travailliste*" based on "the Mouride brotherhood's understanding of work as the means of becoming a follower and disciple of God" (Fatton 1987: 130). According to PDS ideology, a new diversified mode of agricultural development based on peasant self-reliance is the only way out of Senegal's present state of dependency on foreign financial inputs (Fatton 1987: 129–134).[16] One can see why the PDS ideology would appeal to the Jola. Whereas, for example, Fatiya was a PS village (Parti Socialiste, the government party) in 1981, by 1985 slightly more than 50 percent of all the mature men had switched to the PDS. In the 1988 national elections, the entire *arrondissement* of Tangori, voted PDS. It will be interesting to see what happens next, now that M. Wade has joined (in March, 1991) the government as Minister of State.

Despite the existence of a vigorous opposition, it is the view of some experts that Senegal is still dominated by a metropolitan ideology making strong government and political stability prerequisites for development (Sow 1984: 42–54). It is argued that for many decades an administrative elite has monopolized, not only political posts and the groundnut trade, but also the oil and phosphate industries and the banking system. The power of the Senegalese State and its personnel is enormous; it is felt from top to bottom. It is against this feeling of being "dominated" by the predominantly Wolof *nordistes* originating north of the Gambia that some recent developments in the Basse Casamance must be understood.

For the past ten years, the Basse Casamance has been in political turmoil. Expressions of unrest in the form of cessationist movements and anti-government demonstrations have ended up in violence. Thus, when a *coup d'état* was organized in 1981 to depose the Senegalese supported president of Gambia, the leader was a Jola Foñi from the Kajamutay. On December 26, 1982, what began as a sizeable demonstration in the streets of Ziguinchor by a group of *séparatistes* or *indépendantistes*, advocating the separation of the Casamance from the rest of Senegal, ended up a few days later in massive arrests by the forces of order (Geschieri and Van der Klei 1987: 314, 318). Amidst those arrested were a well-known *abbé* and numerous other persons, in their majority Jola. Violence again erupted in December 1983 on the aftermath of the trial of those remaining from the arrests made the year before.[17] At dawn, on the eighteenth of December, Ziguinchor was invaded by groups of *indépendantistes*, some of them armed with guns, knives, bows and arrows. The affair has been described by Darbon 1984: 125. Their clash with the armed forces/police left a considerable number of dead and many wounded, on both sides.[18]

Following this date, other individuals, again Jola, were arrested, some to be pardoned by presidential decree.[19] The Senegalese government all along accused the MFDC (Mouvement des Forces Démocratiques de Casamance) – an organization which it declared illegal – of being behind the bloody events.[20]

In the Spring and Summer of 1990, violence erupted again.[21]

By the summer of 1991, however, calm had returned to Casamance. Nearly 350 presumed *indépendantistes* had been released from jail, the National Assembly had passed a law granting them amnesty, and a cease-fire treaty had been signed (on May 31, 1991, in Bissau) between the Senegalese government and the MFDC leadership.[22]

Underlying all the unrest is a persistent contradiction. The Jola feel at once neglected by the central government and "colonised" by the *nordistes*. In the words of Trincaz (1984: 166), "This has created in the Casamance population a real feeling of being dominated by strangers who occupy all the posts in the administration, in education and private enterprise". At the same time, it should be noted that since 1982 the Senegalese government has done a great deal for the Casamance: "Millions have been injected in that zone and considerable investments continue to take place" (*La Temoin*, No. 5, 5 June: p. 1). Witness the developments that have taken place in the communities where I have worked.

What the future will bring to Lower Casamance and its substantial economic potential is hard to predict. Much will depend upon the success with which the Jola rural population is engaged directly in the development process.[23] The Jola must be made to feel that they partake of power, that they are in control of their own destiny. Given the right political climate and favorable conditions, Lower Casamance could still become "the granary of Senegal."

Notes

Introduction: ideology and agrarian change
1. Thomas (1959, vol. 1, pp. 119–20) is actually rather ambivalent about what he refers to as "the role of fetishism in agriculture": At one point he states that "aucun interdit, aucune superstition ne règlement les divers taches de l'homme où de la femme" . . . and at another point he adds "Mais, dans son principe, la culture est religion . . . acune technique agricole n'a plus d'efficience où de signification religieuse que la riziculture." Pélissier (1966: 706–8), in turn, is quite conscious of the role that religion plays in the social life of the Jola: "La religion diola est donc à la fois un puissant ciment social et un precieux trait d'union entre l'homme et le milieu." But her prefers not to deal with it: "L'étude de cette religion qui tient un grand role dans la vie diola ne releve pas de notre recherche", and then refers the reader to Thomas' work on the subject. Even though their studies are remarkable for their breadth and detail, they are incomplete. Baum's 1987 study of Esudadu (Esulalu) religious and social history probes more deeply into Jola religious concepts, and hence is more useful to us here - especially because he is conversant with the Kasa variant of the Jola language and he *does* try to relate Jola ideology to the agrarian system. But he only deals with the beliefs of one Jola sub-group and mainly as a historian. As valuable in its own right as his study doubtless is, it is not informed by the same anthropological theory that informs the present study.
2. The lower figure is estimated as follows. Cheneau-Loquay (1988: 116) talks about 231,00 rural peoples living in Basse Casamance in 1982, to whom can be added 100,000 town-dwellers in Ziguinchor and some 20,000 town-dwellers in Bignona, bringing the total up to 280,000. At the present growth rate of 2.2 percent, the total population of Basse Casamance would be 328,000 in 1990, of which 80 percent, or 262,000 would be Jola. The upper figure is estimated as follows. Van Loo and Star (1973: 9) talk about 290,000 persons living in Basse Casamance in 1972 (this figure includes the population of the two large towns of Ziguinchor and Bignona). At the present growth-rate of 2.2 percent for the area, the population in 1990 would have been 428,000 persons, of whom 80 percent (342,000 would be Jola).
3. The three communities discussed in this book form a sort of open triangle. The

distances between them, by roads that have been greatly improved in the last decade, are 90 kilometers between communities A and B, and 38 kilometers between communities B and C (see also fig. 1, p. 12).

1 The power of the spirit-shrines

1. The previous census (1964) lists three Esudadu villages as having between 1,000 and 3,000 inhabitants each. The subsequent 1972 census, however, breaks down the population of these three "villages" by its constituent wards. This amounts to a statistical recognition that the wards, containing between 200 and 500 persons, rather than the village, is the basic organizational unit in Esudadu society. Sambujat, the community I will be concerned with, is roughly the size of one of the wards in the larger Esudadu villages. As such, villages were an artificial creation of the French administration.
2. These risks include salinization, locust plagues, bird depredation, and, of course, drought. The latter is the subject of another book, currently under preparation, in which I deal with the interface between social organization and material conditions. The tentative title of the book is *Wet Rice in Dry-years: Jola Social Organization under Duress*.
3. The labor-intensive nature of the Esudadu rice-growing system is nowhere more evident than in the effort put into the carving out of a new paddy field from the mangrove vegetation. The formation of a mangrove field (a *kahint*) takes at least three seasons. First, the men must cut down the thick and hardy mangrove trees at the base, leaving part of the trunk and the prop-roots standing. The women, in turn, must come into the parcel to take out the wood and carry it home. At this point, the big dike (*egaatuk*), which girdles the deep fields keeping saline waters out, is extended to protect the new field. Next, the newly cleared parcel is surrounded by a dike one or two-meters high and very thick, requiring much moving of earth. The field is then allowed to flood during several rainy seasons. In this manner, the remaining trunks and prop-roots decompose, allowing the field to be ridged and furrowed. After putting in stakes to make sure the ridges are straight, the owner, often with help from one of the men's work associations, prepares the newly created mangrove field for planting. For subsequent years, the parcel is desalinated by flushing out salts in the soil. Rainwater is impounded, then allowed out through a duct or sluice made from the hollow trunk of the Borassus palm. The sluice is plugged or opened by means of a large stopper made from banana leaves and reeds. Hundreds of man-hours have to be spent before a mangrove paddy can be cultivated.
4. These calculations were made by following various individuals with a stop-watch in hand during each step in the cultivation cycle. The fields on which they performed the various tasks had been measured and mapped beforehand.
5. The spirit-shrines of the Esudadu Jola, including those of Sambujat, have played a major historical role in maintaining continuity and promoting adjustment to new productive practices and relationships (Baum 1987). From the fifteenth to the nineteenth centuries, new political and economic conditions were ushered in by the trade in slaves, by "legitimate commerce" and by precolonial encounters with the French (see also Mark 1985; Linares 1987). Yet the Esudadu Jola were able to deal with these powerful new forces on their own

terms. Their ability to do so can be attributed in part to the nature of their production system, and in part to the limited trading activities that they were willing to engage in. But, as Baum (1987) has convincingly argued, their faith in the ability of their shrines to meet new challenges and changed conditions was a decisive factor contributing to their cultural and economic survival.

6. It is especially difficult for women to learn about the shrines that men control (and the reverse). For this reason, I have complemented my own information with the excellent account of Esudadu religion given by Baum (1987).

7. Baum (1987: 383) has described the shrines as follows:

   these *ukiin* are "human in form, both white and black in color, very hairy, and physically deformed. Like people, these spirits are said to age, marry, have children, die, and be reincarnated (though always as spirits). These spirits can be either male or female. Like people, their moods may change without reason. They must be coaxed, pleaded with, and supplicated in order for prayers to be answered."

8. A spirit (*bakiin* sing., *ukiin* pl.) is attracted by setting up a shrine, usually the pointed end of a bull's horn, or perhaps a forked stick buried in the sand, and sacrificing to it. In themselves, these structures are hardly impressive. But the shrines also contain "the ritual objects associated with the spirits (like earth from an older shrine, medicines, and other secret objects)" (see Baum 1987).

9. During the eighteenth and nineteenth centuries, *Hupila* became involved in regulating the sale or ransoming of captives (Baum 1987: 167–192). The growing commerce in captives "radically altered the nature of the shrines, its priesthood and its accessibility." It encouraged the emergence of several different forms of the shrines associated with different aspects of the trade in slaves. Once the trade disappeared, however, *Hupila* went back to being the family shrine *par excellence*.

10. *Hupila* is not Sambujat's only corporate symbol, however. The village is divided into two wards. These are named, territorial units (*kalol* or *kajong*), each identified with a sacred forest where the boys' initiation takes place. During initiation, one of the two wards always enters the sacred forest first. Each of the wards also has its own spirit-shrine. The one in ward A is called Enak; the one in ward B, Kalembekin. When ward A propitiates Enak, members of ward B are always invited. When Kalembekin is being propitiated, the reverse is true. Members of the invited ward contribute palm wine at the other ward's ceremonies and all present eat and drink together. At this level, the shrine is concerned with things not being right within the ward, especially when there are many deaths and witchcraft is suspected. Strangers from a nearby village may come to a ward's propitiatory rituals, but only after the keeper of the shrine (the *awasen*) has "talked" and done the libation – that is, after the liturgical or canonical part of the ritual is over – and only to drink palm wine.

11. The meat from the *kaalok* pigs is distributed by the young man to married men, boys, and girls about thirteen years of age, before "they have breasts." Adult married women are forbidden from eating the sacrificial meat, or from tasting the *bunuk* (palm wine) used on these occasions. In fact, they should not even be present.

12. It has been suggested by Beattie (1980: 30–31) that the term "sacrifice" should be restricted to "the killing, immolation of a living victim." He excludes from

consideration such practices as the pouring of libations and the offering of food and drink at a shrine. He further suggests that the "animal" being sacrificed should stand for (symbolize) the person who is making the sacrifice, or the person on whose behalf the sacrifice is being made. Finally, he remarks that this animal is usually domestic because it is identified with the home, rather than with nature. Esudadu Jola beliefs do not fit Beattie's definition of sacrifice very well. Cattle or pigs, two of the most common sacrificial animals, are not considered to be particularly "domestic." And whereas bulls are identified with human strength and wealth, pigs or chickens do not possess human-like traits. Whether one calls it an "offering" rather than a sacrifice, pouring palm wine libations at a shrine is an intrinsic, if not *the*, defining symbol of the *kawasen* rite. It is not simply a type "of symbolic gift-giving" as Beattie would have it. Rather, it is *the* principal instrument for "bringing up" (invoking, attracting) a spirit and talking to it. Without it, the officiant cannot ask the shrine to let go of a sick person's body; or to bestow children or riches upon another person who has sacrificed generously.

13. At these they cannot be present, nor eat the meat and drink the wine. Nonetheless, in many instances, such as the sacrifices that precede taking over the *bukut* or boys' circumcision shrine, they can be given meat from an animal sacrificed for that purpose. And there are some major, male-controlled shrines at which women and children can, and do, eat.

14. One of the most important redistributive occasions, when large amounts of comestibles are circulated, is during the *bukut* or boys' initiation. *Bukut* is unmatched in sheer size and elaboration. *Bukut* refers exclusively to the male initiation ceremony, as well as to the spirit-shrine that constitutes its central symbol. The *bukut* takes place approximately every twenty-five years. The Sambujat *bukut* enforces cooperation in productive endeavors by requiring the mobilization of enormous labor reserves and material resources. The ceremony draws hundreds of visitors from faraway villages. Sambujat holds its *bukut* ceremony in conjunction with two other small Esudadu villages so they can share expenses. Each village has its own *kareŋ* or sacred forest, where the boys are, in principle, secluded for at least three months. The last Sambujat *bukut* took place in 1962 and was attended by upwards of 2,000 persons. Hence, the initiation rite or *bukut* encourages the temporary retention of surpluses, followed by their conspicuous consumption. It stimulates over-production and serves as an important mechanism enforcing the re-distribution of resources.

15. According to Baum (1987: 84, 120), the office of priest-king (*ai*, he spells it *oeyi*) evolved from the sixteenth-century institution of kinship among the Fulup (Floup), the ancestors of the Jola. During the eighteenth century, when the distinctive Esudadu religious tradition began to emerge, the priest-king worked hard to maintain peace. When the *ai* arrived at the scene of a fight between two villages, or between two wards within the same village, he would raise his sacred broom and the contenders had to stop lest they, and all their family, would die. Moreover, I was told that, when a dispute between two or more residents broke out, the *ai* would call together the entire village and ask for witnesses to give testimony on either side: "Then he would decide who was the guilty party and tell him to stop." The guilty person then sacrificed to the *bakiin* through the *ai*'s

good offices. When I asked what would happen if a culprit refused to behave, the answer was that "he wouldn't dare"; "the whole village would oblige him". In Baum's words, the *aï*'s peace-keeping role "does illustrate the fundamental opposition of the priest-king to warfare that would endanger Esudadu's spiritual unity."

16. According to Baum (1987: 133–135), in the late eighteenth century the *aï* was effectively forbidden from cultivating the land or participating in the council of elders (the *Huteendukay*). Barred from participation in factional politics, including land disputes, meant he could not use his extensive powers for private purposes.

17. The burial rite itself does not usually end the cycle of prestations associated with the death of a famous elder (male or female). A ceremony (the *kasinten*, meaning "to grieve") may be held three or four years after the actual burial. On this occasion, forty or more head of cattle might be sacrificed. Members of the agnatic corporation will contribute up to five head a piece, with each bull being tied in the courtyard where the deceased lived, to be admired and remarked upon by hundreds of visitors. This is one of the few contexts in which people will boast about what they have; they won't say exactly how many cattle they own, for this would be to incite envy and risk bewitchment, but they will make indirect references to their large herds. It is also the time when a man who has inherited the "staff" (a stick with cords and wood pieces called a *banaab*) that is passed down among members of families reputed to have great stores of rice, will tie it around his head and dance to show that he is someone "who has something." Because wealth may bring envy, and with it the witchcraft of others, it is something to be displayed with caution and not boasted about except on these occasions.

18. Using oral histories, Baum (1987: 303–307) has reconstructed how the two *Sihuñ* shrines were brought to Esudadu during the middle of the nineteenth century. The first shrine (called *Jeketi*) was brought from a community south of Oussouye by a man who is said to have been concerned with the problems his people were facing with drought, infertility and witchcraft. (Incidentally, men are often said to have introduced female shrines in whose rituals they are forbidden from participating. The reverse is also true; for example, the *bukut*, or exclusively male initiation shrine, is said to have been brought to Esudadu by a woman).

The second *Ehuñ* shrine (called *Teŋo*) was brought by a woman from the communities of Hitou and Niomoun across the Casamance River first to Kagnout. The origins of the third *Ehuñ* shrine, called *Aisissen*, and which brings together all the women in the community, is more obscure. It seems to have been "created' locally. Each of the shrines has different ritual requirements.

19. Baum (1987: 306) mentions that at the second kind of *Ehuñ*, the one brought to the Esudadu from Hitou and Niomoun, "men can partake of the palm wine and meat of sacrifice after the rituals have been concluded." He is talking about Kajinol, the Esudadu community where he worked. In Sambujat, a married man cannot eat meat or drink palm wine sacrificed at either of the female shrines. There are many other details of ritual in which two versions of the same ritual may vary from one Esudadu community to another.

20. However, in some other Jola or related areas women do have rights of disposition over rice paddies; they do so among the Bandial described by Snyder (1981) and among the Ehing described by Schloss (1988).

2 Rice fields and labor relations

1. To begin with, the groom signals his intentions to marry by sending 10 to 20 liters of palm wine to the male members of the bride's *hank* or courtyard group (described later). The wine may be accepted or refused, but if it is accepted, the marriage is approved in principle. The bride's agnates must then agree upon an additional quantity of wine that the groom should contribute in order to propitiate the pertinent shrines at the bride's place of residence. This sometimes amounts to hundreds of liters which the groom has collected himself with the help of his cohorts living in the same *hank*. The next thing to be agreed upon is the size of the pig that must be sent to the girl's father. The animal again is destined to be used for ritual purposes. It is sacrificed at the bride's *Hupila* shrine, in order to secure her health and future procreation of children.
2. A son and his wife must cook and eat their own rice and, if possible, should live in their own house. Thus, if a son has *sembe* (power, strength), he will, as soon as he can, build a house for himself and his wife. The new couple may have to live in the husband's parental home for a while, but they cook for themselves and occupy separate quarters (Linares 1983).
3. Baum (1987: 408), who worked in another of the Esudadu communities, mentions that divorce cannot occur during the planting or harvesting stages because it "would seriously disrupt the family unit of production." This may be so in Sambujat also, even though a friend once remarked to me that divorce was so common that "one wife may transplant and another be there for the harvest." Actually, statistics indicate that divorce is really not that common at all, certainly not by Western standards.
4. Very few women who had been widowed in the years spanning my sundry visits to Sambujat actually remarried. Of the 9 women whose husbands died between 1965 and 1977, 7, or 78 percent, had not remarried by 1981; they were all living with their sons. Both women who had re-married had done so to Sambujat men, one of them by the widow-remarriage or *kataor* convention. Of the four more recently (between 1977–1981) widowed women, half had re-married (one by the *kataor*, one to a man from another village). In short, only a third of the women widowed since 1965 had re-married by 1981; most had chosen to remain single. If a widow chooses instead to remarry, she often does so nearby, with a classificatory *hank* brother of her deceased husband. She may re-marry by the *kataor*, or by any other convention, even though she may be too old to bear children. It is said that, "though elderly, the new spouses will still be able to help each other with agricultural work."
5. Baum (1987: 409) mentions a second form of re-marriage in the community he studied. It is called *Boodji* and takes place every five years or so. On these occasions, widowed or divorced women who are still of child-bearing age are required to choose a husband within the community; they cannot refuse to do so, neither can men refuse to accept them. Otherwise, the elders of the particular shrine associated with the community council will fine them.

6. Because the labor of the youth is so crucial, their exodus from the countryside to the cities is beginning to cause serious problems (de Jonge *et al.* 1978; Van Loo and Star 1973). In fact, in her recent study of the energetic problem in the Casamance, Cheneau-Loquay (1988. 118) asserts. "en pays diola, le manque de main-d'ouvre constitue le principal blocage, le principal problème énergétique." She estimates that 15 percent of the population migrates seasonally to the cities. Young men initially go to the cities in search of an education. And young women go to work as domestics in the households of French, Lebanese and Wolof families (less than 10 percent go there to be educated). Their migration is supposed to be seasonal. Both groups are expected to go back to their natal villages to help their parents with agricultural work. Yet, according to de Jonge *et al.* (1978), not everyone returns seasonally. Within the region of Oussouye, not far from Sambujat, 23 percent of the girls who were away in 1975 returned too late and went back too early. A few girls did not come back at all. As a consequence, the area of rice fields that was regularly transplanted had to be decreased by at least 14 percent. My own census data on Sambujat's youth confirms these estimates. In 1985, one quarter of the Sambujat boys and girls who were away in school or working in Dakar did not come back. But 75 percent did, which is already quite a lot. A very small number of the youth actually find permanent employment in the cities. But those who do, often send home remittances to help their parents hire extra labor.
7. It has become customary in the household literature to put households into some sort of typology and then compare the number of households in each category which live together, eat together, and so forth. This procedure is expected to reveal patterns of familial cooperation. In Sambujat, residence and consumption are quite straightforward; all Sambujat households live in non-extended (i.e. solitary and elementary) households and customarily eat alone. With co-production, however, classification is more tricky. If a household is classified as "elementary," it means that a conjugal family unit regularly cultivates alone. But in "multiple" households a father and his married son, or a deceased brother's son, or two brothers, ordinarily work together.
8. Scholars of different persuasion often remark, somewhat offhandedly, that the Jola kinship system is organized on the basis of patrilineal descent units, which they call patrilineages. The question of what "really" constitutes "descent" has been vigorously debated by anthropologists, so I will not repeat their arguments here. Enough to say that, with Scheffler (1966: 548), I understand descent to be "a generic label for a variety of forms of *genealogical continua*." For Scheffler (1972, 1973), the aspect of continuity, of linked ties to a common ancestor, is crucial to the construction of descent ideologies. He distinguishes descent-based constructs from kinship, the latter involving the recognition of successive filial steps.
9. All Jola, and most especially the Esudadu, maintain close ties with their mothers' kin. A mother's real or classificatory brother can lend land to his sister's son, can protect her children from witchcraft, can contribute rice for his sister's daughter's dowry. A young man is prohibited from marrying his mother's brother's daughter. A man (and his family) moves to his mother's brother's compound if he suspects that one of his agnates is killing his children.

Everyone has an animal double (an *awuum*) which lives in the mother's brother's compound (Sapir 1977); and so forth. It may thus be affirmed in passing (without forcing the data) that an important cognatic element is present in Sambujat social life. Indeed, given the practice of in-marriage, it would be surprising if it were otherwise. And yet, men who are related through matrilateral links do not regularly cooperate in agricultural tasks.

10. Within each courtyard unit or *hank* a single patronym, or at most two patronyms (say Asiin and Jaata, or Baaben), predominate. This might be the reason why scholars (e.g. Thomas 1963, Pélissier 1966, Marzouk-Schmitz 1981) writing on the Jola have often been misled into assuming that members of the same courtyard group or *hank* constitute a patrilineage, that is a descent-based corporation. If we subscribe to the accepted definition of lineage as a group in which the actual relationship between members can be demonstrated (Radcliffe-Brown and D. Forde 1950: 39–40; Fox 1967: 49), then Sambujat's courtyard groups do not qualify as patrilineages, even though the *buaju* units do. Put differently, tracing descent to a common ancestor is not relevant for defining relationship among those persons living around a single courtyard or *hank* (c.f. Schloss 1988 on the Ehing House). Patronyms do not function as descent constructs. They are recent, some persons refuse to adopt them altogether, or they change them in mid-life.

    Patronyms do not regulate marriage either; for marriage between persons sharing the same patronym is regularly permitted so long as the potential spouses were born in different courtyards. The children of a man who has moved from *hank* A to *hank* B cannot marry within either of these two groups. It is said that if this happened it might "ruin friendship." In addition, all men who reside within a courtyard enclosure share responsibility for helping to marry off each other's daughters with a proper "dowry," and for burying each other's dead with the proper prestations. Male members of a *hank* tap wine in a common grove, tend their cattle together, and often cultivate as a group. Female agnates, members of a *hank*, often marry out together, usually into a neighboring *hank*. Furthermore, though the members of a courtyard group do not own rice fields in common, they nonetheless hold residual rights to land; the last surviving member of a *hank* inherits the land.

11. To do so, the tapper goes up the palm with the aid of a hoop made from the central stem of a palm frond, trimming the fronds as he goes along. He makes a round incision at the base of each bunch of fruit, inserts a funnel made from a palm leaf, and attaches a bottle or calabash to it. He goes up in the morning to harvest the wine collected during the night. At that time, he throws away the funnels and lets the incisions breathe. In the afternoon he climbs again, cleans out the incision, and places new funnels and new containers.

12. In the Huluf region, for example, tappers are allowed to tap a particular palm for no longer than ten days in succession. In other areas, "foreign" tappers are allowed to come in every other year, so the palms can rest. In yet other areas, a section of the village groves may be reserved for gathering fruit, and not for tapping. And, finally, in still other areas, only the male inflorescence from the palm, and not the higher-yielding female fruit bunch, may be tapped.

Conclusions to Part I

1. In this connection, one may take notice of the Esudadu custom (called *kanabor*), whereby one of the work-associations takes in charge a poor person or an orphan. Every time a member of the group gets sacrificial meat, he must share it with the fostered person (Thomas 1959: 224).
2. Nowadays, not only young girls, but also large numbers of married women go off to Dakar to work as domestics (*Conseil National*, 1983). While they are absent, their husbands must do domestic work and, if their wives are absent during the rainy season (which is still rare), they must pay for having the women's *etondiŋ* do the transplanting and harvesting.

3 Islamization and the introduction of a cash crop

1. The Bañuñ and the Jola had lived together, or in adjacent areas, in uneasy relations of symbiosis or hostility for many years. Parallels between the *hatichira* ritual and contemporary Esudadu rituals have been analyzed by Baum (1987: 54–55) and Mark (1985: 13–14) in some detail and need not be repeated here. The religious institutions of the Jola and Bañuñ had many features in common. This situation was both a cause and a consequence of the Jola policy of incorporation of Bañuñ groups. In fact, Mark (1985: 50–51) has suggested that Jola–Bañuñ relations may have actually involved a great deal of intermarriage and assimilation.
2. The Portuguese crown had prohibited its nationals from settling on the mainland to trade privately. Some Portuguese did take up residence among some African groups on the coast, receiving the name of *lançados* because they thrust themselves upon the natives. The *lançados* were often married to African wives, a fact that gave them a definite trading advantage. Their offsprings are referred to as the Luso-Africans (Brooks 1980b). By and large, the Jola forbade *lançados* from ever settling in their territory (Brooks 1983: 13). On several occasions, the *lançados* attempted, with little success, to establish garrisons or forts as a protection against Jola hostilities.
3. Brooks (1980a: 32) points out that, during the seventeenth century, Ziguinchor had become the principal *entrepôt* (trading post) for Bañuñ and Luso-African commerce along the Casamance River and its tributaries. In fact, "While the Cassanga to the east and the Banyun north of the Casamance were being ranted, the Banyun around Ziguinchor maintained the position until the second half of the nineteenth century" (Lauer 1969: 56).
4. Wet-rice agriculture is an ancient system in the Upper Guinea Coast. When the Portuguese first arrived in the fifteenth century, rice was widely grown in the region between Guiné Bissau and the Gambia (Portères 1950; Pélissier 1966: 710–716; 731–734). Its cultivation probably dates from many centuries, if not millennia, before European contact (Portères 1950; Linares 1971). The Jola (called Fulup by the Portuguese) were themselves growing rice in inundated fields that were diked and transplanted upon when first contacted. The species of rice being grown was *Oryza glaberrima* or "red rice," which is indigenous to Africa, being descended from the wild species *Oryza brevilugata*. In fact, as Portères has argued, the Casamance was an important early center for the

diversification of the *O. glaberrima* species. It is impossible to know exactly when the Asian species *Oryza sativa* was introduced into the Jola area, however. Pélissier (1966: 733–734) is probably correct when he suggests that *O. sativa* was introduced by the Portuguese much earlier on in the areas south of the Casamance River (such as the Esudadu area), than in the areas north of the Casamance River (such as the Kajamutay), which had less Portuguese influence, and where it was introduced by the Manding. To this day, the Jola of Jipalom, who still grow some *O. glaberrima* varieties, call these *adiola* rice, whereas they call the *O. sativa* varieties *amanding* rice. The elders I interviewed in 1964 still remembered when the *O. sativa* varieties were first grown in Jipalom, placing their introduction into this area sometime in the 1920s.

5. The European need for palm products, mostly oil, was an outcome of the Industrial Revolution. Oil was widely used in Europe as a lubricant for machinery, and the excedent was utilized in making candles and soap. From the nut or kernel margarine was made, and what remained was used as fodder.

6. That such hostilities interfered with peaceful trading activities is confirmed by the fact that French commercial houses had felt the need to hire Wolof and Sarakole *traitants* who would go into Jola villages to buy latex from individual collectors. When one of these firms decided to reduce the number of *traitants* that they hired, the Jola refused to go personally to the trading houses to sell their latex. The Jola were justified in not wanting to come out of their villages, for the Manding and the Fulani were carrying on a prosperous trade in captives deep into Foñi territory (Roche 1976: 197).

7. Besides Fodé Kaba, other warrior-marabouts also attacked the Foñi. Fodé Silla (or Sylla) Ture, a Fula by tradition, concentrated on converting by force the Jola living in the Kombo region close to Gambia. In 1887, Fodé Silla pillaged Kabaline, a village a scant 30 km west of Jipalom. To this end, he built mosques in the Kombo and also forbade palm wine tapping by the Jola under his control (Leary 1970: 112). After he was defeated, many of his followers settled in the area. The Wolof Ibrahima N'Diaye (also spelled Birahim N'Diaye) went deeply into Jola territory. N'Diaye attacked the villages of Tobor (1887) and Unionk (1884) in the Kalunay region (part III). He also pillaged Jinaki (Djinaki) in 1886, some 25 km. from Jipalom. For fifteen years, he ravaged the regions of the Kombo and Foñi. His slave-raiding operations put a temporary end to the groundnut and rubber trades.

8. In Senegal, the main propagator of the Qadiriyya faith at the end of the nineteenth century was Cheik Bou Kounta, born in Cayor, in Wolof country. The *cheik* could neither read nor write Arabic, but he had the reputation as a *thaumaturge* or worker of miracles. He made water spring out in Nidiassene (near Tivaouane, north of Dakar), where he settled in 1885. This is now the capital of the brotherhood. When Islam first took hold in Senegal, the Qadiriyya was the dominant brotherhood. Since then, however, it has been losing adepts to Tijanism and the Murid movement. Nonetheless, the Qadiriyya is still dominant in Casamance, thanks to the activities of Chérif Younous who in 1910 established the village of Banghere as a center from where other sub-branches of the Qadiriyya could spread. From the 1970s to the mid 1980s, when his fortunes waned, the town of Sindian in the Kajamutay, not far from

Jipalom, was the seat of a colorful personage, Cheik Ousmane Sountou Badji, who was a particularly active Qadiriyya proselytizer (Magassouba 1985: 56).
9. Groundnuts (*Arachis hypogaea*) are a lowland South American crop (Pickersgill and Heiser 1977). They were brought into West Africa, as early perhaps as the sixteenth century, by the Portuguese, probably via Brazil. In the Gambia and Casamance regions groundnuts were adopted relatively late. Prior to 1830s, groundnut cultivation in the Gambia and Casamance regions was negligible (Brooks 1975). After this date, Gambia took the lead in producing and exporting groundnuts to Britain. In England, as well as later on the United States and France, the oil and fat were used to manufacture soap and candles. They may also have substituted for olive oil in some places.
10. In and around the *comptoir* (trading house) of Sedhiou in Middle Casamance, groundnuts were initially cultivated mostly by the Sarakole, a Mande group related to the Manding who migrated to Sedhiou every season from the region of Bakel, in the Senegal River (Roche 1976: 120). Once introduced, groundnuts took no time at all to spread to the rest of the Middle Casamance population, in its large majority Manding. By the 1910s, this cash crop covered a large surface of the Middle and Upper Casamance regions, but a large part of the harvest was sold in Gambia. In 1904, groundnuts had also begun to be grown in Lower Casamance near Oussouye (Roche, 1976: 319–320). Between 1905 and 1910, groundnut seed was distributed, "*sans grand resultat*" (without much success) from the European posts of Karaban (Carabane island) and Oussouye (Pélissier 1966: 780). All the Kujamaat Jola I have ever asked reported that they learned to grow groundnuts from the Manding. Mark (1985: 103–104) also remarks that the inhabitants of Tionk Essil in the Buluf say the same thing. But there is still a possibility – albeit slight – that groundnuts spread to the Jola north of the River from Oussouye and Karaban.

4 The impact on social and productive relations
1. The history of Jipalom's resident adult population between 1965, when I made the first census, and 1981, the date of my last census is as follows. In this sixteen-year period, the initial male married population had lost 33 members due to absence or death. Although in this same period 45 young men had married and founded new conjugal family units, only 26 had stayed to live in the village. This means, then, that the resident male married population of Jipalom is not replacing itself. Information on total fertility and mortality rates also show the population to be stagnant, declining, or emigrating.

The "natural" growth of Jipalom's population is also negative, or at least less positive than often-quoted figures make it appear to be. A random sample I took of 24 women past child-bearing age revealed that fertility was high, but so was child mortality. Though small, the sample represented 17 percent of the village in-married female population.

Despite an overall total fertility rate (mean number of live births) of 8.33, nearly half (0.49) of all children born died, many before age three. Thus the average number of live offspring per woman at the end of her reproductive cycle was 4.25. This represents a moderate population growth, at least in comparison with a high fertility rate. Mortality rates are also high for adults (more than 20

per 1,000 per year). These rates, combined with out-migration, put a continuous stress on the supply of labor available for agriculture. It has been calculated (Berger report, 1981: table 8.6) that, in Upper Baila, 33.4 percent of all women, and 32.5 percent of all male students and workers in the age-group 11–35, migrate out of the Baila area during the dry season.
2. At that time, the younger married women had to bring in an experienced Fulani woman all the way from Bulok, in the Gambia, to perform the operation. She charged them a handsome sum. Twenty years later, in 1985, the operation was being performed by an *aseek* or in-married woman from the Bojas ward of Jipalom. Her skills ran in the family; she was one of four sisters who knew how to *eñak*. Held every few years, the *eñakey* is a moderate form of excision. It involves removal of the labia minora, with a two to three week stay in the forest.

5 Ideology and legitimation

1. Thus, Cadamosto (in Crone 1937: 67), during his second voyage to the Gambia River in 1456, was informed about a "principal lord" Farosangoli who was "subject to the Emperor of Melli [Mali], the great Emperor of the Blacks." Farosangoli lived nine to ten days' journey to the south-east. According to Brooks (1980b: 16), this would place him in the upper Geba river in Guiné Bissau. In the Gambian river itself, Cadamosto visited a "lesser lord," Batimaussa [Batimansa], who lived about 60 miles upriver. The same person had been visited by Diogo Gomes (in Monod *et al.* 1959) shortly before. Teixeira da Mota (1972: 199) places Batimansa's "domain" along the Bintang *marigot*. It should be noted that *mansa* is the Manding word for an important and rich man, such as a "ruler" or "king." Hence, when Cadamosto sailed south, he encountered "the river of a negro chief named Casamansa [*mansa* again], who dwelt about thirty miles upriver, but this chief was not to be found there, having gone to war against another" (Crone 1937: 75). This would place "lord" Casamansa – who could have been Kassanga, and hence a Bañuñ, or a Manding, or a son of a Bañuñ woman and a Manding father (Brooks 1980b: 27) – at about the entrance to the Soungrougrou river. In addition to Bautimassa (see above), Diogo Gomes (in Monod *et al.* 1959: 32) also talks about the Rio Francasso, which is the actual Geba river, where he trades with the inhabitants (he calls them *mouros*, i.e. moors). Again, according to Teixeira da Mota (1972: 188) these *mouros* were Manding or "Mandingized" Biafadas.
2. Valentim Fernandes (1506–1510) talks once more about the "Casamansa" kingdom, located 18 leagues (*ca.* 108 km) from the mouth of the Casamance River, and under the rule of a Manding "king." Pacheco Pereira (1506–1508) says of the Gambian groups that all spoke Manding and were Muslims. Further south, the Geba region was inhabited by Guogolis (Cocolis or Landumas) and Beafares (or Biafada), all of who were said to be subjects of the king of the Manding. In 1594, Almada (in Brásio 1964: 70) described a chain of command whereby the Casamance "king" obeyed a Farim further upstream, and this one in turn obeyed another until they reached the Mandimansa who was "the emperor of all blacks."
3. Could it be, he asks, that: "Over centuries of what may have been substantial commercial contact with Mandinka people from the Western Sudan (some or

even most of whom may have themselves adopted their ethnic identity) and of political influence from the strong Mandinka polities on the upper Niger, the Senegambian Mandinka adopted as their own the Mandinka language, Mandinka political system, and many aspects of Mandinka culture" (Wright 1985: 341). Mark (1985: 63) also agrees that: "The history of the northern Diola also appear to conform to Wright's thesis." But he was talking mainly about the process of "forced adoption" – i.e. elders making captives of persons who could not pay fines – as a means to "achieve the ethnic transferral and cultural assimilation that Wright describes." I am more concerned with asymmetrical power relations, uneasy coexistence and subtle forms of religiously defined identity shifts.
4. In the generalized account of Manding social organization that follows, I have relied on the descriptions about the Gambian Malinké by Weil (1971, 1981) and Dey (n.d.), both social anthropologists. The area where Weil has worked (and also Haswell 1963, 1981) is in the Lower River Division, in the Kiang district of the Gambia. The village studied by Dey is further east, in the MacCarthy Island Division. For the Middle Casamance, I have used the descriptions by Schaffer and Cooper (1980), who are also anthropologists. On the Manding of Guiné Bissau there is a general discussion by Carreira (1947), but it is too general to serve our purposes here.
5. During the short time between two of my sundry trips (1977 and 1981), the adult village population had grown in this fashion: 5 adult married men had gone away or died, 8 young men had married and settled down, and 5 new immigrants had arrived with their families.
6. In order to grasp the extent to which the recently Islamized Jola conformed to the practices predicated by the orthodox and the knowing, I interviewed selected persons for their views on correct Muslim behavior. To this end, I designed a questionnaire based on Guèye's (1977) remarkable guide to the practices allowed or prohibited by the Koran.
7. The tradition "of direct descent from founder–settler ancestors" claiming paramount rights over land goes back to at least the seventeenth century, and was a structure of pre-Islamic "animist" Manding society (Quinn 1972: 17).
8. Table IIIa lists the combination of CFU's living under the same roof. It indicates that 30 out of 49 (or 61 percent) CFUs are complex, involving more than one conjugal family unit. In the same year (1981), there was not a single instance of two co-residing CFUs in Sambujat, and only one in the (albeit small) Jipalom ward where I lived (though there were a few more complex units in 1965). As might be expected, more Fatiya founders (13 out of 15, or 87 percent) live in complex, co-residing units, than do immigrants (23 out of 35, or 66 percent). The chief of the village, with his 5 wives, lives in a huge house which he shares with his 3 monogamously married sons, plus a brother's son and his wife, a wife's sister, an unmarried son and a friend, and several cultivators from the region of the Buluf.

6 Social relations of production re-structured
1. There are two kinds of school in Fatiya. The Koranic school, which charges students 200 CFA francs monthly, has 26 students, 5 of them girls. More girls

used to attend, but they were taken out during the years of drought to cut down on expenses.
2. The position of women in the male-dominated world of Fatiya is not, of course, a simple by-product of their having embraced Islam. It is true that Muslim women are considered to be unfitted for public duty. Although entitled to own property, women cannot dispose of it at will. Muslim law also encourages such practices as high bridewealth payments, divorcing a wife without giving justification, keeping women out of the mosque, and so forth (Levy 1957: 91–134). But the women of Jipalom are also Muslim, as are the Wolof and Sereer, and yet they enjoy a relatively high status. Again, it is important to separate Islam from the particular way it is practiced by the Manding, and by those they have influenced.
3. Among the Manding themselves, the boys' initiation takes place frequently, every three or four years, and is a fundamental aspect of the age–class system. Those who have been circumcised together are bound for the rest of their lives by obligations of mutual aid and reciprocity (Charest 1971). Within his own age class, a young Manding boy learns to perform agricultural work and, later on, to participate in collective work.
4. During the late sixties, it was common for some Fatiya men to produce two-and-a-half tons of groundnuts selling for 40,000 francs CFA (about 160 US dollars). A man could also produce up to 40 bundles of millet that he sold at 300 CFA each, for a total of 12,000 CFA (about 48 US dollars). However, during the height of the drought (1971–1974; 1979–1984), some men, in some years, did not grow groundnuts at all, keeping all the millet they produced for home consumption. For those years, the price of groundnuts had gone up, but production had fallen. In addition, in the 1980s, the price per bundle of millet had fallen by about 50 francs from its 1970s price, and with it had fallen the incentive to produce it. By 1981, the rice harvest was slightly up, but the millet, and also the sorghum, were in bad shape. Insects had eaten a good deal of the crop; called "flower abortion," small insects eat the sap at the flowering stage and the seeds fail to develop (J. Posner, personal communication). Thus, when the rains are all right, the insects are out. And when the prices are up, production is down, or the reverse.
5. Not surprisingly, the Manding of Upper Casamance also share a concept based on marriage between hamlets which they refer to by the term *sanao* (Schaffer and Cooper 1980: 50). The same term is also used for cross-cousin as well as for a partner in a joking relationship. It carries the general connotation of alliance between hamlets in the same or different villages.
6. The following example will illustrate how this actually works out in practice:

Abdulai, the chief of Fatiya, comes from the House called Balok. He has five married children, three daughters and two sons. The two sons married their extended patrilateral cross-cousins: they married sisters from the same *fank* in Jitikubon, where the boys' father's father had given a sister; in diagrammatic form, the boys had married their FFZSD. The first of Abdulai's daughters, a girl named Kadi, married her father's brother's wife's brother's son (FBWBS), who came from the village of Kulai, from the House called Bamak. Thus, Kadi married into the same House which two generations before had given a woman in marriage to Balok. The second of Abdulai's daughters, Kaamba, married the brother's son of her father's wife (FWBS). Again, she married an affine born to a House that in the previous generations had donated a wife to her own father. Now, if we take a look at chief Abdulai himself, we see that two of his wives were classificatory sisters, for they had the same father's father. In addition, Abdulai's brother Dauda had married a wife called Janga; Janga's brother, in turn, had married Dauda's sister. This, then, was an example of sister exchange.

7. This can be actual sister exchange as in the case of Dauda, sisters marrying brothers as in the case of Abdulai, taking a wife where a man's father, or a close agnate of his, gave a sister (hence FZD marriage), as in the case of the chief's two sons, or marriage to a removed matrilateral kin (a *kasalanken*), as in the case of the chief's two daughters, Kadi and Kamba. Obviously, the husbands of these two girls were marrying their classificatory patrilateral cross-cousin, that is they were marrying women who stood in the relationship of father's sister's classificatory daughters.

Epilogue
1. In 1974–75, the whole of the Casamance had 15 percent of its population involved in migratory processes. Using data on Lower Casamance migrants coming from four villages, de Jonge *et al.* (1978) attempted to determine who the migrants were and what their departure implied for the agricultural system. Like other researchers before them (van Loo and Star 1973; Journet 1976), they found that the bulk of the migrants were either young unmarried Jola women working as domestics in Dakar, or young bachelor men in the 15–29 age bracket attending schools in town. Their migration was seasonal; both groups were expected to go back to their natal villages to help with agricultural work during the rainy season. In reality, however, not everyone did so. Within the region of Oussouye alone, 23 percent of the girls who were away in 1975 returned too late and went back too early; a few did not return at all. As a consequence, the area of rice fields that was regularly transplanted had to be decreased by at least 14 percent (de Jonge *et al.* 1978: 16).
2. In fact, European missionary efforts have had a long history in the Pte. St. Georges–Esudadu area (Baum 1990). As far back as 1880, members of the Congregation de Saint-Esprit had established a mission in the nearby island of Karabane. It became the spearpoint of missionary efforts in the area. By the first decades of the twentieth century, a fairly sizeable mission was functioning in a nearby Esudadu community. It was there in 1964, under the new leadership of Spanish priests; and there were several Jola cathecists among them. However, the residents of Sambujat had continued to resist all missionary efforts. A chapel which had been built years before layed abandoned. The elders with their shrines were in full control. And in the two decades that followed there were no noticeable changes.
3. The road was built thanks to the efforts of a Jola *Ministre*, who comes from the area. It is maintained in good condition by being barred to traffic after particularly heavy rains.
4. The *garderie* or nursery was built thanks to the efforts of a member of the Baptist mission in Bignona. "Robeer" (as he is called) has done a great deal for the community. Jipalom's women take turns overseeing the children and cooking for them the regular food supplies that "Robeer" brings. This means that most mothers can go to work in the fields without worrying about their

small children. The children must be weaned and walking before they are admitted.
5. As "Robeer's" assistant, she rides around in a *mobilette*, weighing the children of several villages, reporting to him on their nutritional state.
6. The male-nurse is a Jola from the Kasa area south of the Casamance River. He charges 25 francs CFA (less than US $0.10) for treating the children, and twice that to adults. He seems to be doing an excellent job.
7. The tractor that was hired in July, 1989, to do the women's rice fields was run by a Japanese mission, who came to the area in 1986. It charged 1.7 francs CFA a square meter (300 CFA francs equal one US dollar in 1989), compared with 2.05 francs charged for the tractor belonging to DERBAC, the Senegalese government agency that replaced PIDAC. Almost half of all Fatiya's women had at least one of their fields prepared by the tractor. For example, the wives of M. regularly worked six fields together, lent to their husband by several of the village founders. Each wife had one large field prepared by tractor. Two others were prepared by an ox-plough which one of the wives' father lent M. The remaining two fields were hand-hoed by the wives themselves, with the help of a *fusaleŋaf* (a group of women who help each other for free). No man paid for the tractor to do all the fields that his wives cultivated, however. Even if he could afford it, the tractor stayed only four days before it had to move on to another village. Hence, the aim was to prepare at least a portion of all the Fatiya's women's fields, to relieve them somewhat from the heaviest work.
8. "During the era of colonial conquest, they [the brotherhoods] represented a *contre société* resisting the implantation of alien forces" (Fatton 1987: 97). Some maraboutic colonies even offered asylum to individuals who refused to serve in the French army, or to follow the instructions of a *chef de canton*, or a *commandant du cercle* (Coulon 1983: 30). In short, as Coulon has shown, the marabouts served as deterrents to the exercise of tyrannical power by the colonial authorities. However, this did not prevent them from becoming very much involved in the colonial economy. "Once colonialism firmly established its roots, however, they [the marabouts] accommodated themselves to the colonial authorities and eventually became powerful economic and political forces" (Fatton 1987: 97). (See also Harrison 1988, Robinson 1988.)
9. Schumacher (1975: 4–5) puts the matter thusly:

> Concentrated in the densely populated peanut-growing zone of central and western Senegal, maraboutic families grew increasingly wealthy and powerful under the colonial regime. Religious leaders assumed social and political roles previously held by traditional chiefs and aristocrats. They acquired land tenure prerogatives over huge areas newly introduced to cash farming and became active entrepreneurs in commercial networks. Marabouts also benefited from gifts, subsidies, loans, and other forms of aid provided by French colonial officials in exchange for their assistance in the collection of taxes, labor and military recruitment, the maintenance of order, and the promotion of peanut cultivation.

10. Gellar (1982: 46) has noted, however, that, despite their owning large estates, the marabouts of Senegal control less than 1 percent of the farmland. The large majority of Senegal's farms are small and worked by family labor.
11. The price was raised from 23.10 francs CFA per kilo in 1973, to 43 francs CFA per kilo in 1974–1975.

12. Thus, Senegal is a country where groundnut production has always been associated with national political power, maraboutic influence and dependence upon metropolitan France:

> For the State, maraboutic Islam has for a long time functioned, and still does so to a large extent, as an *ideological apparatus* enabling the cultivation of groundnuts at little cost and organizing an original political order, based on an indirect administration, a veritable security valve for the ruling class (Coulon 1981: 297).

In every corner of Senegal, marabouts have played a predominant role in pushing groundnut production among their *talibés* or disciples. The government, in turn, has given important concessions to the marabouts in the form of land grants, subsidies for the construction of Mosques, facilities to obtain government loans and jobs for their followers. The marabouts have also received special treatment from government-run development agencies and, most important, higher prices for their groundnut crop (Gellar 1982). This has meant that they have acquired an independent financial base in the form of sometimes extensive landholdings which they could develop into prosperous groundnut farms, thanks to contributions in cash and labor from their congregations.

13. According to Fatton (1987: 91–121), patron–client relationships involve the unequal exchange of resources between patron and client on an individualized basis. These relationships are grounded in values and behaviors emphasizing paternalism, resource control and divine authority on one side, dependence, submission and exploitation on the other side. Through their claim to divine powers and virtues, the marabouts extract allegiance, devotion and service from their *talibés* in exchange for organizational skills, material assistance and political protection. However, not everyone would subscribe to Fatton's opinion that in Senegal patron–client relationships support class rule and reinforce "existing structures of wealth and privilege." Cruise O'Brien (1975), for example, has argued that even the Murid brotherhood provides a measure of "relative social advancement" and "economic emancipation" to disadvantaged Wolof farmers.

14. Not long after this date, Senegal's rulers were pressured into seeking complete independence from France. They achieved it by 1960, in federation with Mali (Gellar 1982: 20–21). Lasting less than five months, the Mali federation broke apart, and Senegal became a constitutional nation under the presidency of the well-known figure of M. Léopold Senghor, a Serer and a Catholic. For the 20 years that Senghor was in power (1960–1980), he enjoyed the full support of the heads of the major Muslim brotherhoods, who constituted "the most influential group in the country, largely because of their hold over their mass following" (Gellar 1982: 34).

15. In 1976 the Constitution was modified to allow for the existence of three parties representing different ideological positions. In the same year, the UPS or government party was re-named the PS (Parti Socialiste). In January 1982, Léopold Sédar Senghor stepped down voluntarily and M. Abdou Diouf, his Prime Minister and head of the PS became president. With him a multiparty democracy became firmly installed in Senegal. Today, there are seventeen political parties, represented at the national assembly among its 120 deputies,

six opposition newspapers, and a lively if increasingly acrimonious debate over the role of Islam in a secular state.

16. "For the PDS, African countries are rich in manpower, and poor in capital; from the beginning, and as long as national funds are weak, they should choose an economic policy favoring manpower in order to avoid increasing their dependence upon foreign owners of capital" (Nzouankeu 1984: 62–63).

17. On the 6th of December 1983, the police tried to interrupt a demonstration by the *indépendantistes*. The army was called in. At least three *gendarmes* were killed and a number of persons wounded. On December 14, 1983, the *Cour de Sûreté de l'Etat* delivered what was seen as a harsh sentence against the so-called *séparatistes* accused of attempting against the security of the State (nine condemned to 5 years in prison, ten to 3 years, thirteen to 2 years). A few days later, violence again erupted, worse than ever.

18. The number of casualties estimated varies greatly, from the official figure of 19 dead and 80 wounded, to estimates putting the death toll at more than 100 (Geschieri and Van der Klei 1987).

19. For example, following another clandestine meeting of the MFDC in October of 1986, which took place in the Jola village of Thionk-Essil (Conk-Esil), the police made 152 arrests; over half of those arrested were put into provisional liberty a few months later (*Le Monde*, April 11, 1987, p. 4). New arrests were made at the beginning of 1987 and 1988, and again in April 1989. An *Amnesty International Report* of May 23, 1990 entitled "La Torture au Sénégal: le Cas de la Casamance" discusses in detail some of the treatment these prisoners received. The report was made public by the opposition weeklies (*SOPI*, No. 135, June 1, 1990; *Wal Fadjri*, No. 213, June 1–7, 1990), which are allowed to circulate widely without censorship. See also the pro-government weekly *Carrefour Républicain* No. 41, May–June, 1990, p. 5. A second Amnesty report came out in January 1991.

20. The MFDC was created in 1947 by "Casamance nationalistes." It joined the BDS led by President Senghor the year after, and it disappeared from view after Independence, to surface again in 1982 with a pamphlet advocating the cessation of Casamance from the Senegalese nation (see *Amnesty International*, 1990: 3). Some writers see the MFDC and the events of 1982–1983 as indicating a clash within Islamicized Jola villages between the elders, who are the traditional politico-religious leaders and the new Muslim leaders (Glaise, 1990). I see little foundation for this view. There are few "animist" elders left in Jola Muslim villages and those that are still alive have very little religious power left.

21. This time the violence was set off by the death in the first week of May of a young Jola man near Kouring, south of Nyassa, presumed to be a member of the MFDC, and presumably assassinated by the forces of order. All through May, while I was in Basse Casamance doing research on Jola migrants, there were bomb and grenade attacks on a customs house, a *sous-préfecture*, a *gendarmerie*, and public places in Bignona and Ziguinchor. The result was several dead and numbers wounded. In addition, two Wolof *instituteurs* (teachers) were attacked in two villages in the Dept. of Niaguis, where they had been posted, and one was killed, setting off a flight of all rural non-Jola teachers into Ziguinchor for protection. As a response to the situation, the civil governor of

Casamance was replaced early on in June by a *Générale de Brigade* who once served as commander in chief of the southern military zone.
22. The detainees, who were amnestied by presidential decree, were released on May 27, 1991. This, and the peace treaty signed in Bissau four days later, followed months of negotiations in which the *députés* from Casamance played an important mediatory role. According to M. A. Camara of the Senegalese weekly, the *Sud-Hebdo*: the peace treaty creates the proper climate "to find a statute for the Casamance intermediate between the present situation, which is at the root of the present problems, and independence, which is neither in the interest of Senegal nor in the interest of the Casamance" (extracted from *Sub-Hebdo* in *Libertitres: Selection de la Presse Africaine*, Paris, No. 4, p. 4, July–August 1991; my translation).
23. Despite being accused of "*dirigisme excessive*," government agents involved in rural "development" schemes have failed to engage the rural population directly in the development process (Sy 1988). Aware of this situation, the Senegalese government in 1984 launched the Nouvelle Politique Agricole (the NPA) with the aim of increasing the farmers' control of their own future, while at the same time decreasing State interference in rural affairs.

References

Abélès, M. and Chantal Collard. 1985. *Age, Pouvoir et Société en Afrique Noire.* Editions Karthala, Paris.
Almada, André Álvares de. 1594. *Tratado Breve dos Rios de Guiné do Cabo Verde,* António Brásio, ed. Editorial LIAM (1964), Lisboa.
Augé, Marc, 1977. *Pouvoirs de Vie, Pouvoirs de Mort.* Flammarion, Paris.
Badiane, A. D. and J. L. Doneaux. n.d. Document de travail pour un Syllabaire Jola. Délégation Générale à la Promotion Humaine, Dakar.
Barnes, J. A. 1962. "African Models in the New Guinea Highlands," *Man* 62(2): 5–9.
Barry, Boubacar. 1981. "Economic Anthropology of Precolonial Senegambia from the Fifteenth Through the Ninteenth Centuries," in L. G. Colvin, *et al., The Uprooted of the Western Sahel. Migrants' Quest for Cash in the Senegambia,* pp. 27–57. Praeger Scientific, New York.
Barth, Frederick (ed.). 1969. *Ethnic Groups and Boundaries.* Little, Brown and Co., Boston.
Bates, Robert H. 1983. *Essays on the Political Economy of Rural Africa.* Cambridge University Press, Cambridge.
Baum, Robert M. 1987. A Religious and Social History of the Diola-Esulalu in Pre-Colonial Senegambia. PhD Dissertation, Dept. of History, Yale University. University Microfilms International, Ann Arbor.
1990. "The Emergence of a Diola Christianity," *Africa* 60(3): 370–398.
Beattie, J. H. M. 1980. "On understanding sacrifice," in M. F. C. Bourdillon and M. Fortes, eds., *Sacrifice.* Academic Press, London and New York, pp. 29–44.
Bérenger-Féraud, L.-J.-B. 1879. "Les Mandingues," in Leroux, E., ed., *Les Peuplades de la Sénégambie. Histôire-Ethnographie-Moeurs et Coutumes, Legendes, etc.,* Chapter 5, pp. 199–228. Libraire de la Société Asiatique, Paris.
Berry, Sara. 1968. "Christianity and the Rise of Cocoa-Growing in Ibadan and Ondo." *Journal of the Historical Society of Nigeria,* 4(3): 439–451.
Bertrand-Bocandé, M. 1856. "Carabane et Sedhiou: Des Réssources que Présentent dans leur Etat Actuel les Comptoirs Français sur les Bords de la Casamance," *Revue Coloniale,* Série 2e., pp. 398–421.

Bledsoe, Caroline H. 1980. *Women and Marriage in Kpelle Society.* Stanford University Press, Stanford.
Boserup, Esther. 1965. *The Conditions of Agricultural Growth: The Economics of Agrarian Change under Population Pressure.* Aldine Publishing Co., Chicago.
— 1970. *Women's Role in Economic Development.* St. Martin Press, New York.
Bourdieu, Pierre. 1977. *Outline of a Theory of Practice.* Cambridge: Cambridge University Press.
— 1980. *Le Sens Pratique.* Paris: Les Éditions de Minuit.
Bradburd, Daniel A. 1983. "National Conditions and Local-Level Political Structures: Patronage in Prerevolutionary Iran." *American Ethnologist* 10(1): 23–40.
Brásio, António (ed.). 1964. *Tratado Breve dos Rios de Guiné do Cabo Verde,* by André Álvares de Almada, 1594. Editorial LIAM, Lisbon.
Bray, Francesca. 1986. *The Rice Economies: Technology and Development in Asian Societies.* Oxford: Basil Blackwell.
Brooks, George E. 1975. "Peanuts and Colonialism: Consequences of the Commercialization of Peanuts in West Africa, 1830–1870," *Journal of African History* 16(1): 29–54.
— 1980a. "Perspectives on Luso-African Commerce and Settlement in the Gambia and Guinea-Bissau Region, 16th–19th Centuries." Working Paper No. 24, Boston University, African Studies Center.
— 1980b. "Kola Trade and State-Building: Upper Guinea Coast and Senegambia, 15th–17th Centuries." Working Paper No. 38, Boston University, African Studies Center.
Brown, Judith. 1970. "A note on the division of labor by sex". *American Anthropologist* 72: 1073–1078.
Bulletin de la Congrégation de Saint-Esprit; archives de la Congrégation; Tomes XII (1880–1882), XIII (1883–1886), XIV (1887–1888), XVI (1891–1893), XXVI (1911–1912), XXX (1921–1922). Paris.
Burnham, Philip. 1980. *Opportunity and Constraint in a Savanna Society: The Gbaya of Meiganga, Cameroon.* Academic Press, New York and London.
Burton, Michael L. and D. R. White. 1984. "Sexual Division of Labor in Agriculture", *American Anthropologist* 86: 568–583.
Cadamosto, Alvise. 1455–1456. (see G. R. Crone 1937).
Camara, Sory. 1976. *Gens de la Parole. Essai sur la Condition et le Rôle des Griots dans la Société Malinké.* Mouton, Paris and La Haye.
Carreira, António. 1947. *Mandingas da Guiné Portuguesa,* Centro de Estudos da Guiné Portuguesa, No. 4, Publição Comemorativa do V Centenário da Descoberta da Guiné.
Charest, Paul. 1971. "Les Classes d'Age chez les Malinké Animistes de Kédougou (Sénégal Oriental)," in D. Paulme, ed., *Classes et Associations d'Age en Afrique de l'Ouest,* pp. 131–156, Recherches en Sciences Humaines, No. 35. Librairie Plon, Paris.
Cheneau-Loquay, Annie. 1988. "Les Relations entre l'Espace et l'Énergie en Casamance. In *Énergie et Espace au Sénégal.* Ph. Grenier and Cheneau-Loquay, eds., tome 2, pp. 109–243. Travaux et Documents de Géographie Tropicale, No. 62. CEGET-CNRS, Bordeaux.

Clammer, John. 1985. *Anthropology and Political Economy: Theoretical and Asian Perspectives*. London: The Macmillan Press Ltd.

Cleave, John H. 1974. *African Farmers: Labor Use in the Development of Smallholder Agriculture*. New York: Praeger Publishers.

Coelho, Francisco de Lemos. 1669. *Duas Descrições Seiscentistas da Guiné*. In Peres, Damião, ed. Manuscritos Inéditos Publicados. Lisboa 1953.

Cohen, Abner. 1969. *Custom and Politics in Urban Africa: A Study of Hausa Migrants in Yoruba Towns*. Berkeley and Los Angeles: University of California Press.

Comaroff, John L. 1980. "Introduction," in J. L. Comaroff, ed., *The Meaning of Marriage Payments*, pp. 1–47. Academic Press, London and New York.

Comaroff, Jean. 1985. *Body of Power, Spirit of Resistance: The Culture and History of a South African People*. Chicago: The University of Chicago Press.

Conseil National des Femmes Noires Americaines, 1983. "Les Femmes Migrantes Casamançaises à Dakar," Vol. No. 3, US Agency for International Development, Report No. 3. Dakar.

Copans, Jean. 1980. *Les Marabouts de l'Arachide: la Confrérie Mouride et les Paysans du Sénégal*. Le Sycomore, Paris.

Coulon, Christian. 1981. *Le Marabout et le Prince. (Islam et Pouvoir au Sénégal)*, Centre d'Étude d'Afrique Noire, Série Afrique Noire No. 11. Editions A. Pedone, Paris.

1983. *Les Musulmans et le Pouvoir en Afrique Noire*. Éditions Karthala, Paris.

1984. "Sénégal." In Decraene, P. ed. *Contestations en Pays Islamiques*, pp. 63–88. Paris: Centre National de la Recherche Scientifique (CNRS). Cheam.

Crone, G. R. (tr.). 1937. *The Voyages of Cadamosto and other Documents on Western Africa in the Second Half of the Fifteenth Century*, by Alvise Cadamosto, 1455–1456. Hakluyt Society, London.

Cruise O'Brien, Donald B. 1971. *The Mourides of Senegal*. Clarendon Press, Oxford.

1975. *Saints and Politicians*. Cambridge University Press, Cambridge.

1979. "Ruling Class and Peasantry in Senegal, 1960–1976: The Politics of a Monocrop Economy," in D. B. Cruise O'Brien, ed., *The Political Economy of Underdevelopment: Dependence in Senegal*, pp. 209–227. Sage Publications, Beverly Hills and London.

Cultru, P. (ed.). 1913. *Premier Voyage du Sieur de La Courbe, Fait à la Côte d'Afrique en 1685*, by Sieur Jajolet de la Courbe, 1685. Édouard Champion and Émile Larose, Société de l'Histoire des Colonies Françaises, Paris.

Curtin, Philip. 1975. *Economic Change in Precolonial Africa: Senegal in the Era of the Slave Trade*, 2 vols. Madison: the University of Wisconsin Press.

Dalby, David. 1971. "Distribution and Nomenclature of the Manding People and their Language," in C. T. Hodge, ed., *Papers on the Manding*. Indiana University Publications, African Series, Vol. 3, pp. 1–13. Mouton and Co., The Hague.

Darbon, D. 1984. "Le Culturalisme Bas-Casamançais," *Politique Africaine* 14: 125–128.

Decraene, Philippe. 1985. *Le Sénégal*. Presses Universitaires de France, Paris.

de Jonge, Klaas, J. van der Klei, H. Meilink, and R. Storm. 1978. *Les Migrations en Basse Casamance*. Rapport Final, Afrika Studiecentrum, Leiden.

Dey, Jennie. 1981. "The Socio-Economic Organisation of Farming in the Gambia and its Relevance for Agricultural Development Planning," Overseas Development Institute: *Agricultural Administration Networks Papers* 7: 1–42. London.
  1983. (Ms.) The Social Organization of Production, Annex C. in Dey, J., The Rice Industry of the Gambia, Food and Agricultural Organization, Rome.
Diop, Abdoulaye-Bara. 1981. *La Société Wolof. Tradition et Changement. Les Systèmes d'Inégalité et de Domination*. Éditions Karthala, Paris.
Direction de la Statistique. 1972. *Répertoire des Villages*. Dakar, Sénégal.
Doneaux, Jean L. 1975. "Hypothèses pour la comparative des Langues Atlantiques." In *Annales du Musée Royal de l'Afrique Centrale*, Sciences Humaines No. 88, pp. 43–129. Tervuren: Belgium.
Donelha, André. 1625. *Descrição da Serra Leoa e dos Rios de Guiné do Cabo Verde*. A. Teixeira da Mota, ed. Notes and English Translation by P. E. H. Hair, Centro de Estudos de Cartografiá Antiga, no. 19. Lisbon.
Donham, Donald L. 1981. "Beyond the Domestic Mode of Production," *Man* 16: 515–541.
  1985. "Culture, Contradictions et Histoire: Analyse des Anciens Mallé (Ethiopie)," in Abélès and Collard, eds., *Age, Pouvoir et Société en Afrique Noire*, pp. 19–38. Éditions Karthala, Paris.
Durkheim, Emile 1984. *The Division of Labour in Society*, with an introduction by Lewis Coser. MacMillan Publishers Ltd., London.
Eisenstadt, S. N. and L. Roniger. 1984. *Patrons, Clients and Friends: Interpersonal Relations and the Structure of Trust in Society*. Cambridge: Cambridge University Press.
Epstein, A. L. 1978. *Ethos and Identity: Three Studies in Ethnicity*. Tavistock Publications, London.
Ewane, Michel L. 1985. "Le Montée du Discours Fondamentaliste Musulman au Sénégal," *Le Monde Diplomatique*, April 1985: 15.
Fatton Jr., Robert. 1986. "Clientism and Patronage in Senegal." *The African Studies Review* 29(4): 61–78.
  1987. *The Making of a Liberal Democracy: Senegal's Passive Revolution, 1975–1985*. Lynne Rienner Publishers, Inc., Boulder.
Fernandes, Valentim. 1506–1510. *Description de la Côte Occidentale d'Afrique (Sénégal au Cap de Monte, Archipels)*, ed. by Th. Monod, A. Teixeira da Mota et R. Mauny. Centro de Estudos da Guiné Portuguesa No. 11, (1951), Bissau.
  1506–1507. *Description de la Côte d'Afrique de Ceuta au Sénégal*, P. de Cenival and Th. Monod, eds., Librairie Larose (1938), Paris.
Fisher, Humphrey J. 1973. "Conversion Reconsidered: Some Historical Aspects of Religious Conversion in Black Africa," *Africa*, 43(1): 27–40.
  1985. "The Juggernaut's Apologia: Conversion to Islam in Black Africa." *Africa* 55(2): 153–173.
Fox, Robin. 1967. *Kinship and Marriage: an Anthropological Perspective*. Penguin Books Ltd., Middlesex, England.
Friedl, Ernestine. 1975. *Women and Men: An Anthropologist's View*. Holt, Rinehart and Winston, New York.
Gaudio Attilio, and R. Pelletier. 1980. *Femmes d'Islam ou le Sexe Interdit*. Éditions Denoël/Gonthier, Paris.

Geertz, Clifford. 1984. "Culture and Social Change: the Indonesian case." *Man* 19(4): 511–532.
Gellar, Sheldon. 1982. *Senegal: An African Nation Between Islam and the West.* Westview Press, Boulder.
Geschieri, Peter and J. Van der Klei. 1987. "La Relation État-paysans et ses Ambivalences: Mode Populaires d'Action Politique chez les Maka (Cameroun) et les Diola (Casamance)," in E. Terray, ed. *L'Etat Contemporain en Afrique.* Paris: Éditions L'Harmattan.
Giddens, Anthony. 1979. *Central Problems in Social Theory: Action, Structure and Contradiction in Social Analysis.* University of California Press, Berkeley.
  1981. *A Contemporary Critique of Historical Materialism.* Vol. I: *Power, Property and the State.* London: the MacMillan Press Ltd.
  1984. *The Constitution of Society. Outline of a Theory of Structuration.* The Polity Press, Cambridge.
Glaise, Joseph. 1990. "Casamance: la Contestation Continue." *Politique Africaine* 37: 83–89.
Godelier, Maurice. 1984. *L'idéel et le Matériel.* Librairie Arthème Fayard, Paris.
Gomes, Diogo. See Monod, Mauny and Duval, eds.
Goody, Jack. 1973. "Polygyny, Economy and the Role of Women," in Goody, J., ed., *The Character of Kinship,* pp. 175–190. Cambridge University Press, Cambridge.
  1976. *Production and Reproduction: a Comparative Study of the Domestic Domain.* Cambridge Studies in Social Anthropology No. 17. Cambridge University Press, Cambridge.
Gourou, Pierre, 1984. *Riz et Civilisation.* Fayard, Paris.
Grist, D. H. 1965. *Rice.* Longmans, London.
Guèye, Moustapha. 1977. *Le Droit Chemin dans la Pratique Islamique Parfaite.* Les Nouvelles Éditions Africaines, Dakar-Abidjan.
Guyer, Jane I. 1984a. "Naturalism in Models of African Production," *Man* 19(3): 371–388.
  1984b. *Family and Farm in Southern Cameroon.* African Research Studies No. 15. Boston University: African Studies Center.
Hamer, Alice. 1983. Tradition and Change: A Social History of Diola Women (Southwest Senegal) in the Twentieth Century. Ph.D. dissertation. University Microfilms International, Ann Arbor.
Harms, Robert. 1975. "The End of Red Rubber: a Reassessment," *Journal of African History* 16(1): 73–88.
Harrison, Cristopher. 1988. *France and Islam in West Africa, 1860–1960.* Cambridge University Press, Cambridge.
Hart, Keith. 1982. *The Political Economy of West African Agriculture.* Cambridge University Press, Cambridge.
Haswell, Margaret R. 1963. *The Changing Pattern of Economic Activity in a Gambia Village.* Department of Technical Co-Operation, Overseas Research Publication No. 2. Her Majesty's Stationary Office, London.
  1981. *Energy for Subsistence.* The MacMillan Press, London.
Hesseling, Gerti. 1985. *Histoire Politique du Sénégal.* Editions Karthala, Paris.
Horton, Robin. 1971. "African Conversion," *Africa* 41(2): 85–108.

1975a. "On the Rationality of Conversion, Part 1," *Africa*, 45(3): 219–235.
1975b. "On the Rationality of Conversion, Part 2," *Africa*, 45(4): 373–398.
Jajolot de la Courbe, Sieur. 1685. *Premier Voyage du Sieur de la Courbe fait à la Cote d'Afrique en 1685*, ed. by P. Cultru. Champion, Larose (1913), Paris.
Journet, Odile. 1976. "Rôles et statuts des femmes dans la société Diola (Basse Casamance)." Thèse du 3e. cycle. Lyon.
Keesing, Roger M. 1975. *Kin Groups and Social Structure*. Holt, Rinehart and Winston, New York.
Kertzer, David. 1988. *Ritual, Politics and Power*. New Haven: Yale University Press.
Kopytoff, Igor. 1971. "Ancestors as Elders in Africa," *Africa* 41(2): 129–142.
La Courbe, Sieur Jajolet de. 1913, see Jajolet de la Courbe, Sieur.
La Fontaine, J. S. 1978. *Sex and Age as Principles of Social Differentiation*. London: Academic Press.
1985. *Initiation*. Penguin Books, Middlesex, England.
Lancaster, Chet S. 1976. "Women, Horticulture and Society in Sub-Saharan Africa." *American Anthropologist*. 78(3): 539–564.
Lauer, Joseph J. 1969. Rice in the History of the Lower Gambia-Geba Area. Master's thesis. Department of History, University of Wisconsin, Madison.
Leary, Frances A. 1970. "Islam, Politics and Colonialism. A Political History of Islam in the Casamance Region of Senegal (1850–1914)." Ph.D. dissertation. Northwestern University, University Microfilms International, 1971. Ann Arbor.
1971. "The Role of the Mandinka in the Islamization of the Casamance, 1850–1901," in Carleton T. Hodge, ed., *Papers on the Manding*. Indiana University Publications, African Series, Vol. 3, pp. 227–248. Mouton and Co., The Hague.
Levy, Ruben. 1957. *The Social Structure of Islam*. Cambridge University Press, Cambridge.
Lewis, I. M. 1968. "Introduction," in Lewis, I. M., ed., *History and Social Anthropology*, pp. 9–28. Tavistock Publications, London and New York.
(ed.) 1980. (First published in 1966.) *Islam in Tropical Africa*. London: Hutchinson Library for Africa.
1986. *Religion in Context: Cults and Charisma*. Cambridge University Press, Cambridge.
Lewis, John van Dusen. 1979. "Descendants and Crops: two Poles of Production in a Malian Peasant Village." Ph.D. dissertation, Yale University, University Microfilms International, Ann Arbor.
1981. "Domestic Labor Intensity and the Incorporation of Malian Peasant Farmers into Localized Descent Groups," *American Ethnologist*, 8(1): 53–73.
Linares, Olga F. 1970. "Agriculture and Diola Society," in P. F. M. McLoughlin, ed., *African Food Production Systems: Cases and Theory*, pp. 195–227. The John Hopkins Press, Baltimore.
1971, "Shell middens of Lower Casamance and problems of Diola protohistory." *West African Journal of Archaeology* 1:23–54.
1981. "From Tidal Swamp to Inland Valley; on the Social Organization of Wet Rice Cultivation Among the Diola of Senegal," *Africa*, 51(2): 557–595.

1983. "Social, Spatial and Temporal Relations: Diola Villages in Archaeological Perspective," in E. Z. Vogt and R. M. Leventhal, eds., *Prehistoric Settlement Patterns*, pp. 129–163. University of New Mexico Press, Albuquerque, and Peabody Museum, Cambridge, Massachusetts.

1984. "Households among the Diola of Senegal: should Norms Enter by the Front or the Back Door," in R. Netting and R. Wilk, eds., *Household Changes in Space and Time*, pp. 407–445. University of California Press, Berkeley and Los Angeles.

1985. "Cash Crops and Gender Constructs: the Jola of Senegal," *Ethnology* 24: (2) 83–93.

1986. "Islamic 'Conversion' Reconsidered." *Cambridge Anthropology* 11(1): 4–19.

1987. "Deferring to Trade in Slaves: the Jola of Casamance in Historical Perspective," *History in Africa* 14: 113–139.

1988. "Kuseek and Kuriimen: Wives and Kinswomen in Jola Society." *Canadian Journal of African Studies* 22(3): 472–490.

In preparation. *Wet Rice in Dry Years: Drought and Social Change among the Jola of Casamance, Senegal.*

1990. "Natal versus conjugal households: the *Ebune* ritual among the Kujamaat Jola of Senegal." Paper presented at the 89th Annual Meeting of the American Anthropological Association. New Orleans, special session on Rituals and the Reproduction of Domestic Groups.

Long, Norman. 1968. *Social Change and the Individual: a Study of Social and Religious Responses to Innovations in a Zambian Rural Community*. Manchester: Manchester University Press.

Loquay, Annie. 1979. "Thionck-Essyl en Base – Casamance. Evolution Recente de la Gestion des Ressources Renouvelables." Thèse de Doctorat de 3e Cycle. Centre d'Etudes de Géographie Tropicale, Université de Bordeaux (see also Cheneau-Loquay).

Lowith, Karl. 1982. *Max Weber and Karl Marx*. George Allen and Unwin, London.

Magassouba, Moriba. 1985. *L'Islam au Sénégal: Domain des Mollahs?*. Paris: Éditions Karthala.

Mair, Lucy. 1962. *Primitive Government*. Indiana University Press, Bloomington and London.

Mark, Peter J. 1976. "Economic and Religious Change among the Diola of Boulouf (Casamance), 1890–1940: Trade, Cash Cropping and Islam in Southwest Senegal." Ph.D. dissertation, Department of History, Yale University. University Microfilms International, Ann Arbor.

1977. "The Rubber and Palm Produce Trades and the Islamization of the Diola of Boulouf (Casamance), 1890–1920," *Bulletin de l'I.F.A.N.*, Tome 39(2): 342–361.

1978. "Urban Migration, Cash Cropping, and Calamity: the Spread of Islam among the Diola of Boulouf (Senegal), 1900–1940," *African Studies Review* 21(2): 1–14.

1985. *A Cultural, Economic, and Religious History of the Basse Casamance since 1500.* Studien zur Kulturkunde, no. 78. Franz Steiner Verlag Wiesbaden GMBH, Stuttgart.

Martin, Susan. 1988. *Palm Oil and Protest: An Economic History of the Ngawa*

Region, South Eastern Nigeria 1800–1980. Cambridge: Cambridge University Press.

Marty, Paul. 1916. "Les Mandingues, Élément Islamisé de Casamance," *Revue du Monde Musulman*, 30: 443–468.

Marzouk Schmitz, Yasmine. 1981. "Stratégie et Aménegement Paysans – deux Eco-Types Humains en Basse Casamance à Partir des Monographies de Kamoubel et Niamdame," Mimeographed report for US Agency for International Development, p. 119. Dakar.

Meillassoux, Claude. 1964. *Anthropologie Economique des Gouro de Côte d'Ivoire.* Mouton and Co., Paris.

—— 1975. *Femmes, Greniers et Capitaux.* Librairie François Maspero, Paris.

—— 1981. *Maidens, Meal and Money: Capitalism and the Domestic Community.* Cambridge University Press, Cambridge, (Translation of Meillassoux, 1975).

Michaelson, Karen L. 1976. "Patronage, Mediators, and the Historical Context of Social Organization in Bombay." *American Ethnologist* 3(2): 281–295.

Michie, Barry H. 1981. "The Transformation of Agrarian Patron–Client Relations: Illustrations from India." *American Ethnologist* 8(1): 21–40.

Middleton, J. 1960. *Lugbara Religion: Ritual and Authority among an East African People.* London: Oxford University Press; Reprinted in 1985, Smithsonian Institution Press.

—— 1977. "Ritual and Ambiguity in Lugbara Society," in S. F. Moore and B. G. Myerhoff, eds., *Secular Ritual*, pp. 73–90. Van Gorcum, Amsterdam.

Monod, Th.A., Teixeira da Mota et R. Mauny (eds.) 1951. *Description de la Côte Occidentale d'Afrique (Sénégal au Cap de Monto, Archipels), by Valentim Fernandez, 1506–1510.* Centro de Estudos da Guiné Portuguesa No. 11, Bissau.

Monod, Th., R. Mauny and G. Duval (eds). 1959. *De la Première Découverte de la Guinée (1459–1460)*, by Diogo Gomes. Bissau: Centro de Estudos da Guiné Portuguesa. No. 21. Bissau.

Morris, Brian 1987. *Anthropological Studies of Religion: an Introductory Text.* Cambridge: Cambridge University Press.

Muller, Jean-Claude. 1985. "Initiation, Chefs et Aînés/Cadets chez de Rukuba du Nigeria Central." In Abélès et Collard (eds.) *Age Pouvoir et Société en Afrique Noire*, 131–148.

Netting, Robert McC. 1965. "Household Organization and Intensive Agriculture: the Kofyar Case." *Africa* 35(4): 422–429.

—— 1968. *Hill Farmers of Nigeria: Cultural Ecology of the Kofyar of the Jos Plateau.* Seattle and London: University of Washington Press.

Nzouankeu, Jacques M. 1984. *Les Partis Politiques Sénégalais.* Dakar: Éditions Claireafrique.

Oboler, Regina Smith. 1985. *Women, Power and Economic Change: the Nandi of Kenya.* Stanford University Press, Stanford.

Ortner, Sherry B. 1984. "Theory in Anthropology Since the Sixties," *Comparative Studies in Society and History*, 26(1): 126–166.

Pacheco Pereira, Duarte. 1506–1508. *Esmeraldo de Situ Orbis: Côte Occidentale d'Afrique du Sud Marocain au Gabon.* R. Mauny, ed., Centro de Estudos da Guiné Portuguesa No. 19, (1956), Bissau.

Parkin, David. 1972. *Palms, Wine and Witness: Public Spirit and Private Gain in an*

African Farming Community. San Francisco: Chandler Publishing Company.
Parkin, Frank. 1982. *Max Weber*. Chichester, Sussex: Ellis Horwood Ltd; London Tavistock Publications.
Pélissier, Paul. 1966. *Les Paysans du Sénégal. Les Civilisations Agraires du Cayor à la Casamance*. Imprimerie Fabrègue: Saint-Yrieix, France.
Pickersgill, B. and C. B. Heiser. 1977. "Origin and Distribution of Plants Domesticated in the New World Tropics," in Reed, Charles A., ed., *Origins of Agriculture*, pp. 803–835. Mouton, The Hague.
Portères, Roland. 1950. "Vieilles Agricultures de l'Afrique 'Intertropicale'." *Agronomie Tropicale*, 5(9–10): 489–507.
Quinn, Charlotte A. 1971. "Mandingo States in Nineteenth-Century Gambia," in C. T. Hodge, ed., *Papers on the Manding*. Indiana University Publications, vol. 3, pp. 205–225. Mouton and Co., The Hague.
  1972. *Mandingo Kingdoms of the Senegambia*. Northwestern University Press, Evanston.
Radcliffe-Brown, A. R. and Forde (eds.). 1950. *African Systems of Kinship and Marriage*. London: Oxford University Press.
Rapport d'Ensemble sur la Situation Politique, Administrative, Financière et Economique. 1900–1902. Gouvernement Général de l'Afrique Occidentale Française. Imprimerie du Gouvernement. St. Louis, Senegal.
Rapport Politique Annuel. 1915, 1925. Gouvernement Général de l'Afrique Occidental Français. Imprimerie du Gouvernement. St. Louis, Sénégal.
Ray, Benjamin C. 1976. *African Religions: Symbol, Ritual, and Community*. Prentice Hall, Englewood Cliffs, New Jersey.
Richards, Paul. 1983. "Ecological Change and the Politics of African Land Use," *The African Studies Review*, 26(2): 1–72.
  1984. "Spatial Organization as a Theme in African Studies." *Progress in Human Geography* 8(4): 551–561.
Robinson, David. 1988. "French 'Islamic' Politics and Practice in late nineteenth-century Senegal." *Journal of African History* 29(4): 415–435.
Roche, Christian. 1976. *Conquête et Résistance des Peuples de Casamance (1850–1920)*. Les Nouvelles Éditions Africaines, Dakar and Abidjan.
  1985. *Histoire de la Casamance. Conquête et Résistance: 1850–1920*. Éditions Karthala, Paris (Reprinted from the 1976 edition).
Rodney, Walter. 1970. *A History of the Upper Guinea Coast 1545–1800*. Oxford University Press, Oxford.
Rogers, Barbara, 1980. *The Domestication of Women. Discrimination in Developing Societies*. London and New York: Tavistock Publications.
Rueschemeyer, Dietrich. 1986. *Power and the Division of Labour*. Cambridge: Polity Press.
Runciman, W. G. (ed.) 1978. *Weber: Selections in Translation*. Cambridge: Cambridge University Press.
Sahlins, Marshall. 1972. *Stone Age Economics*. Aldine-Atherton, Inc., Chicago.
Sall, S., J. Posner, M. Kamuanga et al. 1985. *Recherches sur les Systèmes de Production en Basse-Casamance*. Rapport Annuel d'Activités, No. 2. Institut Sénégalais de Recherches Agricoles. Document No. 1985–13. Ziguinchor and Dakar.
Sanneh, Lamin O. 1979. *The Jakhanke*. International African Institute, London.

Sapir, J. David. 1970. "Kujaama: Symbolic Separation among the Diola Fogny," *American Anthropologist* 72(6): 1330–1348.
1971. "West Atlantic: An Inventory of the Languages, Their Noun Class Systems and Consonant Alternation," in T. Sebeok, ed. *Current Trends in Linguistics*, vol. 7: 45–112. Linguistics in Sub-Saharan Africa. Mouton Publishers, The Hague and Paris.
1977. "Fecal Animals: an Example of Complementary Totemism". *Man* 12(1): 1–21.
1983. (unpublished). Spirits and the Female Agnates in Kujamaat Thought. Paper presented to the American Anthropological Association Meetings, Chicago, 1983.
Schaffer, David M. 1976 (Ms.) "Pakao: A Study of Social Process among the Mandingo People of the Senegambia." Ph.D. dissertation, Department of Anthropology and Geography, Oxford University, Oxford.
Schaffer, David and C. Cooper. 1980. *Mandinko: The Ethnography of a West African Holy Land*. Holt, Rinehart and Winston, New York.
Scheffler, Harold W. 1966. "Ancestor Worship in Anthropology: or, Observations on Descent and Descent Groups," *Current Anthropology* 7(5): 541–551.
1972. "Systems of Kin Classification: a Structural Typology." In: Reining P. (ed), *Kinship Studies in the Morgan Centennial Year*, pp. 113–133. Washington: The Anthropological Society of Washington.
1973. "Kinship, Descent and Alliance." In Honigmann, J. J. (ed). *Handbook of Social and Cultural Anthropology*, ch. 17, pp. 747–793. Chicago: Rand McNally.
Schloss, Marc R. 1988. *The Hatchet's Blood: Separation, Power and Gender in Ehing Social Life*. The University of Arizona Press: Tucson.
Schumacher, Edward J. 1975. *Politics, Bureaucracy and Rural Development in Senegal*. Berkeley and Los Angeles: University of California Press.
Service de l'Agriculture, Rapport Annuel. 1905, 1907, 1920, 1925, 1930. Gouvernement de l'Afrique Occidental Français. Imprimerie du Gouvernement. St. Louis, Sénégal.
Sillitoe, Paul. 1985. "Divide and No One Rules: the Implications of Sexual Divisions of Labour in the Papua New Guinea Highlands." *Man* 20(3): 494–522.
Snyder, Francis G. 1981. *Capitalism and Legal Change: an African Transformation*. Academic Press, New York and London.
Sow, Fatou. 1984. In Pathé Diagne, ed. *Quelle Démocratie Pour le Sénégal?* pp. 41–54. Éditions PFD Sankore, Langres, France.
Staniland, Martin. 1985. *What is Political Economy? A Study of Social Theory and Underdevelopment*. New Haven: Yale University Press.
Swindell, Ken. 1985. *Farm Labour*. Cambridge: Cambridge University Press.
Sy, Cheikh Tidiane. 1988. "La Crise du Développement Rural et Désengagement de l'Etat au Sénégal. C. T. Sy (ed). *Les Nouvelles Éditions Africaines*. Dakar-Abidjan-Lome.
Teixeira da Mota, Avelino. 1972. *Mar, Além Mar. Estudos e Ensaios de História e Geografia*, Vol. I (1944–1947). Pedrulha, Coimbra, Portugal: Atlântida Editora.
Teixeira da Mota *et al*. 1977. Introduction to Donelha, André *Descrição da Serra*

Leoa e Dos Rios de Guiné do Cabo Verde (1625). Junta de Investigações Cientificas do Ultramar, Centro de Estudos de Cartografia Antiga, 19: 1–329, Lisbon.

Thomas, Louis-Vincent. 1959, Parts I and II. *Les Diola*. Memoire de l'Institut Français d'Afrique Noire, 55. Dakar.

―― 1963. "Essai sur Quelques Problèmes Relatifs au Régime Foncier des Diola de Basse-Casamance (Sénégal)," in Biebuyck, D., ed., *African Agrarian Systems*, pp. 314–330. Oxford University Press, Oxford.

―― B. Luneau and J. Doneux. 1969. *Les Religions d'Afrique Noire: Textes et Traditions Sacrés*. Paris: Fayard/Daniel.

Trimingham, J. Spencer. 1959. *Islam in West Africa*. Oxford University Press, London.

Trincaz, Jacqueline. 1981. *Colonisations et Religions en Afrique Noire. L'Exemple de Ziguinchor*. Éditions L'Harmattan, Paris.

Trincaz, Pierre Xavier. 1984. *Colonisation et Régionalisme. Ziguinchor en Casamance*. ORSTOM, Travaux et Documents 172, Paris.

Van Binsbergen, W. H. J. 1981. *Religious Change in Zambia: Exploratory Studies*. Kegan Paul International, London.

Vansina, Jan. 1978. *The Children of Woot: a History of the Kuba Peoples*. Madison: The University of Wisconsin Press.

Van Loo, Henk L. and Nella J. Star. 1973. *La Basse Casamance, Sud-Ouest du Sénégal. Données de Base Démographiques et Socio-Économiques, 1972*. Afrika Studiecentrum, Leiden.

Webster, J. B. 1963. "The Bible and the Plough". *Journal of the Historical Society of Nigeria* 2: 418–434.

Weil, Peter M. 1971. "Political Structure and Process among the Gambia Mandinka: the Village Parapolitical System," in Hodge, C. T., ed., *Papers on the Manding*, Indiana University Publications, African Series, vol. 3, pp. 249–272, Mouton and Co., The Hague.

―― 1980. "Mandinka Adaptation to Colonial Rule in the Gambia," in *Cultures et Dévoloppement*, 12(2): 295–318.

―― 1981. (unpublished). "Human Resources and Socio-Economic Constraints: the Lower Casamance Master Plan Project," Mimeographed report for Harza Engineering Corporation, 88pp. Chicago.

―― 1984. "Slavery, Groundnuts, and European Capitalism in the Wuli Kingdom of Senegambia, 1820–1930," *Research in Economic Development*, 6: 77–119.

White, Douglas R., M. L. Burton, M. M. Dow. 1981. "Sexual Division of Labor in African Agriculture: a Network Autocorrelation Analysis". *American Anthropologist* 83: 824–849.

Wright, Donald R. 1977. *The Early History of Niumi: Settlement and Foundation of a Mandinka State on the Gambia River*. Papers in International Studies, African Series No. 32, Ohio University, Athens.

―― 1985. "Beyond Migration and Conquest: Oral Traditions and Mandinka Ethnicity in Senegambia," *History in Africa* 12: 335–348.

Index

Abélès et Collard, 77, 166
age, *see* elders, division of labor
agnate, *see* descent
agriculture: extensive (bush-fallow) versus intensive (wet-rice), 5, 9, 15–16 *see also* groundnut cultivation, labor, rice cultivation
agricultural tools: 3–4; *kajandu* 19, 21pl.2top, 59pl.7, 66pl.8, 125, 30pl.13, 132, 133pl.14, 189; *kanata* 19; *kaŋom* 22; *eronkatoŋ* 189, 190pl.19top, 192pl. 20a; *ebara* 137pl.15, 194pl.21, 195. *See also* ox-plough
aí, ritual elder, *see* elders
ajawáati, host, 92, 107, 129, 169
ancestor(s): 63, 76, 105, 229n8; in Fatiya 162; among Lugbara 75; among Manding 235n7; in Sambujat 24, 33, 35, 230n10
animals: animal doubles 230n9; in sacrifices 29, 31, 32, 45, 48, 50, 68, 70, 255n11, 226n12; 228n1; pig epidemic 213; and Islamic prohibitions against eating or raising pigs 97, 159, 175. *See also* cattle
Augé, M., 166
awasen, shrine-keeper, see spirit-shrines

Badiane and Doneaux n.d., xviii
Baila: *marigot* 89, 92, 104; region 140; road 100; village 125–126
bakiin/ukiin, see spirit-shrines
Balanta, ethnic group of Guiné Bissau, 5, 89
Banjal, a Jola sub-group, 40
Bañuñ, ethnic group in Casamance, 85, 86–87fig.2, 88–89, 90, 167, 231n1, 231n3
Barnes, J.A., 63
Barry, B., 90, 149
Barth, F., 148

Bates, R. H., 10
Bathurst, capital of Gambia, 92, 12fig.1, 86fig.2
Baum, R., 5, 17, 25, 29, 30, 32, 42, 49, 51, 53, 54, 69, 74, 212, 224n5, 225n6–n9, 226n15, 227n16, 227n18, 227n19, 228n3, 228n5, 231n1, 237n2
Beattie, J. H. M., 225–226n12
Berger Report, 184, 134n1
Berry, S., 9
Bertrand-Bocandé, M., 99
Bignona (town), xviii, 3, 5, 89, 100, 154, 212, 214, 237n4
Bignona *marigot*, 104
Bintang (Vintang), *marigot* in Gambia, 85, 234n
Bledsoe, C., 182
Boserup, E., 9, 78, 138, 168, 191, 196
Bourdieu, P., 74
Bradburd, D., 169–170
Brásio, A., 85, 234n2
Bray, F., 16
bridewealth, *see* marriage
Brooks, G., 85, 88, 89, 149, 231n2, 231n3, 233n9, 234n1
Brown, J., 9
buaju, patriline, *see* descent and filiation, Sambujat
bunuk, see palm wine, trade in forest products
Burnham, P., 70
Burton, M., *et al*, 9
butoŋ, *see* households (Sambujat)
Buwinko, *see* spirit-shrines (female, in Sambujat)

Cacheu: region, 89; River 85, 86fig.2, 149
Camara, S., 152, 173
capitalism: impact on gender 196;

253

capitalism (cont.)
    penetration of 83, 142; and religion. See also wage labor
captives, see slaves
Carreira, A., 253n4
Casamance: see Lower Casamance, Middle Casamance
Casamance River, 6, 7, 11, 19, 28, 79, 83, 85, 86–87fig.2, 88, 89, 90, 94, 101, 149, 150, 151
cash crops, see groundnuts, palm wine, rice crop, vegetable gardens
cattle: general role in Sambujat 34–35, 38, 40, 43, 47, 52, 54, 61, 147, 230n10, ownership by women 45, 51; bulls in rituals and symbols 32, 46, 48, 226n12, 227n17
Charest, P., 176
Cheneau-Loquay, A., 6, 145, 223n2, 229n6
chief: in Esudadu (Sambujat) 42–44; in Kajamutay 125; in Kalunay (Fatiya) 163–164, 168–169, 189
Christianity: Africans converts 8; Catholicism 96, 99; Catholics in Esudadu (Sambujat) 212–213, 237n2
circumcision (boys' initiation): *bukut* in Sambujat 32, 43, 226n13, 226n14; *futamp* in *Jipalom*, 112–113, 138; *futamp* in Kalunay (Fatiya) 178; 236n3; relation to girls' excision rites 177. See excision, girls' initiation rite
Clammer, J., 10
Cleave, J. H., 199
Coelho, F. de L., 89
Cohen, A., 8
Comaroff, Jean, 75
Comaroff, John, 55
conjugal family, see household, labor (division of), marriage
conscripted (corvée) labor: see French administration
Conseil National de Femmes Noires Americaines, 231n2
contradictions, see ideology, contradictions in
conversion, and economic change, 8–9. See Islamization
cooking, eating and the conjugal family: in Fatiya 179, in Jipalom 141, in Sambujat 59, 228n
Copans, J., 98, 219
Coulon, C., 97, 98, 218, 219, 238n8, 239n12
Crone, G. R., 149, 234n1
Cruise O'Brien, D. B., 98, 219, 239n13
Cultru, P., 88
cultural: constructs 4; patterns 7, symbols 74. See ideologies
Curtin, P., 149

Dalby, D., 150
Darbon, D., 222
Decraene, P., 154
de Jonge, K. et al, 57, 229n6, 237n1
descent and filiation: approaches to 229n8; *buaju* and *hank* in Sambujat 63–65, 230n10, see spirit-shrines; *eluup* and *fank* in Jipalom 105–107; patrilineal descent in Fatiya 161–163. See also uterine kin
Dey, J., 153, 235n4
Diop, A. B., 110
division of labor: *see* labor, division of
Doneaux, J., 5, 85
Donham, D., 76, 77, 166
dowry; see marriage

Ebune, female agnatic shrine, *see* spirit-shrines
education, *see* schooling
Ehuñ/Sihuñ, female agnatic shrine, see spirit-shrines
Eisenstadt, S. N., 170
ekáf/sikáf, *see* labor (associative)
elder(s)/elderhood: age as a social principle 9–10, 165–166; *ai* or ritual elder in Sambujat: 30, 38–39, 40–42, 76, 226n15, 227n16; female *ai* 45; Esudadu elders in general 28–31, 32–33, 38, 76–78; Kajamutay elders of Jipalom 84, 116, 123, 126, 132–135, 201, 240n20; women elders of Jipalom 115; Kalunay elders of Fatiya 156, 165, 170, 179–180, 187–188, 203
eluup, see descent and filiation, Japan
Epstein, A. L., 147
ethnicity: 147–148, 150; Manding identity 152
Ewane, M., 220
excision or female circumcision, 109–111, 176–177, 234Ch.4n2

Fatton Jr., R., 169, 218, 220, 221, 238n8, 239n13
female farming, theories, 9, 196–197
Fisher, H. J., 118
Fodé Kaba, *jihad* leader 93; *see also* Islam, Holy Wars
Foñi: area 85, 92; dialect 6; invasion of 93, 232n7; and Manding kingdoms 151
founders in Fatiya, 161–164, 166–169, 239n8; among Manding 153, 235n7
Fox, R., 230n10
French colonial administration: and groundnuts 99, 100–101, 218; and conversion to Islam 94–96, 99, 238n8, 238n9; and Senegalese independence 220
Friedl, E., 45, 51
Fulani (Peul, Fula), 17; Fodé Silla Ture

232n7; and female excision 234n2
Fulup, Portuguese name for Jola, 85, 89, 90, 231n4
funerals, 28, 45–47, 46pl.6, 174, 227n17

Gambia, 3, 6, 92
Gambia River 85
Gaudio A. and Pelletier, 158, 177
Geertz, C., 205
Gellar, S. 100, 238n10, 239n12, 239n14
gender: associated principles 8–10, 186; and cultural constructs of 179, 198; in Esudadu (Sambujat) 24, 50–51, 52, 61, 71; in the Kajamutay (Jipalom): 92, 130–132, 201, *see* spirit-shrines; in the Kalunay (Fatiya): 172–173, 236n2. *See also* excision, Islam, labor (social division of), marriage
Geschieri, P., 221, 240n18
Giddens, A., 11, 23, 84–85
Glaise, J., 240n20
Godelier, M., 4
Goody, J., 55, 181
Gouro (Guro), ethnic group, Ivory Coast, 77, 90
Gourou, P. 205
groundnut(s): as symbol 75, 98–99, 140–41
Groundnut Basin 6, 170, 212, 218
groundnut cultivation: absence from Sambujat 71, 207; adoption in Lower Casamance, 98–101, 233n10; adoption in other regions 211; groundnuts in the Kajamutay (Jipalom): access to plateau lands 127, 129, and associative labor 133pl.14, 135, 137pl.15, and field distribution 128fig.4, and time invested in 131, 138, 139tabl.IIc, sale of crop in recent years 213–214; and women 131, 137, 139; groundnuts in the Kalunay (Fatiya): and the extended family 187–189, and groundnut cooperative 164, and land ownership 168–169, and Manding settlers 158, 187, 206, and marabouts 189, 190pl.19, 203, and sale of crop 180, 184, 236n4, 238n11, and women 168; in Senegalese–Murid economy 218–219, 239n12; slaves and groundnuts among the Manding 93–94. *See also* labor (division of)
Guèye, M., 159, 160, 173, 235n6
Guiné Bissau 5, 35, 72, 85, 151
Guyer, J., 58, 70, 197

Hamer A., 79, 90, 91, 92
hank, patrigroup in Sambujat: *see* descent and filiation, labor (associative), spirit-shrines, witchcraft
Harms, R., 91

Harrison, C., 238n8
Hart, K., 10
Haswell, M. R., 235n4
Hesseling, O., 96, 97, 218
Horton, R. 95
households: classification 229n7; comparison between 3 communities 235n8; in Esudadu (Sambujat): 57, 62, 63Tabl.Ic, 65; in Kajamutay (Jipalom) 105, 119, 132; in Kalunay (Fatiya): 179–180.
Huteendukay, the Sambujat labor shrine, and *ai* 41, 227n16, functions of 53–54, 69

ideology(ies): as belief or religion 7; and economic processes 4, 9, 11, 15, 16, 74, 79; contradictions in 7, 103; Islamic (Murid) ideology and the State 219–221. *See also* Islam
indépendantistes, 221–222, 240n17, 240n18, 240n19, 240n20, 240n21
initiation, *see* circumcision (for boys), excision (for girls)
instruction, *see* schooling
Islam: and brotherhoods (Qadiriyya, Muridiyya or Murid, Tijaniyya or Tijani) 97–98, 117, 159, 218–219, 232n8, 239n14; and Koran 156, 158–160, 235n6; and meaning for Jola 97; mosques: in Fatiya 156, 173–174, in Jipalom 116–117; percent of Muslims in population 217; Islam in Jipalom 84, 116–118, 142, 217; role of Islam in Fatiya society 156, 158–160
Islamic clerics; *atalibao* (Koranic instructor) 116, 138, 156, *alaak* (curer) 113, 161, *awadani* (person who calls to prayer) 117, 174, *imam* 117, 152, 174, marabout(s): 158, 174–175, 203, 218–220, 238n8–10
Islamization: conversion to Islam 94–97, 118; and groundnuts (general) 98–99, 101, and Holy Wars 92–93, 151

Jakhanke, Mande group 93
jihads, see Islamization: Holy Wars
Jola language 5–6, 104
Journet, O., 79, 237

kajandu, see agricultural tools
kalol/ulol, wards: in Fatiya 162, 189; in Jipalom 104, 121
Kaneewak, agnatic family shrine: in Fatiya 160–161; in Jipalom 111–112
Karabane island 99
Kassangas, people 88
kawaw, palm wine tapping, see trade in palm products

Keesing, R., 182
Kertzer, D., 42
Kombo region: kingdom of 151, migration to 92, population density 6
Kopytoff, I., 63
Koran, see Islam
Kru (people from Sierra Leone) 91
kurimen pl./*arimen* sing.: female agnates in Fatiya, and *Ebune* 178, and brothers' wives 186, 195; female agnates in Jipalom, and *Ebune* 113–115, 201, and land 122–123, rights of 106, 109, and work groups 136
kuseek pl./*aseek* sing., wives/wife 108–109, 121–122

labor, access to by women: in Fatiya 193, 195, in Jipalom 136, in Sambujat 70; associative labor in Sambujat by men 65–69, by women 69–70, in year 1990 213; associative labor in Jipalom by men 132–136, 134 Tabl.IIb, 138, by women 136–137, 141; associative labor in Fatiya: demise among men 189, by women 193–195, 215; summary of associative labor in 3 communities 199–203; division of labor: in Fatiya 186–189, 198–199, 202, in Jipalom 130–132, in Sambujat 58–62; division of labor in nineteenth-century trade 92; flow of labor 107, 134–135, 203; labor inputs by women in the 3 villages 196Tabl.IIIb, in Fatiya 199, in Jipalom 131, in Sambujat 23; labor and the rural exodus 229n6
la Courbe, Jajolet de, 88
La Fontaine, J. S., 9, 110, 177
Lancaster, C., 9
land: in Esudadu (Sambujat): curses on 37–38, and transmission of 56, 228Ch.1n20; in Kajamutay (Jipalom): access to extra fields 127–129, 140–141, conflicts over land 124–126, ownership and tenure 119, 121–122, and pledging 123, and the State 124, 126 and women 129; in Kalunay (Fatiya): clearing land 169, and founders versus immigrants, 154, 166–168, 169, and Manding 171, and women 168
Lauer, J., 89, 149, 231n3
Leary, F. A., 93, 94, 152, 154, 232n7
Levy, R., 236
Lewis, J. V. D., 76, 167
Lewis, I. M., 95, 143, 175
Linares, O. F., 19, 56, 62, 65, 83, 89, 94, 95, 105, 119, 129, 139, 141, 147, 163, 179, 181, 200, 224n5, 228n2
Long, N., 8
Loquay, A., *see* Cheneau-Loquay
Lower Casamance: location 3, 11; population 5, 223n2; surface 6
Luso-Africans: 88, 89, 231n2, 231n3

Magassouba, M., 233n8
Mair, L., 165, 170
Manding: Dyula 91; ethnic divisions 150, and female excision 110, at first European contact 149–150, 234–235n1–3, and the French administration 95–97, and Holy Wars 92–93, 151, and introduction of groundnuts 99, and Islamic revolution 152, location *vis à vis* Kalunay 151, and social organization 5, 151–153, 235n4, 236n5, in Pte. St. Georges 17, westward expansion of 89
"Mandingization": as a process: 147–149, 204–205, 206–207. *See also* Islamic clerics
Manjaku, ethnic group of Guiné Bissau, 5
marabout, *see* Islamic cleric
maraboutic wars, *see* Islam, Holy Wars
marigot(s), tidal creek, 17, 18, 19
Mark, P., 88, 90, 91, 92, 94, 95, 96, 98, 99, 100, 101, 224n5, 231n1, 233n10, 235n3
marriage: in Esudadu (Sambujat), 55–57, 77, 228n1, 230n10; in Kajamutay (Jipalom) 107–109; in Kalunay (Fatiya) 181–186, 236n6, 237n7; among the Manding 236n5; re-marriage in Esudadu (Sambujat) 9–10, 58, 228n4, 228n5, in Kajamutay (Jipalom) 122, in Kalunay (Fatiya) 185
Martin, S., 8, 198
Marty, P, 95, 96
Marzouk-Schmitz, Y., 61, 119, 204
matrilateral kin: *see* uterine kin
Meillassoux, C., 43, 77, 90, 134, 166
Michaelson, K. L., 170
Michie, B. H., 169
Middle Casamance: 3, 99, 101, 150, 152, 154, 233n10
Middleton, J., 24, 75–76
migration: to Gambia in nineteenth century 92, 151. *See also* wage-labor migration
millet, cultivation: in Kajamutay (Jipalom): 130, 131, 139t.IIc; in Kalunay (Fatiya) 187, 202; millet beer, 99, 159; sale of millet in Fatiya 180, 184
Monod, Th. *et al*, 85, 88, 234n1
Morris, B., 7, 103
Muller, J. C., 77

Netting, R., 16
Ngoram, village in Kalunay, 158
Nzouankeu, J., 240n16

Oboler, R. S., 58, 130, 196, 197
oral traditions, 104–105
Ortner, S., 4

Oussouye xviii, 3, 17
ox-plough: absence of in Esudadu 23, 199; presence in Kajamutay (Jipalom) 131, 138-139, 139Tabl.IIa, 142; presence in Kalunay (Fatiya) 189, 191, 192Pl.20b, and women 193, 215

palm wine: among Esudadu: and *ai* 41, and *Huteendukay* 54; libations of 24, 26, 31; and marriage 55; symbolic dimension 75, 99; and trade 71-73; and women 79
Parkin, D., 8
patron–client relationships: definition 169, 239n13; in Fatiya 148, 161, 170-171; among Manding 153; in other groups 170; in the Senegalese countryside 220
Pélissier, P., 4, 6, 61, 119, 147, 211, 223n1, 231-232n4, 233n10
Pickersgill, B. 233n9
Pointe St. Georges, 3, 17, 18
political economy: definition 15; in Esudadu (Sambujat) 24, 38, 55; in Kajamutay (Jipalom) 83, 84; in Kalunay (Fatiya), 207; and Senegalese State: 6-7, 217-220
population: of Esudadu region 17, 224n1; of Fatiya 154, 235n5; of Jipalom 233n1; of Lower Casamance 223n2
Portères, R., 231n4
power: definitions and concepts, 5, 10, 15, 16, 23-24. *See also* resources, spirit-shrines, labor power
pray/prayer: in Sambujat: and *Ehuñ* 48-49, at other times 24, 33, 68, 225n7; in Kajamutay (Jipalom): and female excision 111, and Koran 94, 97, and mosque 116, 117, and women 139, and men 141; in Kalunay (Fatiya): and gender 156, and ablutions 159, and women 173-174, 175; and Manding 153. *See also* Islamic clerics, mosques
production: 4, 5, 11, 16, 79; *See also* labor, division of, spirit-shrines

Quinn, C. A., 151, 235n7

Radcliffe-Brown, A. R., 230n10
Ray, B., 55
resources: allocative and authoritative, definitions of 23-24
rice crop: milling machine 61, 213, 215-216; imports of 215; in rituals: *charité* 180, 216, conversion and curing 94, 113, in Sambujat funerals 46, and shrines 55; rice sale 61, 70, 78; rice storage 52, 62, 180
rice-cultivation: antiquity in Upper Guinea Coast 231n4; in Esudadu (Sambujat): general 17, 19, 22, 23, steps in 20Tabl.Ia, 21Pl.2, yields 16, 23; in the Kajamutay (Jipalom) 118-119, 130, 214-215; in the Kalunay (Fatiya), 191, 193-196. *See also* labor, social division of
rice fields: layout 18-19, 118, 120, 155pl.16
Richards, P., 138, 148
rituals: in Esudadu (Sambujat): *kawasen* (to sacrifice) 24, 31-34, 225n12, and *Ehuñ* 227n19, *kaalok* (participatory ritual) 29, 225n11; *kanabor* (sharing of ritual meat) 231Concl.n1; in Jipalom: *Kaneeawak* shrine 111; in Fatiya 161. *See also* Islam, pray/prayer, spirit-shrines
roads: and conscripted labor 100; and Fatiya 156; and Jipalom 214-215, 237n3
Robinson, D., 238n8
Roche, C., 88, 91, 93, 97, 100, 232n6, 233n10
Rodney, W., 149
Rogers, B., 61
Rueschmeyer, D., 10

sacrifice, see animals (sacrifice), rituals
Sall, S., 65
salt-making, 215
Sanneh, L. O., 93
Sapir, J. D., xvii, 5, 6, 85, 113, 114
Schaffer, D. and Cooper, 152, 167, 176, 235n4
Scheffler, H. W., 229n8
Schloss, M. R., 228n20
schools/schooling: in Fatiya 156, 174, 235Ch.6n1; in Jipalom 117-118; in Sambuja 213
Schumacher, E. J., 218, 238n9
Senegalese State, 217-218, 221
seniority, *see* elder/elderhood
Sillitoe, P., 9
Sindian, community in the Kajamutay: xviii, 93, 118, 154, 167, 189, 232-233n8
slaves: and the *ai* 40, and groundnut production among Manding 93-94, 167; in Pte. St. Georges villages 17; slave trade 89, 211, 225n9, 232n6, 232n7
Snyder, F. G., 7, 68, 228n20
Soninke (Mande group, lapsed Muslim), 93
Soungrougrou River, dividing Lower from Middle Casamance: 3, 6, 85, 88, 89, 93, 154
Sow, F., 221
spirit-shrine(s) in Esudadu (Sambujat): under female control (*Sihuñ*) 47-50, 227n18, 227n19, under male control 24-27, 225n6-n10, *see also* elders; spirit-shrine(s); in Kajamutay (Jipalom): under female control 113-115, under male control 111-113; spirit-shrine(s) in Kalunay (Fatiya): under female control

spirit-shrine(s) in Esudadu (Sambujat) (*cont.*)
178, under male control 160–161
Staniland, M., 15
"strangers": in Esudadu (Sambujat) 17; in Kajamutay (Jipalom) 107, 135; in Kalunay (Fatiya) 163, Lobé 164, Manding 153
Swindell, K., 67, 196
Sy, Cheikh T., 241n22

talibé (disciple), 7, 97, 98, 156, 157pl.17
Teixeira da Mota *et. al.* 88, 234n1
Thomas, L. V., 4, 31, 37, 38, 39, 45, 48, 54, 74, 78, 119, 147, 223n1, 231n1
Tionk-Essil, Jola community, 93, 94, 98, 99, 240n19
tractor 215, 238n7
trade: and gender 91–92, 198; in beeswax 88; in palm products 90–91, 151, 211, 232n5, *see also* palm wine; in red rubber 91, 151, 211, 232n6. *See also* slave-trade
Toucoulers, 5, 98, 164
Trimingham, J. S., 94

urban migration, 212, 213, 237n1. *See also* wage-labor migration
uterine (matrilateral) kin: 47, 108, 112–113, 121–122

Van Binsbergen 148
Van Loo, H. L., 237
vegetable gardens, 198, 216

wage-labor migration: 69, 70, 78–79, 211, 231n2 (concl.)
wards, village units, in Fatiya 189, in Jipalom 104, in Sambujat 225n10
Webster, J. B., 8
Weil, P., 93, 151, 152, 153, 235n4
West Atlantic languages, 5
wet-rice, *see* rice cultivation
White, D. R., 9
witchcraft, 36–39, 49, 52, 109, 212
Wolof, 5, 6, 17, 97, 110, 219, 221, 232n6–7, 241n21
women, *see* gender
Wright, D. R., 149, 150, 151, 235n3

Ziguinchor, xvii, 3, 88, 89, 100, 212, 214, 231n3

Cambridge Studies in Social and Cultural Anthropology

Editors: ERNEST GELLNER, JACK GOODY, STEPHEN GUDEMAN, MICHAEL HERZFELD, JONATHAN PARRY

1 The Political Organisations of Unyamwezi
  R.G. ABRAHAMS
2 Buddhism and the Spirit Cults in North-East Thailand*
  S.J. TABIAH
3 Kalahari Village Politics: An African Democracy
  ADAM KUPER
4 The Rope of Moka: Big-Men and Ceremonial Exchange in Mount Hagen, New Guinea
  ANDREW STRATHERN
5 The Majangir: Ecology and Society of a Southwest Ethiopian People
  JACK STAUDER
6 Buddhist Monk, Buddhist Layman: A Study of Urban Monastic Organisation in Central Thailand
  JANE BUNNAG
7 Contexts of Kinship: An Essay in the Family Sociology of the Gonja of Northern Ghana
  ESTHER N. GOODY
8 Marriage among a Matrilineal Elite: A Family Study of Ghanaian Civil Servants
  CHRISTINE OPPONG
9 Elite Politics in Rural India: Political Stratification and Political Alliances in Western Maharashtra
  ANTHONY T. CARTER
10 Women and Property in Morocco: Their Changing Relation to the Process of Social Stratification in the Middle Atlas
  VANESSA MAHER
11 Rethinking Symbolism
  DAN SPERBER, translated by Alice L. Morton
12 Resources and Population: A Study of the Gurungs of Nepal
  ALAN MACFARLANE
13 Mediterranean Family Structures
  EDITED BY J.G. PERISTIANY
14 Spirits of Protest: Spirit-Mediums and the Articulation of Consensus among the Zezuru of Southern Rhodesia (Zimbabwe)
  PETER FRY
15 World Conqueror and World Renouncer: A Study of Buddhism and Polity in Thailand against a Historical Background*
  S.J. TAMBIAH
16 Outline of a Theory of Practice*
  PIERRE BOURDIEU, translated by Richard Nice
17 Production and Reproduction: A Comparative Study of the Domestic Domain
  JACK GOODY

18 Perspectives in Marxist Anthropology
   MAURICE GODELIER, translated by Robert Brain
19 The Fate Shechem, or the Politics of Sex: Essays in the Anthropology of the Mediterranean
   JULIAN PITT-RIVERS
20 People of the Zongo: The Transformation of Ethnic Identities in Ghana
   ENID SCHILDKROUT
21 Casting out Anger: Religion among the Taita of Kenya
   GRACE HARRIS
22 Rituals of the Kandyan State
   H.L. SENVIRATNE
23 Australian Kin Classification
   HAROLD W. SCHEFFLER
24 The Palm and the Pleiades: Initiation and Cosmology in Northwest Amazonia*
   STEPHEN HUGH-JONES
25 Nomads of Southern Siberia: The Pastoral Economies of Tuva
   S.I. VANSHTEIN, translated by Michael Colenso
26 From the Milk River: Spatial and Temporal Processes in Northwest Amazonia*
   CHRISTINE HUGH-JONES
27 Day of Shining Red: An Essay on Understanding Ritual*
   GILBERT LEWIS
28 Hunters, Pastoralists and Ranchers: Reindeer Economies and their Transformations*
   TIM INGOLD
29 The Wood-Carvers of Hong Kong: Craft Production in the World Capitalist Periphery
   EUGENE COOPER
30 Minangkabau Social Formations: Indonesian Peasants and the World Economy
   JOEL S. KAHN
31 Patrons and Partisans: A Study of Two Southern Italian Communes
   CAROLINE WHITE
32 Muslim Society*
   ERNEST GELLNER
33 Why Marry Her? Society and Symbolic Structures
   LUC DE HEUSCH, translated by Janet Lloyd
34 Chinese Ritual and Politics
   EMILY MARTIN AHERN
35 Parenthood Social Reproduction: Fostering and Occupational Roles in West Africa
   ESTHER N. GOODY
36 Dravidian Kinship
   THOMAS R. TRAUTMANN
37 The Anthropological Circle: Symbol Function, History*
   MARC AUGE, translated by Martin Thom
38 Rural Society in Southeast Asia
   KATHLEEN GOUGH
39 The Fish-People: Linguistic Exogamy and Tukanoan Identity in Northwest Amazonia
   JEAN E. JACKSON
40 Karl Marx Collective: Economy, Society and Religion in a Siberian Collective Farm*
   CAROLINE HUMPHREY
41 Ecology and Exchange in the Andes
   edited by DAVID LEHMANN
42 Traders without Trade: Responses to Trade in two Dyula Communities
   ROBERT LAUNAY
43 The Political Economy of West African Agriculture*
   KEITH HART
44 Nomads and the Outside World
   A.K. KHAZANOV, translated by Julia Crookenden

45 Actions, Norms and Representations: Foundations of Anthropological Inquiry*
   LADISLAV HOLY and MILAN STUCHLIK
46 Structural Models in Anthropology*
   PER HAGE and FRANK HARARY
47 Servants of the Goddess: The Priests of a South Indian Temple
   C.J. FULLER
48 Oedipus and Job in West African Religion*
   MEYER FORTES
49 The Buddhist Saints of the Forest and the Cult of Amulets: A Study in Charisma, Hagiography, Sectarianism, and Millennial Buddhism*
   S.J. TAMBIAH
50 Kinship and Marriage: An Anthropological Perspective (available in paperback/in the USA only)
   ROBIN FOX
51 Individual and Society in Guiana: A Comparative Study of Amerindian Social Organization*
   PETER RIVIERE
52 People and the State: An Anthropology of Planned Development*
   A.F. ROBERTSON
53 Inequality among Brothers; Class and Kinship in South China
   RUBIE S. WATSON
54 On Anthropological Knowledge*
   DAN SPERBER
55 Tales of Yanomami: Daily Life in the Venezuelan Forest*
   JACQUES LIZOT, translated by Ernest Simon
56 The Making of Great Men: Male Domination and Power among the New Guinea Baruya*
   MAURICE GODELIER, translated by Rupert Swyer
57 Age Class Systems: Social Institutions and Polities Based on Age*
   BERNARDO BERNARDI, translated by David I. Kertzer
58 Strategies and Norms in a Changing Matrilineal Society: Descent, Succession and Inheritance among the Toka of Zambia
   LADISLAV HOLY
59 Native Lords of Quito in the Age of the Incas: the Political Economy of North-Andean Chiefdoms
   FRANK SALOMON
60 Culture and Class in Anthropology and History: A Newfoundland Illustration
   GERALD SIDER
61 From Blessing to Violence: History and Ideology in the Circumcision Ritual of the Merina of Madagascar*
   MAURICE BLOCH
62 The Huli Response to Illness
   STEPHEN FRANKEL
63 Social Inequality in a Northern Portuguese Hamlet: Land, Late Marriage, and Bastardy, 1870–1978
   BRIAN JUAN O'NEILL
64 Cosmologies in the Making: A Generative Approach to Cultural Variation in Inner New Guinea*
   FREDRIK BARTH
65 Kinship and Class in the West Indies: A Genealogical Study of Jamaica and Guyana
   RAYMOND T. SMITH
66 The Making of the Basque Nation
   MARIANNE HEIBERG
67 Out of Time: History and Evolution in Anthropological Discourse
   NICHOLAS THOMAS

68 Tradition as Truth and Communication: A Cognitive Description of Traditional Discourse
   PASCAL BOYER
69 The Abandoned Narcotic: Kava and Cultural Instability in Melanesia
   RON BRUNTON
70 The Anthropology of Numbers
   THOMAS CRUMP
71 Stealing People's Names: History and Politics in a Sepik River Cosmology
   SIMON J. HARRISON
72 The Bedouin of Cyrenaica: Studies in Personal and Corporate Power
   EMRYS L. PETERS, edited by Jack Goody and Emanuel Marx
73 Property, Production and Family in Neckerhausen
   DAVID WARREN SABEAN
74 Bartered Brides: Politics, Gender and Marriage in an Afghan Tribal Society
   NANCY TAPPER
75 Fifteen Generations of Bretons: Kinship and Society in Lower Brittany, 1720–1980
   MARTINE SEGALEN, translated by J.A. Underwood
76 Honour and Grace in Anthropology
   Edited by J.G. PERSTIANY and JULIAN PITT-RIVERS
77 The Making of the Modern Greek Family: Marriage and Exchange in Nineteenth-Century Athens
   PAUL SANT CASSIA and CONSTANTINA BADA
78 Religion and Custom in a Muslim Society: The Berti of Sudan
   LADISLAV HOLY
79 Quiet Days in Burgundy: A Study of Local Politics
   MARC ABELES, translated by Annella McDermott
80 Sacred Void: Spatial Images of Work and Ritual Among the Giriama of Kenya
   DAVID PARKIN
81 A Place of Their Own: Family Farming in Eastern Finland
   RAY ABRAHAMS

* available in paperback